School's Out!

BRIDGING OUT-OF-SCHOOL LITERACIES WITH CLASSROOM PRACTICE

Edited by
GLYNDA HULL
KATHERINE SCHULTZ

Foreword by Shirley Brice Heath

Teachers College
Columbia University
New York and London

Published by Teachers College Press, 1234 Amsterdam Avenue, New York, NY 10027

Library of Congress Cataloging-in-Publication Data

Schools out!: bridging out-of-school literacies with classroom practice / edited by Glynda Hull, Katherine Schultz ; foreword by Shirley Brice Heath.
      p. cm. — (Language and literacy series)
   Includes bibliographical references and index.
   ISBN 0-8077-4190-6 — ISBN 0-8077-4189-2 (pbk.)
      1. Literacy—Social aspects—United States.   2. Socially handicapped—Education—United States.   3. Language arts—United States.   4. Compensatory education—United States.   I. Hull, Glynda A.   II. Schultz, Katherine. III. Language and literacy series (New York, N.Y.)
   LC151 .S29 2002
   370.11′1—dc21   2001049466

ISBN 0-8077-4189-2 (paper)
ISBN 0-8077-4190-6 (cloth)

LANGUAGE AND LITERACY SERIES

Dorothy S. Strickland and Celia Genishi, SERIES EDITORS

ADVISORY BOARD: RICHARD ALLINGTON, DONNA ALVERMANN, KATHRYN AU,
EDWARD CHITTENDEN, BERNICE CULLINAN, COLETTE DAIUTE,
ANNE HAAS DYSON, CAROLE EDELSKY, JANET EMIG,
SHIRLEY BRICE HEATH, CONNIE JUEL, SUSAN LYTLE

School's Out! Bridging Out-of-School
Literacies with Classroom Practice
    GLYNDA HULL and KATHERINE SCHULTZ,
    Editors

Building Family Literacy in an Urban
Community
    RUTH D. HANDEL

Children's Inquiry: Using Language to
rld
?ORS

cesses, Practices,
ıs
ı
NN, Editors

/hole Language
ſ and
itors

ism, and ESL in the

and PAULA WOLFE,

nd Literate Practices
ɩicano Community

Resistance and
g of Literature
Z and

ing Literature and

teracy, Language,
ɩryday Life
MARY BETH
MPHILL, and
ſT DeMARRAIS
ds: Early Learning
ɩunities

ractices

BARBARA M. TAYLOR, MICHAEL F.
GRAVES, PAUL van den BROEK, Editors
Writing in the Real World: Making the
Transition from School to Work
    ANNE BEAUFORT
Young Adult Literature and the New
Literary Theories: Developing Critical
Readers in Middle School
    ANNA O. SOTER
Literacy Matters:
Writing and Reading the Social Self
    ROBERT P. YAGELSKI

HANNA ARLENE FINGERET and
CASSANDRA DRENNON
Children's Literature and the Politics of
Equality
    PAT PINSENT
The Book Club Connection: Literacy
Learning and Classroom Talk
    SUSAN I. McMAHON and TAFFY E.
    RAPHAEL, Editors, with VIRGINIA J.
    GOATLEY and LAURA S. PARDO
Until We Are Strong Together:
Women Writers in the Tenderloin
    CAROLINE E. HELLER

(Continued

Contents

v

Foreword

This book makes us look to the past and future.

The editors and contributors have stepped courageously to the forefront of what will surely become a fundamental phenomenon characterizing civil societies in the coming decades. They have laid out principles and practices of learning as a full-time human activity without physical barriers of walls, doors, and fences or arbitrary limits imposed by age, gender, race, class, and geography. This is a big step forward within the profession of education that has for the past millennium "housed" teachers, students, texts, and tests to protect, promote, and privilege them. Upon the orders of the State—whether communist, socialist, or capitalist—education has implemented laws upholding age-grading and divisions based on categories of identity: sexual, ethnic, economic, and sociodemographic. For professional education, then, this book is ahead of its time, and points us toward a positive future.

However, outside the physical barriers and arbitrary limits of education, the concept of learning unrestricted by time and place is an ancient and instinctive one. As long as human memory has been recorded, individuals and groups have represented in visual, musical, dramatic, and choreographic terms their indebtedness to learning without direct instruction or written authorized texts and imposed tests. Such learning, and its forms of celebration, have been a core theme of the literary arts across all societies. Scientists and inventors, as well as explorers, have recorded with astonishment and gratitude their revelations resulting from observing, experimenting, and learning from mistakes. Notice to the smallest and most unexpected details and patterns of change have led to major advances in medicine, engineering, artistic production, and countless other fields.

Within the past two decades, scientists wishing to understand beyond philosophical and theological terms what it means to be human have taken the brain and the body as unexplored territories that can tell us much about how cognitive, linguistic, and physical knowledge changes. Much of this work, particularly that which depends on crossing disciplines, has had minimal impact on time-honored professions such as medicine, law, and education. Effects have moved rapidly, however, at the edges, in worlds we have come to call "alternative," in arenas that have little or no professional standing. In health practices, neuroscientists now work with art historians to grasp visual and spatial learning. Teaching hospitals, prisons, and entrepreneurial cooperatives depend on seminars, workshops, and mixed-media to demonstrate ways to control pain, to release anger, and to make profit, not only financially but also socially. These benefits extend individual lives and improve the quality of life in communities.

It is worth reflecting on contemporary forces that may be critical to the current appeal of "alternative" learning strategies, contexts, and agents. These same forces, no doubt, lie also behind the creation of this book. At least three such forces are simultaneously converging on professional education. The first seems to be a sense of extraordinary effort by individuals, groups, and governments to generate improvement. The desire here is not only the more rapid and effective learning of more information and skills by more of us, but also a better means of putting people and knowledge to work on critical societal problems.

A close second among forces drawing us to new means of spreading learning environments is the atmosphere of desperation driven by the realization that technological challenges, health crises, environmental deterioration, and group hatreds far outstrip current skills and accumulated information. Formal education cannot, and should not, be the prime source of the will and the wisdom to imagine and sustain the means necessary to have a significant positive influence on the sources of our desperation. Complementary and alternative environments and motivations, as well as ends of learning, have to be available in powerfully attractive and sustaining shapes. These are certain to work in different combinations for every individual at particular points along the life-span, and through the various changes in health, employment, self-interests, and community identity we all face at one time or another.

Finally, perhaps the most critical force pushing us to alternative ways of learning is the quickening pace of change and mutation properties of the ills that mark contemporary societies. Institutions have always been created to withstand change and hence do not learn or adapt with speed; inertia protects and sustains institutions and their members and must always do so to provide core stability for governments. Taken together, these three forces outstrip the capacity of professional or formal education to address them. They are not likely to diminish or disappear, so we can be sure that the push toward alternatives is likely to accelerate.

The editors and authors of this book demonstrate just how often and how well learning goes on beyond institutional walls. The learning documented and theorized here bears qualities of generativity, inclusion, and dynamism that is difficult to maintain within institutions of formal education. But most important, though only a beginning, these accounts illustrate possibilities of extension and expansion. Much more can, and indeed must, be done to guide communities toward taking responsibility for ensuring healthy, challenging learning as part of everyday life. Entire nations, such as England, and numerous communities, such as those engaged in the international learning communities movement, have already moved ahead to ensure that learning has no physical or temporal boundaries. The capacity of this learning is certainly of great need in the United States for generating health awareness, information absorption and adaptation, and peaceful productive cooperation.

This book as a first step will, we hope, inspire not a march or any such regimented forward movement. Instead, an ideal response would be something more akin to a grand series of newly inspired dances, absorbing hikes, and pleasurable jaunts—the effects of which will be felt in the quickened pulse, broadened experience, and deepened curiosity of learners when they cross the thresholds of formal education.

Shirley Brice Heath
Bread Loaf School of English, Middlebury College
Departments of English and Linguistics, Stanford University

Introduction

Negotiating the Boundaries Between School and Non-School Literacies

GLYNDA HULL and KATHERINE SCHULTZ

School's out! School's out!
Teacher let the fools out!
No more pencils, no more books!
No more teacher's dirty looks!
    (Knapp & Knapp, 1976)

During the last two decades researchers from a range of disciplines have documented the considerable intellectual accomplishments of children, youth, and adults in out-of-school settings, accomplishments that often contrast with their poor school-based performance and suggest a different view of their potential as capable learners and doers in the world. Much of this work has dealt with the practice of mathematics—for example, young candy-sellers in Brazil who, despite being unschooled, develop flexible methods for arriving at correct answers to math problems important to their vending (Saxe, 1988; see also Cole, 1996). Worlds away, southern California suburbanites have shown a comparable competence in real-world arithmetic problem-solving—figuring out the best bargain in supermarkets or calculating precise portions as part of weight-watching activities (Lave, 1988). Like the children in South America, these adults provide the illusion of incompetence in their performance on formal tests of the same mathematical operations.

In literacy research, too, there has been much interest in recent years in documenting and analyzing the writing and reading activities that go on out of school, activities diverse in function, form, and purpose. Some of these studies have highlighted the kinds of writing that adults do as part of everyday life (Barton & Hamilton, 1998; Barton & Ivanic, 1991). Others have high-~~ted~~ the literacy-related activities that many adolescents do on their own, ~~ding~~ diaries and plays (e.g., Camitta, 1993; Finders, 1997), as well as the ~~acies~~ that accompany engagement in sports and hobbies (e.g., Mahiri, 1998). Some researchers, while also focusing on youth culture, have centered their analyses of literate activity on notions of "text" more broadly conceived—the graffiti produced by youth in gangs (Cintron, 1991), for example, or Internet-related surfing and chat (e.g., Cohen, 2000; Knobel, 1999; Lankshear, 1997). In addition to personal literacy practices and those that flourish in friendship or peer networks, some researchers have noted the high levels of literacy and language use that anchor a variety of community-based activities (e.g., Ball, 2000; Cushman, 1998; Heath & McLaughlin, 1993; Moss, 1994).

Others, notably Flower and colleagues (Flower, in preparation; Flower, Long, & Higgins, 2000) and Cole (e.g., Cole, 1996), have designed and organized theory-driven after-school programs. Others, researchers and teachers in the field of composition studies, have linked out-of-school literacy activities with in-school writing instruction, developing "service-learning" courses in which college students volunteer their time in a variety of organizations in exchange for real-world practice in writing (e.g., Adler-Kassner, Crooks, & Watters, 1997). Still another branch of out-of-school research on literacy has been attentive to the considerable pressures on recent immigrants to learn and put to use the literate practices of their adopted countries (e.g., Weinstein-Shr, 1993). And finally, first spurred by worries about the economy and then inspired by features of our "new capitalism," researchers and corporate leaders alike have become interested in the role of literacy in the context of work (e.g., Hart-Landsberg & Reder, 1997; Hull, Jury, Ziv, & Katz, 1996).

In this edited volume we feature research on literacy in out-of-school settings—homes, after-school programs, and community-based organizations—where literacy practices flourish. This work was conducted with children, youth, and adults in quite different contexts and cultural worlds—an after-school program in Chicago, a YMCA in the California Bay Area, a community center in Pittsburgh, and the homes of immigrants from Mexico and Cambodia—yet it shares a focus on non-school practices. Why, we have wanted to know, does literacy so often flourish out of school? We hope the chapters in this volume will begin to answer this question through their rich and detailed histories, descriptions, and analyses of literate activities.

A second goal of the book is to imagine a range of possible relationships between school and non-school contexts. Could research on literacy and out-of-school learning help us think again and anew about literacy teaching and learning in the schoolroom—in formal, "traditional" educational settings? And if so, how? Interest in research on out-of-school learning is currently keen, and we are beginning to have portraits of children and adults performing successfully in a variety of out-of-school tasks that they've not been able or eager to complete in the schoolroom. But we are troubled by a tendency we have noticed to build and reify a great divide between in school and out of school. Sometimes this dichotomy relegates all good things to out-of-school contexts and everything repressive to school. Sometimes it dismisses the engagement of children with non-school learning as merely frivolous or remedial or incidental. What we want to argue in this volume is that, rather than setting formal and informal education systems and contexts in opposition to each other, we might do well to look for overlap or complementarity or perhaps a respectful division of labor. Dewey (1899/1998) argued many years ago that there is much we can learn about successful pedagogies and curricula by foregrounding the relationship between formal education and ordinary life. "From the standpoint of the child," he observed, "the great waste in the school comes from his inability to utilize the experiences he gets outside of the school in any complete and free way within the school itself; while, on the other hand, he is unable to apply in daily life what he is learning at school" (pp. 76–78).

In this edited volume we bring together a number of researchers and educators who have made important contributions to understanding literacy learning through ethnographic or field-based studies in homes, community organizations, and after-school programs. The chapters pay particular attention to instances in which adults, youth, and children engage successfully in language and literacy practice and performance out of school. Yet they don't romanticize out-of-school contexts, but try instead to acknowledge the complexities, tensions, and opportunities that are often born there—when, to take one example, participants from different cultural worlds come together to learn, work, and play in after-school organizations. To signal the importance of building bridges between school, home, and community, we include responses to each chapter by classroom teachers and teacher educators. We intend these responses to shed light on what seems noteworthy or problematic to school-based educators about research on literacy out-of-school.

The Organization of This Book

The collection begins with two introductory chapters jointly written by the editors. Despite the fact that there exists a growing body of research on literacy in a variety of out-of-school contexts, to our knowledge no one has yet synthesized this work. The first chapter reviews three theoretical traditions that have significantly informed research on literacy in out-of-school settings: the ethnography of communication; Vygotskian perspectives and activity theory; and the New Literacy Studies. We report here on our discovery that most of the conceptual advances in thinking about literacy in the last two decades have come from research on out-of-school literacy. The second chapter features recent research with children, adolescents, and adults engaged in literacy-related, non-school-based activities. We use vignettes drawn from this research to test the boundaries between out-of-school and in-school literacy and to draw attention to tensions, complementarity, overlap, and possible divisions of labor.

Part II, Literacy at Home and in the Community, begins with a chapter by Ellen Skilton-Sylvester that features her 3 years of comparative participant observation in homes and schools. Skilton-Sylvester highlights the striking differences between the home literacy practices of a Cambodian girl and her writing at school in order to reveal the often hidden and untapped linguistic and social resources of immigrant students. Situating this examination of literacy, peer culture, and identity within the context of the Cambodian refugee experience, Skilton-Sylvester describes Nan's home literacies. Rather than arguing that there is a mismatch between home and school cultures, Skilton-Sylvester suggests that Nan chose popularity rather than academic success at the same time that she brought to school abundant, but largely unnoticed, capabilities. She concludes by outlining some of the ways in which teachers might discover their students' invisible resources in the context of a peer culture that can mitigate against academic success.

Chapter 4, by Juan C. Guerra and Marcia Farr, describes the writing of two Mexicanas who are part of a social network the two researchers came to know over the course of 10 years of research and collaboration. They examine spiritual and autobiographical writings in order to reveal and understand cross-cultural misunderstandings in college composition classrooms. Guerra and Farr conclude with a discussion of the possibilities for writing classrooms, suggesting that instructors both respect students' approaches and insist on essayist literacy in place of taking just one of these stances. In addition, they argue for the development of a more flexible conception of academic writing.

Part III, Literacy in After-School Programs, begins with a chapter by Elenore Long, Wayne C. Peck, and Joyce A. Baskins in which they offer a model for the use of computer technology in community centers, one which has at its heart building human capacity and fostering community renewal. They call their model STRUGGLE, and they introduce it through their work with community members at a modern-day settlement house in Pittsburgh. Like many community activists, Long, Peck, and Baskins worry about the "digital divide" that separates lower-income communities from many of the resources associated with an information age, but we find their conception of how to cross that divide as different from standard fare as it is lyrical and thoughtful. Drawing variously on recent notions of cultural production theory, a Freirean-inspired commitment to personal and social transformation, and cognitively oriented research on rhetoric and problem-solving, they interweave portraits of young people and adults who come together "at the table" to shape responses to both personal and community dilemmas. Writing, they remind us, is at the heart of STRUGGLE, although the tool itself is an example of multimedia computer technology. Long, Peck, and Baskins thus offer an example of community-based literacy practices that build on both university-inspired research and community talents and resources, and that move young people toward views of themselves as agents of their own life choices.

The Fifth Dimension is an after-school "activity system" initially developed by Mike Cole and his colleagues at the University of California, San Diego, to bring computer technologies into after-school settings in a manner carefully organized to support students' academic growth, especially literacy. It has spread to sites across the United States and internationally, including, as Gillian Dowley McNamee and Sarah Sivright show us in Chapter 6, an after-school computer lab serving African American children in Chicago. These authors focus on writing development and explore how children who were struggling in school benefited from participation in written dialogues with peers across a variety of contexts and under the guidance of a playful and caring adult figure known as "the Wizard." Drawing on test scores and qualitative case studies based on a year of data collection, McNamee and Sivright concluded that this instantiation of the Fifth Dimension, with its incorporation of play and its attention to the personal interests of the children, supported children's literacy learning across multiple dimensions. However, their chapter also reveals the many complexities and challenges of helping children develop their voices through writing after school.

Ellen Cushman and Chalon Emmons use their fieldwork at a San Francisco Bay Area YMCA to characterize those literacies that resulted when college students and children worked and played together and developed relationships of mutual trust and support. The instructors of a university-based course, Cushman and Emmons describe their efforts to promote stronger connections between their campus and a nearby community by giving children in an after-school program access to material, informational, and human resources, and by encouraging them to imagine a variety of futures and selves. Introducing readers both to undergraduates and to children from the Y, they offer a winsome portrait of the resulting collaborations and relationships, but they also highlight the tensions that arose—the pull in one direction, for example, to teach "standard" English, and in the other, to encourage children's creativity. Running as a thread through this chapter is the authors' construct of "hybrid literacies," a term they use to refer to the literacy practices developed by the children and the undergraduates. These hybrid literacies, say Cushman and Emmons, combine elements of oral and written discourse, multiple genres, and several forms of representation. Most importantly, they stand apart by giving primacy to social relationships; that is, literacy provided occasions for young people from different worlds to come to know and learn from each other.

In sum, Part I is our review of theory and research on out-of-school literacy, and Parts II and III, researchers' reports of their recent after-school or out-of-school research and teachers' and other educators' responses to that work. We hope in these chapters to have crossed boundaries between school and non-school understandings of literacies. But, as Elyse Eidman-Aadahl shows us in the book's final chapter, there is another great divide to be bridged—that between policy and research and practice. In particular, she introduces us to policy perspectives on non-school time, youth organizations, and school–community partnerships. In so doing, she reveals how differently, to take one example, after-school time is represented in literacy studies as compared to policy debates, where arguments are cast in terms of the "productivity of youth" or the "value of discretionary time." She urges us, too, to consider carefully the need to develop mutually beneficial partnerships with community-based organizations and borrows Cushman and Emmons's conception of "hybrid literacies" in order to ask for "hybrid organizational work practices." And she warns, given the huge interest in after-school activities these days on the part of so many public and private agencies, that we may lose what makes after-school activities special, as standards and accountability packages seep from school to after-school sites. Yet Eidman-Aadahl's chapter is, in the end, optimistic, celebrating the wealth of opportunities available to those who wish to nurture partnerships with community-based organizations. Through the policy perspectives that she introduces in her chapter, she helps us approach those partnerships more thoughtfully in terms of understanding both constraints and possibilities.

Acknowledgments

This book began by means of a grant from the Research Foundation of the National Council of Teachers of English. We thank that organization for their early recognition of the growing interest in out-of-school literacy. Support for final preparation of the manuscript came via the National Academy of Education, and we gratefully acknowledge this timely aid. We also thank the University of California, Berkeley, for supporting our interest in including teacher's perspectives in this volume. Research assistance was provided by Julie Kalnin, Mira-Lisa Katz, and Deborah Stern, and we thank them for their most able work. This book developed over a long period of time, and many people influenced our thinking along the way. We especially want to acknowledge Fred Erickson, Linda Flower, Jim Gee, Shirley Brice Heath, Nancy Hornberger, Colin Lankshear, Mike Rose, and Brian Street for pivotal conversations. Ed Warshauer, David Paul, and Nora, Danny, and Jenna Paul-Schultz are experts at out-of-school thinking, and we thank them for their inspiration and their patience.

The childhood verse "School's Out" has been recited by generations of North American schoolchildren, and it captures something of their raucous joy in the freedom signaled by the school bell at the end of the day. In this book we celebrate that exuberance, but we also hope to funnel it back into the classroom. Thus we call for researchers and educators to reexamine the boundaries and dispositions that characterize the school/out-of-school divide and to reconfigure our taken-for-granted assumptions about what constitutes rich locations for literacy and learning.

References

Adler-Kassner, L., Crooks, R., & Watters, A. (Eds.). (1997). *Writing the community: Concepts and models for service-learning in composition*. Washington, DC: American Association for Higher Education.

Ball, A. (2000). Empowering pedagogies that enhance the learning of multicultural students. *Teachers College Record, 102*(6), 1006–1034.

Barton, D., & Hamilton, M. (1998). *Local literacies: Reading and writing in one community*. London: Routledge.

Barton, D., & Ivanic, R. (Eds.). (1991). *Writing in the community*. Newbury Park, CA: Sage.

Camitta, M. (1993). Vernacular writing: Varieties of literacy among Philadelphia high school students. In B. V. Street (Ed.), *Cross-cultural approaches to literacy* (pp. 228–246). Cambridge, UK: Cambridge University Press.

Cintron, R. (1991). Reading and writing graffiti: A reading. *The Quarterly Newsletter of the Laboratory of Comparative Human Cognition, 13*, 21–24.

Cohen, J. (2000, November). *Global links from the postindustrial heartland: Mexican American high school girls, literacy and the Internet*. Paper presented at the annual meeting of the American Anthropological Association, San Francisco.

Cole, M. (1996). *Cultural psychology: A once and future discipline*. Cambridge, MA: Harvard University Press.

Cushman, E. (1998). *The struggle and the tools: Oral and literate strategies in an inner city community*. Albany: State University of New York Press.

Dewey, J. (1998). School and society. In *Dewey on Education*. New York: Teachers College Press. (Original work published 1899)

Finders, M. J. (1997). *Just girls: Hidden literacies and life in junior high*. New York: Teachers College Press.

Flower, L. (in preparation). Talking across difference: An activity analysis of situated knowledge, conflict, and construction. In C. Bazerman & D. R. Russell (Eds.), *Activity and interactivity: A collection of research and theory*.

Flower, L., Long, E., & Higgins, L. (2000). *Learning to rival: The practice of intercultural inquiry*. Hillsdale, NJ: Erlbaum.

Heath, S. B., & McLaughlin, M. W. (1993). *Identity and inner-city youth: Beyond ethnicity and gender*. New York: Teachers College Press.

Hart-Landsberg, S., & Reder, S. (1997). Teamwork and literacy: Teaching and learning at Hardy Industries. In G. Hull (Ed.), *Changing work, changing workers: Critical perspectives on language, literacy, and skills* (pp. 359–382). Albany: State University of New York Press.

Hull, G., Jury, M., Ziv, O., & Katz, M. (1996). *Changing work, changing literacy: A study of skill requirements and development in a traditional and a reorganized workplace*. Final Report to the National Center for Research in Vocational Education and the Center for the Study of Writing and Literacy, Berkeley, CA.

Knapp, M., & Knapp, K. (1976). *One potato, two potato: The folklore of American children*. New York: Norton.

Knobel, M. (1999). *Everyday literacies: Students, discourse, and social practice*. New York: Peter Lang.

Lankshear, C. (1997). *Changing literacies*. Buckingham, UK: Open University Press.

Lave, J. (1988). *Cognition in practice: Mind, mathematics, and culture in everyday life*. Cambridge, UK: Cambridge University Press.

Mahiri, J. (1998). *Shooting for excellence: African American and youth culture in new century schools*. Urbana, IL: National Council of Teachers of English.

Moss, B. J. (Ed.). (1994). *Literacy across communities*. Cresskill, NJ: Hampton Press.

Saxe, G. B. (1988). Candy selling and math learning. *Educational Researcher*, August–September, pp. 14–21.

Weinstein-Shr, G. (1993). Literacy and social process: A community in transition. In B. V. Street (Ed.), *Cross-cultural approaches to literacy* (pp. 272–293). Cambridge, UK: Cambridge University Press.

Part I

FRAMING THE ISSUES

1

Locating Literacy Theory in Out-of-School Contexts

KATHERINE SCHULTZ and GLYNDA HULL

In public discourse, literacy has long been associated with schooling. Talk about literacy crises is often accompanied by calls for better schools and more rigorous curricula, and images of reading and writing are closely connected to school-based or essayist forms of literacy. However, when we widen the lens of what we consider literacy and literate activities, homes, communities, and workplaces become sites for literacy use. It was in fact in these out-of-school contexts, rather than in school-based ones, that many of the major theoretical advances in the study of literacy have been made in the past 25 years. Studies of literacy out-of-school have been pivotal in shaping the field. Indeed, to talk about literacy these days, both in school and out, is to speak of events, practices, activities, ideologies, discourses, and identities, and at times to do so almost unreflectively, since these categories and terminology have become so much a part of our customary ways of thinking in academic domains. Through an exploration of three major theoretical traditions that have launched numerous studies of literacy, we show that in large part this new theoretical vocabulary sprang from examinations of the uses and functions of literacy in contexts other than school.

The three theoretical perspectives that we treat in this chapter are the ethnography of communication (e.g., Heath, 1983; Taylor & Dorsey-Gaines, 1988), Vygotskian perspectives and activity theory (e.g., Engeström, 1998; Scribner & Cole, 1981), and the New Literacy Studies (e.g., Gee, 1996; Street, 1993a, 1993b). To be sure, these theoretical categories are not impermeable and current projects often draw on more than one of these traditions. For instance, a study might reflect both certain methodological insights from the ethnography of communication and also the interest in power relations made manifest by the New Literacy Studies. And in some important ways, the more recent theoretical points of view are made possible by, even draw their life from, the earlier ones. However, our categories do provide a useful historical lens for seeing more clearly the pivotal role played by studies of literacy out of school, and they serve as well as a heuristic for mapping the ever-growing territory of research and practice in out-of-school settings, a topic we turn to in Chapter 2.

One other caveat before we begin. There are some ways in which the distinction between in school and out of school sets up a false dichotomy. By foregrounding physical space (i.e., contexts outside the school house door) or time (i.e., after-school programs), we may ignore important conceptual dimensions that more readily account for successful learning or its absence. We may fail to see the presence of school-like practice at home (e.g., Street & Street, 1991) or non-school-like activities in the formal classroom. Such contexts are not sealed tight or boarded off; rather, one should expect to find, and one should look to account for, the movement from one context to the other.

In a related way, Cole (1995) calls our attention to a possible danger in treating the notion of context as a container, as that which surrounds and therefore, of necessity, causes or influences or shapes. Writing primarily about hierarchical levels, Cole worries about the tendency to see a larger context (i.e., the school) as determining the smaller (i.e., the classroom). But his comments can be extended to apply more simply to our case of the adjacent contexts of school and out of school. That is, in any analysis of out-of-school programs, we will want to avoid the temptation to oversimplify the creative powers of context—to assume that successful learning in an after-school program occurs merely or only because it occurs after school.

All of this said, school has come to be such a particular, specialized institution, with its own particular brand of learning (cf. Miettinen, 1999), that it does seem useful to set it in opposition to other institutions and different contexts for learning. Doing so will allow us to consider what we've grown accustomed to taking as natural and normal as actually an artifact of a particular kind of learning that is associated primarily with schooling.

The Ethnography of Communication

We turn first to a series of studies that take what is now known as a sociolinguistic perspective on literacy and schooling. These studies reflect the conceptual leap made by bringing anthropological and linguistic perspectives and research methods to the study of literacy. In the 1960s and 1970s, scholars from traditions outside of education, in particular anthropology and linguistics, looked beyond schools to family and community settings to understand how urban schools might reach students from cultural, socio-economic, and linguistic backgrounds that differed from the mainstream. Educators were concerned that students of color, especially those from low-income families, were not doing well in school. Up until that time, the most prevalent explanations for children's difficulties in school were deficit theories that blamed students and families. Anthropologists interested in the study of language and literacy in schools brought to the study of class-rooms a view of culture as "patterns in a way of life characteristic of a bounded social group and passed down from one generation to the next" (Eisenhart, in press, p. 4). This view of socialization and culture prompted researchers to look to settings outside of schools in order to understand the patterns of school success and school failure across groups of students.

In 1962 Dell Hymes and John Gumperz organized a panel for the American Anthropology Association that brought together researchers from the fields of linguistics and anthropology. In his introduction to the proceedings, Hymes (1964) urged linguists to study language in context and anthropologists to include the study of language in their description of cultures. Hymes proposed the concept of an "ethnography of communication," which would focus on the communicative patterns of a community and a comparison of these patterns across communities. Although Hymes intended the ethnography of communication to include writing and literacy, the early focus on speaking led many to believe his emphasis was on spoken language (Hornberger, 1995).

Then, in 1965, a group of scholars from a range of disciplines, including linguistics, anthropology, psychology, and education, were brought together by the Office of Education to examine the relationship between children's language and school success. Since this came in the midst of Lyndon Johnson's expansive Great Society programs, researchers were asked to consider why schools were failing "low-income and minority" children (Cazden, 1981). The conclusion reached by the group was that many "school problems" of "minority" students could be explained by discontinuities, specifically differences in language use, between a child's home and school communities (Cazden, John, & Hymes, 1972). As a result, the National Institute of Education funded a number of studies to examine these issues. A major finding from this initial work was that children socialized in diverse contexts come to school differentially prepared to respond to the demands of school. As a result they experience school differently, resulting in success for some and failure for others. Hymes's (e.g., 1974) notion of the communicative event, which included components such as the setting, participants, norms, and genres, became a useful framework for the documentation of language use, including literacy, in and out of school settings.

Following this initial work in language and speaking, Basso (1974) suggested that an ethnography of writing should be the centerpiece of ethnographies of communication. He called for studies of writing as it is distributed across a community rather than a single focus on the classroom. Basso introduced the term *writing event*, describing it as an act of writing and characterizing writing, like speaking, as a social activity. Building in turn on Basso's work and prefiguring the theory behind the New Literacy Studies (e.g., Gee, 1996; Street, 1993a), Szwed (1981) argued for an ethnography of literacy and proposed that, rather than a single continuum or level of literacy, we should imagine a variety of configurations or a plurality of literacies.

Although Basso's description seemed to arise out of an academic interest in bringing together sociolinguistics and anthropology, Szwed's focus on an ethnography of writing was a response to the "literacy crisis" of the 1980s. He suggested that despite the claims of a crisis of "illiteracy," we had not yet conceptualized literacy, nor did we know how literacy or reading and writing were used in social life. He linked his research interest directly to schools and explained that the definitions of reading (and we can add writing and speaking) that schools use may not take into account the reading a student does out of school. Thus he called for a study of the relationship between school and the world outside it and specified that the focus should be an inventory of one community's needs and resources. Szwed's call for the cataloguing of how and where literacy occurred in the community was the basis for many studies that sought to document empirically this new concept of multiple literacies (cf., Hornberger, 1995; Shuman, 1986; Weinstein-Shr, 1993; see also Chapters 3, 4, 7, this volume).

Around the same time, Heath (1981) signaled the importance of documenting the social history of writing, for which she coined the term *ethnohistory of writing*. Like Szwed, Heath made explicit links between writing in social or family settings and methods of writing instruction in school. Using preliminary data from what would become a pathbreaking ethnography, Heath described ethnographic research begun in response to complaints made by junior and senior high school teachers that it was impossible to teach students to write. According to the teachers, their classrooms were filled with students who planned to work in the textile mills, where reading and writing were not needed for work. Heath concluded that while there was a debate about how to teach writing in school, there was little systematic description of the functions of writing for specific groups of people. Her study suggested the possibility of using ethnographic studies of writing to reorganize schooling with potentially dramatic results. This early work, followed by her well-known study detailed later in this chapter

(Heath, 1983), supported the notion of teacher and student research and prompted both teachers and students to investigate the functions and uses of literacy in their communities in order to inform classroom practice.

Likewise, Hymes's (1981) ethnographic research funded by the National Institute of Education, which included Heath as a team member, used conversations with teachers about their difficulties in teaching language arts as a starting point. Researchers worked with teachers to uncover the dimensions of their difficulties with students and to understand students' perspectives on their school experiences. The researchers were quickly convinced that any investigation of school phenomena would require the study of classroom and school structures as well as those in children's homes and wider communities. This work became the core of Gilmore and Glatthorn's (1982) collection of educational ethnographies, *Children in and out of School*. Throughout the studies reported in this volume, schools were portrayed as cultures organized around a set of values and beliefs that frequently were not shared by the students and surrounding communities in which they are located. A major finding of this research was that children socialized in different contexts come to school differentially prepared to participate in school, which may result in failure—an argument now referred to as continuity–discontinuity theory (see Jacobs & Jordan, 1993). Heath (1982) explained in this volume that if education is seen as a process of cultural transmission, then formal schooling is only a part of this process. In her chapter on ethnography in education, Heath made an early argument for the need to study schools and classrooms in relation to the broader community or culture. She called for comprehensive, broad-based community studies.

Heath's (1983) long-term examination of and participation with three contiguous communities over a decade in the 1960s and 1970s illustrated how each community—a black working-class community, a white working-class community, and a racially mixed middle-class community—socialized their children into very different language practices. Heath documented each community's "ways with words" and found, for instance, that members of the white working-class community rarely used writing and generally viewed literacy as a tool to help them remember events and to buy and sell items. Although parents collected reading and writing materials so that children were surrounded by print, the parents rarely read themselves and used reading and writing mostly for functional purposes. In contrast, while residents of the black working-class community did not accumulate reading materials, reading was more seamlessly integrated into their daily activities and social interactions. Literacy was jointly accomplished in social settings.

Heath concluded that, "The place of language in the life of each social group [in these communities and throughout the world] is interdependent with the habits and values of behaving shared among members of that group" (1983, p. 11). When children from each of these communities entered school, only the middle-class students, whose language use was similar to that of the teachers, were successful. In this way, Heath demonstrated how children from each of these communities were differentially prepared for school, which promoted and privileged only middle-class ways of using language. This study inspired and paved the way for many other research projects, though most were not as extensive or long term as Heath's own work (e.g., Cochran-Smith, 1984; Gilmore, 1983; Weinstein-Shr, 1993). These studies helpfully documented both the functions and uses of literacy practices in various communities as well as the differential preparation children from different communities brought to school.

Begun as a turn away from schools and toward communities, Hymes's conception of the ethnography of communication gave researchers and educators a frame for noticing the resources students bring to school and provided teachers with a way to imagine changing their pedagogy and curricula rather than assuming students themselves had to adapt and change. Subsequently, many researchers began to catalogue and describe the ways in which young people used language in competent and, indeed, exciting ways, in and out of school, in a manner that their teachers might not have noticed or acknowledged. This work not only reframed and broadened conceptions of literacy, it also gave researchers a new lens for documenting learning in out-of-school contexts.

Vygotskian and Activity Theory Perspectives

If the ethnography of communication grew from the union of two fields—linguistics and anthropology—activity theory was born of the need to reimagine a third discipline, that of psychology. As richly documented in various accounts (e.g., Cole, 1996; Engeström, 1998; Wertsch, 1991), this effort has centered on theorizing about and investigating not the mind in isolation or the mind as automaton, but mind in society or culture in mind. Whereas ethnographies of communication took and continue to have as their main focus the role of language in learning, with a special emphasis on language differences in and out of school, activity theory chooses a different centerpiece, learning and human development. To be sure, activity theory had its origins in the work of the Soviet scholar Lev Vygotsky, who placed a premium on the role of language as the premier psychological tool. He gave pride of place as well to written language. But it is certainly the case that many researchers who adopt an activity theory perspective get along quite well without directing their research toward language or writing per se (cf.

Engeström, Miettinen, & Punamäki, 1999). This is because they are interested instead in honoring "activity" as a unit of analysis, an enterprise that might or might not include an analysis of sign-mediated communication per se as a principle concern.

Thus our discussion in this chapter of Vygotskian perspectives and activity theory represents but a small, if significant, slice of the pie: those pivotal theoretical studies that have examined literacy—literacy, that is, as part of integral units of human life, motivated by human goals, enacted in the course of everyday activities, especially beyond the school. We begin by briefly revisiting Vygotsky's ideas about the importance of writing, move next to attempts to test his claims empirically, and turn finally to a few projects that embody present-day formulations of activity theory. We ask, all the while, why these researchers have been interested in examining literacy out of school and what thereby they have learned.

Vygotsky believed that human sign systems, such as language, writing, and mathematics, have significant consequences for how we think and how we interact with the world. As the products of human history that emerge over time and vary in their nature and use from culture to culture, such sign systems, or psychological tools as Vygotsky called them, structure mental activity, mediating between thought and action and interaction. Writing, Vygotsky reasoned, is a sign system that is especially noteworthy for its far-reaching impacts on thinking. The effects of psychological tools such as writing will vary, he also wagered, depending on the nature of the symbol systems available at particular historical junctures and their uses in particular societies.

In the 1930s, with the help of Alexander Luria, Vygotsky saw the opportunity to test this theory by empirically investigating how intellectual functioning might be affected by cultural change. Mounting a major field-based research project, Luria traveled to Central Asia, where vast and rapid reforms were at that time in progress—reforms requiring nonliterate farmers to take part in collective ownership, for example, to use new agricultural technologies, and to acquire literacy through schooling. Luria found that the participants in his research did indeed respond differently to a variety of experimental tasks related to perception, classification, and reasoning, depending on their exposure to literacy and schooling. This he took as confirmation of Vygotsky's theory that cultural change affects thinking. But given the complexity of the setting, we might ask exactly which change impacted thinking—was it literacy, or schooling, or collective farming, or other major shifts in the organization of everyday life? It is impossible to say. Further, Luria seemed to put too much stock in certain culturally biased test materials, in particular the syllogisms that were for a long time a standard part of the cross-cultural researcher's experimental arsenal. He didn't, that is, take into account that such materials might merely measure an individual's familiarity with school-based types of tasks, rather than a person's ability to think abstractly or logically.

Thus a quick foray into the Soviet landscape of days gone by illustrates the preoccupation with literacy that was at the heart of Vygotsky's work, as well as aspects of his theorizing that still hold sway, especially his focus on writing as a mediational tool or the power of written language as an instrument for thinking. But the excursion also allows us to introduce the first important rationale within this tradition of work for juxtaposing school and non-school environments—that is, as a means (albeit often flawed) for ascertaining the effects of literacy/schooling on thought or cognitive development. If literacy is acquired in school, the reasoning went, and if adults and children differ in the amount of schooling to which they've been exposed, then whatever differences appear on tests of mental activity can be attributed to literacy—or at least to literacy coupled with schooling. A great deal of cross-cultural research during the 1960s was driven by just such reasoning. Although the majority of this work was limited by methodologies with a Western cultural bias, not to mention what now appears to be a naive faith in the efficacy of schooling, one within-culture comparison stands out both for its methodological savoir faire and its contribution to current conceptions of literacy: the monumental analysis of literacy among the Vai conducted by Scribner and Cole (1981).

In the early 1970s, at the same time that linguists and ethnographers had began to apply the approach called the ethnography of communication to problems of language difference in and out of school in the United States, psychologists Sylvia Scribner and Michael Cole were organizing a research project in Liberia. Hoping to pick up where Vygotsky's theorizing had left off, they devised an ambitious plan to investigate the cognitive consequences of literacy but to avoid the methodological confounds that marred Luria's work. In particular, Scribner and Cole drew on local cultural practices in designing the content of their experiments, and they also decoupled the effects of literacy from the effects of schooling. The latter they could accomplish handily, since the Vai boast the unusual distinction of having invented an original writing system, the learning of which takes place out of school. While classes in government-sponsored schools were taught in English, and Qur'anic study was conducted in Arabic, the Vai used their indigenous script for specialized purposes such as record-keeping and letter-writing. Thus this unusual patterning of languages, scripts, and acquisition practices made it possible to find people who were literate but had become so outside schooling, or who were literate through school and biliterate in two scripts acquired informally, and so on. Scribner and Cole's research team gathered ethnographic and survey-based descriptions of language and literacy use, and they also administered a complex battery of experimental tasks designed to tap the cognitive processes traditionally believed to be connected to literacy—abstraction, memorization, categorization, verbal explanation, and the like.

In a nutshell, Scribner and Cole did not find that literacy was responsible for great shifts in mental functioning of the sort the Soviets and many policy makers and educators expect even today. But they did demonstrate that particular writing systems and particular reading and writing activities foster particular, specialized forms of thinking. For example, Qur'anic literacy improved people's performance on certain kinds of memory tasks, whereas Vai script literacy gave people an edge in certain varieties of phonological discrimination. In addition to sorting out the specialized effects of particular literacies, Scribner and Cole identified the equally specialized effects of schooling in and of itself apart from literacy—namely, the enhanced ability of schooled people to offer certain kinds of verbal explanations.

It should be noted that in scaling down the grand claims often made about the effects of literacy on cognition, Scribner and Cole took care to note that Vai literacy was a restricted literacy; it served relatively few, and a noticeably narrow, range of functions. They also made clear that in societies where economic, social, and technological conditions converge to warrant the increased use of literacy, the potential exists for literacy to serve many more functions and therefore to be more deeply implicated in thinking processes. The current moment, we would point out, is just such a time, as communication via the Internet for economic, social, and personal purposes becomes more and more widespread. Yet if we have learned anything from Scribner and Cole, it should be that literacy is not literacy is not literacy. Specialized forms of reading and writing, both in school and out, have specialized and distinctive effects, even in an information age. Scribner and Cole were the very first to teach us this.

In fact, they were the first, to our knowledge, to introduce the now-omnipresent term *practice* as a way to conceptualize literacy. Recently Cole (1995) has written about the current popularity of terms such as *practice* in studies of cognitive development. He attributes this popularity, as well as that of related terms such as *activity, context,* and *situation,* to a widespread desire these days to move beyond a focus on the individual person as a unit for psychological analysis. Cole has also traced the theoretical origins of this new language (1995, 1996). Looking back to Marx, for example, he explains that the notion of practice was a way to get around the separation of the mental and the material. Consulting post-Marxist social theorists such as Giddens (1979), he reminds us that "practice" has also been offered as a construct that avoids the impasse of agency versus determinism.

In *The Psychology of Literacy*, Scribner and Cole (1981) did not reveal the theoretical etymology of their use of the term *practice*. But they did explain in some detail the framework they constructed to interpret their data, a framework centered on the notion of "practice." They defined a practice as "a recurrent, goal-directed sequence of activities using a particular technology and particular systems of knowledge" (p. 236). Literacy, as a socially organized practice, "is not simply knowing how to read and write a particular script but applying this knowledge for specific purposes in specific contexts of use" (p. 236). It follows that, "in order to identify the consequences of literacy, we need to consider the specific characteristics of specific practices" (p. 237).

Central to a plurality of literacies is the notion of practice, with its emphasis on purpose within context and the patterned interplay of particular skills, knowledge, and technologies. Within the Vygotskian tradition, research on out-of-school literacy sprang from the desire to contrast the schooled, and their presumed literacy-enhanced cognitive capabilities, with the non-schooled, who were suspected of thinking differently. Aware of the pitfalls of the tradition of cross-cultural research, Scribner and Cole redirected such efforts through a complex and culturally sensitive research design, and thereby they also changed our thinking in literacy studies. Like ethnographers of communication, they helped the field understand literacy as a multiple rather than a unitary construct, calling attention to the distinctive literacies that can exist beyond the schoolhouse door.

Scribner and Cole's project is an example of early research within a then-burgeoning activity theory perspective (cf. Scribner, 1987). In subsequent years Scribner turned her attention to a major non-school endeavor, that of work, while Cole became invested in establishing sustainable after-school activity systems for children that juxtapose learning and play (see Chapter 6, this volume). In both their new research agendas, Scribner and Cole were interested in studying not the isolated mental tasks that were thought (erroneously) to be elicited by means of laboratory experiments, but thinking as part of ongoing activity. Activities, we learn from the theory by the same name, serve larger goals and life purposes, rather than as ends in themselves.

Thus it makes sense from this theoretical perspective to study thinking as part of a dominant life activity—such as school—but more significantly for our purposes in this essay, as part of play or work. As Scribner pointed out, we would be quite remiss were our accounts of human development to ignore entire realms of activity. For example, "While we are certainly not wholly defined through our participation in society's labor, it is unlikely we can fully understand the life cycle of development without examining what adults do when they work" (1997, p. 299). At its very core, then, activity theory reminds us to look not just in school and in research laboratories but outside them, always with the goal of capturing "human mental functioning and development in the full richness of its social and artifactual texture" (Cole, Engeström, & Vasquez, 1997, p. 13). For literacy, this perspective opens the door to studies of reading, writing, and speaking within the context of a panoply of activities, activities themselves motivated by larger purposes and aims than literacy itself.

The New Literacy Studies

Located at the crossroads of sociolinguistic and anthropological theories of language and schooling and ethnographic and discourse methodologies is the recently conceptualized field of the New Literacy Studies (NLS) (Gee, 1996; Street, 1993a). Characterized by their focus on an understanding of literacies as multiple and situated within social and cultural practices and discourses, these studies point to the central role of power. As compared to the emphasis on language, learning, writing, and development in the studies reviewed in the first two sections, the NLS research has as its focus literacy and discourse. Like the other two theoretical traditions, the New Literacy Studies are noteworthy for their emphasis on literacy in out-of-school contexts. New Literacy Studies build on the ethnographic tradition of documenting literacy in local communities, often adding an analysis of the interplay between the meanings of local events and a structural analysis of broader cultural institutions and practices. Gee, a linguist who has been central to this field, situates the New Literacy Studies—together with the ethnography of communication and studies based on activity theory— within a group of movements that have taken a "social turn" from a focus on the study of individuals to an emphasis on social and cultural interaction (Gee, 2000). He points out that while these movements claim that meaning (or writing or literacy) is always situated, they often fail to articulate the mutually constitutive nature of their contexts.

Most work done under the banner of the New Literacy Studies takes "literacy" as its central unit of analysis. But Gee introduced and popularized a broader category, "discourse," which he defines as "ways of behaving, interacting, valuing, thinking, believing, speaking, and often reading and writing that are accepted as instantiations of particular roles (or 'types of people') by specific *groups* of people. . . . [Discourses] are, thus, always and everywhere *social* and products of social histories" (Gee, 1996, p. viii, emphasis in original). Gee explains further that people use discourses to affiliate and display their membership in particular social groups. Discourses are, in effect, an "identity kit" or a group of behaviors, activities and beliefs that are recognizable by others. Discourses are inherently ideological and, like literacies, are embedded in social hierarchies and reflect the distribution of power. The NLS research often explores the ways in which individual identities, social relationships, and institutional structures are instantiated and negotiated through what people say and do with texts (Maybin, 2000). Gee's discussion of Discourses provides a frame for understanding the connections among literacy, culture, identity, and power. By virtue of turning our gaze to the larger construct of "Discourse," and insisting that literacy is always about more than literacy, Gee's framework draws our attention away from a solitary focus on learning and language use in school settings and positions us to understand learning, literacy, and identity construction in and out of schools and across the life span.

While Gee illustrates how the term *literacy* can be limiting, Street (e.g., 1993a; 1995; Street & Street, 1991) has argued that schooling and pedagogy constrain our conceptions of literacy practices. Street defines literacy as an ideological practice, rather than a set of neutral or technical skills as it is traditionally conceived in schools, adult literacy programs, and mass literacy campaigns (Street 1984, 1993a, 1993b, 1995). Rather than focusing on neutral bits of information, this conception of literacy highlights its embedded or social nature. Thus, according to Street, Western notions of school or academic literacy are one form of literacy among many literacies.

Street's theoretical conceptualization of the New Literacy Studies is derived from his fieldwork in Iran in the early 1970s (1984, 1995). Through a careful examination of and participation in village life, Street identifies three different kinds of literacy practices used by youth and adults in the village where he resided. These include what he terms "maktab" literacy, or literacy associated with Islam and taught in the local Qur'anic schools; "commercial" literacy, or the reading and writing used for the management of fruit sales in the local village; and school literacy, associated with the state schools recently built in both villages and urban areas. Although teaching and learning in the religious schools was based on memorizing portions of religious text and traditional teaching methods, there were local reading groups connected to the "maktab" schools that gathered at members' homes to read passages from the Qur'an and commentary on it, in order to generate discussions and interpretation. Thus Street, through close examination of literacy and learning in the context of village life and culture, paints a portrait that differs from the conventional descriptions of religious training in Islamic schools as consisting exclusively of rote memorization.

Street describes the ways in which the skills students learned through this "maktab" literacy were hidden in relation to Western notions of literacy. Children and adults educated in this manner were considered "illiterate" as compared to those educated in the state schools designed to prepare youth for jobs in the modern sector. However, according to Street, the skills connected with "maktab" literacy were a preparation for the "commercial" literacy that, as it turned out, were key to economic success during the early 1970s, when oil production resulted in an economic expansion. During this time, many students who went to the state-run schools in urban areas found themselves without work, while their peers, educated in the "backward" villages and drawing on their "maktab" literacy practices, prospered from their work selling fruit.

This study, along with others in the NLS tradition, connects microanalyses of language and literacy use with macroanalyses of discourse and power. It also points to the dangers of reifying schooled notions of literacy. As scholars in this field contend, and this study exemplifies, literacy must be studied in its social, cultural, historical, economic, and political contexts both in school and out (Gee, 1996, 2000). In this study Street articulates a conception of literacy as tied to social practices and ideologies, such as economic, political, and social conditions; social structures; and local belief systems. He connects the literacy practices with identity and social positions in a manner that contrasts sharply with the dominant discourse about literacy. He uses his theory, grounded in anthropological research, to argue for research that makes visible the "complexity of local, everyday, community literacy practices," or literacies outside of school settings (Street, 2001).

Over the years, Street has repeatedly raised the question: When there are so many different types of literacy practices, why is it that school literacy has come to be seen as the defining form of reading and writing? He describes the "pedagogization" of literacy, or the defining of literacy solely in terms of school-based notions of teaching and learning while marginalizing other forms of literacy (Street & Street, 1991). This contrasts with historical evidence that suggests that in the past literacy was associated with social institutions outside of school (Street & Street, 1991; see also Cook-Gumperz, 1986). For instance, educated middle-class women in seventeenth-century China wrote poems as a way to construct a community of women (Yin-yee Ko, 1989, cited in Street & Street, 1991). Historically, and across cultural contexts, women have used literacy in informal, nonreligious, and nonbureaucratic domains (Heller, 1997; Rockhill, 1993; Street & Street, 1991). Street and Street (1991) argue that these uses of writing have been marginalized and destroyed by modern Western literacy "with its emphasis on formal, male, and schooled aspects of communication" (p. 146). One conclusion from this analysis is that rather than focusing on the continuities and discontinuities between home and school in ethnographic research, there is a need to focus on ethnographies of literacies more broadly and to document, as the authors do, the ways that school imposes a version of literacy on the outside world (Street & Street, 1991).

Extending Street's (1984, 1995, 1996) framework, Barton and colleagues demonstrate the importance of carefully documenting literacy in everyday lives. Through work conducted primarily in Lancaster, England, they illustrate how everyday literacies involve various media and symbol systems, and they document how different literacies are associated with particular cultures and domains of life within the cultures. Rather than locating literacy solely within the life of individuals, they emphasize the ways in which families and local communities regulate and are regulated by literacy practices (Barton, 1991, 1994; Barton & Hamilton, 1998; Clark & Ivanic, 1997).

In a similar vein, Prinsloo and Breier (1996) have drawn from the theoretical perspectives lent by the New Literacy Studies to look for the meanings of everyday literacy practices in a wide range of contexts in South Africa. Like Street's (1984) early research in Iran, these studies point to the disjuncture between local practices and the new adult literacy programs begun in the post-apartheid era. The authors seek to describe the practices undertaken by people who might be considered "illiterate" by school or state standards. Consonant with the New Literacy Studies, their work documents what people actually accomplish with literacy, rather than judging them as deficient (Street, 1996), and presses for a reconceptualization of literacy that takes it out of the context of school and into the context of local practices (Prinsloo & Breier, 1996).

Most recently, Barton and colleagues have emphasized the interplay of structure and agency, focusing on insiders' perspectives of what constitutes local practices and the ways in which these practices reflect and shape social structures (Barton, Hamilton, & Ivanic, 2000). This focus on the term *literacy practices* draws from the anthropological tradition to describe ways of acting and behaving that reflect power positions and structures. Street (2001) makes a distinction between practices and events, explaining that one could photograph an event but not a practice. Literacy practices, according to Street, embody folk models and beliefs, while events might be repeated occurrences or instances in which interaction surrounds the use of text (cf. Barton & Hamilton, 2000). Hornberger (2001) offers a useful distinction between literacy practices and literacy events, explaining that the reading of a bedtime story in middle-class U.S. homes is a literacy event (Heath, 1986), while these individual and repeated events are explained and undergirded by a set of literacy practices or conventions and beliefs about the value of reading to young children, assumptions about parent–child relationships, normative routines around bedtime, and the like.

It is important to note that, while studies growing from an activity theory tradition and those taking the NLS as a starting point both use the term *practice*, the usage is different in important ways. In Scribner and Cole's early work, for example, *practice* explicitly includes notions of skill, technology, and knowledge as well as patterned activity. In the NLS, on the other hand, the focus is clearly on the ways in which activity is infused by ideology, and there is little interest in specifying the cognitive dimensions of social practices. Thus recent literacy theorists often employ the term *practice* in a narrower sense that is consonant with their focus on culture, ideology, and power, though this specialized use of the term is usually not acknowledged.

While literacy theorists have worked to conceptualize the New Literacy Studies, there has been a parallel and, at times, overlapping focus by researchers and practitioners in an area captured by the term *critical literacy*.[1] Predating the work in New Literacy Studies, much of this field is directly related to schools and pedagogy rather than to everyday practice. While both share a commitment to defining literacy in relation to power and identity, critical literacy has a stronger focus on praxis and schooling. Luke and Freebody (1997) recently defined critical literacy as "a coalition of educational interests committed to engaging with the possibilities that the technologies of writing and other modes of inscription offer for social change, cultural diversity, economic equity, and political enfranchisement" (p. 1). This tradition, noteworthy for its explicit political agenda, owes the most to Paulo Freire (e.g., 1970; Freire & Macedo, 1987), whose teaching methods have been central to several national literacy campaigns around the world. Freire's focus was on the ways in which education and literacy should support people to question and shape their worlds. As he explains, "Reading the world always precedes reading the word, and reading the word implies continually reading the world . . . [and] transforming it by means of conscious practical work" (Freire & Macedo, 1987, p. 35).

Although much of the work in the area of critical literacy is located in school contexts, it has clear implications for thinking about (and rethinking) literacy out-of-school (see Chapter 5, this volume). For instance, Lankshear and Knobel (1997) propose a rereading and rewriting of our impoverished notions of citizenship in order to produce a new discourse of active citizenship that enables students to understand their social positionings in relation to their identity formation and subjectivities. Lankshear and Knobel describe how this new discourse might look in an English class, but their formulation has implications for learning more broadly construed.

In 1996, a group of scholars from the United States, England, and Australia met and spent the following year in dialogue to develop a way of talking about the social context of literacy learning, including the content and form of literacy pedagogy. Calling themselves the New London Group (after the site of their first meeting in New London, New Hampshire), they built this dialogue in part on notions developed by researchers and practitioners identifying themselves with the critical literacy and New Literacy Studies movements as well as researchers from a range of disciplines. Their findings can be summed up by their central term—*multiliteracies*—that signals multiple communication channels, hybrid text forms, new social relations, and the increasing salience of linguistic and cultural diversity. As they explain, "Multiliteracies also creates a different kind of pedagogy, one in which language and other modes of meaning are dynamic representational resources, constantly being remade by their users as they work to achieve their various cultural purposes" (New London Group, 1996, p. 64). In their discussion of multiliteracies and the implications of what Gee and his colleagues have termed "fast capitalism" (Gee, Hull, & Lankshear, 1996), Luke and Freebody (1997) raise persistent questions about who will get access to the new forms of writing and representations and how the traditional fractures of race, culture, class, gender, and sexuality will get reinscribed. As they explain:

> The challenge then is not just one of equity of access (or lack of access) to such technologies and institutions, but also of the possibilities of using discourse and literacy to reinvent institutions, to critique and reform the rules for the conversion of cultural and textual capital in communities and workplaces, and to explore the possibilities of heteroglossic social contracts and hybrid cultural actions. The challenge is about what kinds of citizenship, public forums for discourse and difference are practicable and possible. (p. 9)

Gee and colleagues (1996) take up this challenge in their recent book, *The New Work Order*. They extend the notion of literacy as social practices to include their concept of sociotechnical practices, which they describe as "the design of technology and social relations within the workplace to facilitate productivity and commitment, sometimes in highly 'indoctrinating' ways" (p. 6). These researchers go on to write that while old forms and organizational structures of work may have been alienating, new workplaces are asking workers to invest themselves in their work, merging public and private lives, in ways that might be considered coercive. They raise a number of provocative questions that suggest a blurring of the lines separating literate practices in and out of school. These questions include: "How should we construe learning and knowledge in general in a world where the new capitalism progressively seeks to define what counts as learning and knowledge in a 'knowledge economy' made up of 'knowledge workers' doing 'knowledge work'" (p. 23)?

The New Literacy Studies thus focus our attention to the shifting landscape of home, community, work, and schools and give us a language and set of theoretical constructs for describing the close connections between literacy practices and identities. Perhaps more than any other theoretical tradition, the NLS have embraced out-of-school contexts, almost to the exclusion of looking in schools, and have unabashedly valued out-of-school literacy practices as distinct from those associated with schools. At the same time, the close description of literacy practices in out-of-school contexts and the concurrent focus on how these practices are shaped by power and ideology lead us to look with fresh eyes at what kinds of literacy we teach in school and what we count as literate practices.

What would our conceptions of literacy be like had researchers such as Hymes, Heath, Scribner, Cole, Street, and Gee never ventured in their formulations outside of schools, either literally or figuratively? We believe that our understandings of literacy, literacy learning, and literacy "problems" would be narrower, less helpful and generative. We suspect that what we now acknowledge as appreciable differences in home and school language and literacy practices, we might still treat, knee-jerk fashion, as a lack or a deficit. We might yet be content to see literacy in monochrome, as singular, as neutral, as just a skill. We would surely be less savvy about the rainbow of literate practices that color the world and less aware of how, as social practices, literacies come stitched tight with activities, identities, and discourses. In the next chapter, in order to provide particular, on-the-ground instances of these and other theoretical insights, as well as to think through their implications, we turn to recent research in the traditions of the ethnography of literacy, activity theory, and the New Literacy Studies.

Note

1. We don't review here but want to acknowledge the important scholarship associated with "critical discourse analysis," a field that, like the critical literacy area, is politically alert but uses the tools of discourse analysis to critique and challenge dominant institutional practices. See, for example, Fairclough (1995).

References

Barton, D. (1991). The social nature of writing. In D. Barton & R. Ivanic (Eds.), *Writing in the community* (pp. 1–13). Newbury Park, CA: Sage.

Barton, D. (1994). *Literacy: An introduction to the ecology of written language.* Oxford, UK: Blackwell.

Barton, D., & Hamilton, M. (1998). *Local literacies: Reading and writing in one community.* London: Routledge.

Barton, D., & Hamilton, M. (2000). Literacy practices. In D. Barton, M. Hamilton, & R. Ivanic (Eds.), *Situated literacies: Reading and writing in context* (pp. 180–196). London: Routledge.

Barton, D., Hamilton, M., & Ivanic, R. (2000). *Situated literacies: Reading and writing in context.* London: Routledge.

Basso, K. (1974). The ethnography of writing. In R. Bauman & J. Sherzer (Eds.), *Explorations in the ethnography of speaking* (pp. 425–432). Cambridge, UK: Cambridge University Press.

Cazden, C. B. (1981). Four comments. In D. H. Hymes (Ed.), *Ethnographic monitoring of children's acquisition of reading/language arts skills in and out of the classroom.* Final report for the National Institute of Education, Philadelphia.

Cazden, C. B., John, V. P., & Hymes, D. (Eds.). (1972). *Functions of language in the classroom.* New York: Teachers College Press.

Clark, R., & Ivanic, R. (1997). *The politics of writing.* London: Routledge.

Cochran-Smith, M. (1984). *The making of a reader.* Norwood, NJ: Ablex.

Cole, M. (1995). The supra-individual envelope of development: Activity and practice, situation and context. In J. J. Goodnow, P. J. Miller, & F. Kessel (Eds.), *Cultural practices as contexts for development* (pp. 105–118). San Francisco: Jossey-Bass.

Cole, M. (1996). *Cultural psychology: A once and future discipline.* Cambridge, MA: Harvard University Press.

Cole, M., Engeström, Y., & Vasquez, O. (1997). Introduction. In M. Cole, Y. Engeström, & O. Vasquez (Eds.), *Mind, culture, and activity: Seminal papers from the Laboratory of Comparative Human Cognition* (pp. 1–21). Cambridge, UK: Cambridge University Press.

Cook-Gumperz, J. (1986). Literacy and schooling: An unchanging equation? In J. Cook-Gumperz (Ed.), *The social construction of literacy* (pp. 16–44). Cambridge, UK: Cambridge University Press.

Eisenhart, M. (in press). Changing conceptions of culture and ethnographic methodology: Recent thematic shifts and their implications for research on teaching. In V. Richardson (Ed.), *The handbook of research on teaching* (4th ed.). New York: Macmillan.

Engeström, Y. (1998, April). *Distinguishing individual action and collective activity in the study of organizational literacy.* Paper presented at the annual meeting of the American Educational Research Association, San Diego.

Engeström, Y., Miettinen, R., & Punamäki, R-L. (Eds.). (1999). *Perspectives on activity theory.* Cambridge, UK: Cambridge University Press.

Fairclough, N. (1995). *Critical discourse analysis: The critical study of language.* New York: Longman.

Freire, P. (1970). *Pedagogy of the oppressed* (M. B. Ramos, Trans.). New York: Seabury Press.

Freire, P., & Macedo, D. (1987). *Literacy: Reading the word and the world.* South Hadley, MA: Bergin & Garvey.

Gee, J. P. (1996). *Social linguistics and literacies: Ideology in discourses* (2nd ed.). London: Falmer.

Gee, J. P. (2000). New people in new worlds: Networks, the new capitalism and schools. In B. Cope & M. Kalantzis (Eds.), *Multiliteracies: Literacy learning and the design of social futures* (pp. 43–68). London: Routledge.

Gee, J. P., Hull, G., & Lankshear, C. (1996). *The new work order: Behind the language of the new capitalism.* Boulder: Westview.

Giddens, A. (1979). *Central problems in social theory: Action, structure, and contradiction in social analysis.* Berkeley: University of California Press.

Gilmore, P. (1983). Spelling "Mississippi": Recontextualizing a literacy event. *Anthropology and Education Quarterly, 14*(4), 235–256.

Gilmore, P., & Glatthorn, A. A. (Eds.). (1982). *Children in and out of school: Ethnography and education.* Washington, DC: Center for Applied Linguistics.

Heath, S. B. (1981). Ethnography in education. In D. Hymes (Ed.), *Ethnographic monitoring of children's acquisition of reading/language arts skills in and out of the classroom* (pp. 33–55). Final report for the National Institute of Education, Philadelphia.

Heath, S. B. (1982). Protean shapes in literacy events: Ever-shifting oral and literate traditions. In D. Tannen (Ed.), *Spoken and written language: Exploring orality and literacy* (pp. 91–118). Norwood, NJ: Ablex.

Heath, S. B. (1983). *Ways with words.* New York: Cambridge University Press.

Heath, S. B. (1986). What no bedtime story means: Narrative skills at home and school. In B. Schieffelen & E. Ochs (Eds.), *Language socialization across cultures* (pp. 97–115). Cambridge, UK: Cambridge University Press.

Heller, C. E. (1997). *Until we are strong together: Women writers in the Tenderloin.* New York: Teachers College Press.

Hornberger, N. H. (1995). Ethnography in linguistic perspective: Understanding school processes. *Language and Education, 9*(4), 233–248.

Hornberger, N. H. (2001). Afterword: Multilingual literacies, literacy practices and the continua of biliteracy. In K. Jones & M. Martin-Jones (Eds.), *Multilingual literacies: Reading and writing different worlds* (pp. 353–367). Amsterdam: John Benjamins.

Hymes, D. (1964). Introduction: Toward ethnographies of communication. In J. J. Gumperz & D. Hymes (Eds.), *The ethnography of communication* (pp. 1–34). Washington, DC: American Anthropological Association.

Hymes, D. (1974). *Foundations of sociolinguistics.* Philadelphia: University of Pennsylvania Press.

Hymes, D., (1981). *Ethnographic monitoring of children's acquisition of reading/language arts skills in and out of the classroom.* Final report for the National Institute of Education, Philadelphia.

Jacobs, E., & Jordan, C. (Eds.). (1993). *Minority education: Anthropological perspectives.* Norwood, NJ: Ablex.

Lankshear, C., & Knobel, M. (1997). Critical literacy and active citizenship. In S. Muspratt, A. Luke, & P. Freebody (Eds.), *Constructing critical literacies: Teaching and learning textual practice* (pp. 95–124). Cresskill, NJ: Hampton.

Luke, A., & Freebody, P. (1997). Critical literacy and the question of normativity: An introduction. In S. Muspratt, A. Luke, & P. Freebody (Eds.), *Constructing critical literacies: Teaching and learning textual practice* (pp. 1–18). Cresskill, NJ: Hampton.

Maybin, J. (2000). The New Literacy Studies: Context, intertextuality and discourse. In D. Barton, M. Hamilton, & R. Ivanic (Eds.), *Situated literacies: Reading and writing in context* (pp. 197–209). London: Routledge.

Miettinen, R. (1999). Transcending traditional school learning: Teachers' work and networks of learning. In Y. Engeström, R. Miettinen, & R.-L. Punamäki (Eds.), *Perspectives on activity theory* (pp. 325–344). Cambridge, UK: Cambridge University Press.

New London Group. (1996). A pedagogy of multiliteracies: Designing social futures. *Harvard Educational Review, 66*(1), 60–92.

Prinsloo, M., & Breier, M. (1996). *The social uses of literacy: Theory and practice in contemporary South Africa.* Bertsham, South Africa: SACHED Books.

Rockhill, K. (1993). Gender, language and the politics of literacy. In B. V. Street (Ed.), *Cross-cultural approaches to literacy* (pp. 156–175). Cambridge, UK: Cambridge University Press.

Scribner, S. (1997). Mind in action: Some characteristics of practical thought. In E. Tobach, R. J. Falmagne, M. B. Parlee, L. M. W. Martin, & A. S. Kapelman (Eds.), *Mind and social practice: Selected writings of Sylvia Scribner* (pp. 296–307). Cambridge, UK: Cambridge University Press.

Scribner, S., & Cole, M. (1981). *The psychology of literacy.* Cambridge, MA: Harvard University Press.

Shuman, A. (1986). *Storytelling rights: The uses of oral and written texts among urban adolescents.* Cambridge, UK: Cambridge University Press.

Street, B. V. (1984). *Literacy in theory and practice.* Cambridge, UK: Cambridge University Press.

Street, B. V. (1993a). (Ed.). *Cross-cultural approaches to literacy.* New York: Cambridge University Press.

Street, B. V. (1993b). The new literacy studies: Guest editorial. *Journal of Research in Reading, 16*(2), 81–97.

Street, B. V. (1995). *Social literacies: Critical approaches to literacy in development, ethnography and education.* London: Longman.

Street, B. V. (1996). Preface. In M. Prinsloo & M. Breier (Eds.), *The social uses of literacy: Theory and practice in contemporary South Africa* (pp. 1–9). Bertsham, South Africa: SACHED Books.

Street, B. V. (2001). Literacy 'events' and literacy 'practices': Theory and practice in the 'New Literacy Studies.' In K. Jones & M. Martin-Jones (Eds.), *Multilingual literacies: Comparative perspectives on research and practice.* Amsterdam: John Benjamins.

Street, J. C., & Street, B. V. (1991). The schooling of literacy. In D. Barton & R. Ivanic (Eds.), *Writing in the community* (pp. 106–131). Newbury Park, CA: Sage.

Szwed, J. F. (1981). The ethnography of literacy. In M. F. Whiteman (Ed.), *Writing:*

The nature, development, and teaching of written communication, part 1 (pp. 13–23). Hillsdale, NJ: Erlbaum.

Taylor, D., & Dorsey-Gaines, C. (1988). *Growing up literate: Learning from inner-city families.* Portsmouth, NH: Heinemann.

Weinstein-Shr, G. (1993). Literacy and social process: A community in transition. In B. V. Street (Ed.), *Cross-cultural approaches to literacy* (pp. 272–293). Cambridge, UK: Cambridge University Press.

Wertsch, J. (1991). *Voices of the mind: A sociocultural approach to mediated action.* Cambridge, MA: Harvard University Press.

Yin-yee Ko, D. (1989). *Toward a social history of women in seventeenth century China.* Unpublished doctoral dissertation, Stanford University, Stanford, CA.

2

Connecting Schools with Out-of-School Worlds

Insights from Recent Research on Literacy in Non-School Settings

GLYNDA HULL and KATHERINE SCHULTZ

In Chapter 1 we trace the ways in which examinations of literacy in out-of-school settings have provided pivotal moments theoretically, turning the field toward new understandings of "literacies" and into different lines of research. Indeed, we argue that most of the theoretical advances that have been made in the field of literacy studies over the last 25 years have had their origin in discoveries about literacy and learning not in school, but outside it. To talk about literacy these days, both in school and out, is to speak of events, practices, activities, ideologies, discourses, and identities (and at times to do so almost unreflectively, so much a part of our customary academic ways of thinking have these categories and terminology become). Again, we argue that in large part this new theoretical vocabulary sprang from examinations of the uses and functions of literacy in contexts other than school.

Having outlined a host of conceptual steps and leaps, we begin in this chapter to push at the boundaries between literacy out of school and literacy in school, identifying tensions, complementarity, overlap, and possible divisions of labor. The need is great to marshal the best of our resources in the most powerful combinations toward improving the life chances of those children and adults who have been most poorly served. Surely this can happen most effectively when schools and community organizations, teachers and community activists consciously work together.

As centerpieces for our following discussion, we offer six vignettes of children, youth, and adults engaged in literate activities outside of school, vignettes adapted from recent reports of research growing out of the theoretical traditions of the ethnography of communication, activity theory, and the New Literacy Studies. One reason for providing these accounts is to foreground representations of real people and their activities after, in Chapter 1, a very theoretical journey. A strength of the research conducted in all three traditions is its ability to bring to life literacy activities through fine-grained ethnographic and qualitative accounts of particular lives, contexts, and historical moments. Through such research we come to know, even to feel we know intimately, a panoply of individuals, families, networks, communities, organizations, and institutions. And we also begin to understand some of the multifaceted ways in which literacy connects with learning, doing, and becoming outside of school. Through the following vignettes, then, we hope to at least hint at this richness.

Second, the portraits themselves form a backdrop for thinking through the policy, curricular, and pedagogical insights for schooling and school/non-school partnerships that can be gleaned from recent studies of literacies beyond the schoolhouse door, as well as for raising the questions and problems that still persist for literacy education and research. We begin with a page from Down Under, an account of a cool teenager, reluctant writer, and budding businessman in urban Australia.[1]

Jacques: "I'm not a pencil man."

Jacques is 13 years old and lives with his parents and siblings in a white, affluent neighborhood of Brisbane. A disengaged student in the classroom, one who often "loses" his homework and would die a thousand deaths before volunteering an answer to a teacher's general query, he nonetheless provides a running sotto voce gloss on classroom activity, waxing in turn ironic, humorous, dramatic. This self-designated joker has "great difficulty with literacy" according to his teacher. But he is quite good at derailing attempts to involve him in the classroom milieu. No "writing process" pedagogy for this young man. Rather than use the Writer's Centre to produce and publish a story, Jacques spends days stapling together a miniature book in which he writes, to his teacher's dismay and his peers' delight, a mere 10 words. Made to repeat first grade, Jacques now patiently measures time until he can leave school for good. Neither professing nor demonstrating an interest in reading and writing, he explains: "I'm like my dad. I'm not a pencil man" (Knobel, 1999, p. 104).

Out of school, Jacques participates in two worlds valued by his family:

work and religion. A member of the Jehovah's Witnesses, he ably takes part in a variety of literacy-related religious activities—scriptural exegesis, the distribution on Saturday rounds of church literature such as *The Watchtower*, presentations at a weekly Theocratic School. But it is being a working man, with certain specialized ways of interacting and valuing, that offers Jacques a current identity and a future vision of the person he expects—and wants—to become. His father owns a successful business as an excavator, and it is his potential role in this physically palpable occupation, revolving as it does around machines and action in and upon the world, that captures Jacques's attention and his energy. His involvement in and apprenticeship for the adult world of work also includes some home-based literacy activities. There is, for example, the design and publication with a home computer of an advertisement for Jacques's own neighborhood mowing service. This professional-looking flyer promises "efficiency" and "reliability" and even offers "phone quotes"—turns of phrase we all can recognize as ubiquitous in the world of business advertising. Jacques's out-of-school identity as an aspiring businessman and the social practices that support it, so obvious at home, are invisible in school, where he appears unengaged and less than competent. Yet one might wager that he will nonetheless lead a successful adult life, finding a comfortable economic and social niche, given his cooperative immersion in valued adult worlds.

The vignette of Jacques is adapted from Michele Knobel's (1999) recent book, *Everyday Literacies: Students, Discourse, and Social Practice*, an ethnographic case study of four adolescents coming of age in urban Australia. Framing her study with Gee's discourse theory (e.g., 1996) and methodological insights drawn from Green and the Santa Barbara Classroom Discourse Group (e.g., Green & Harker, 1988), Knobel poses what we believe is the central question raised (but not yet answered) by years of research on out-of-school literacy. She asks: "What *is* the relationship between school learning and students' everyday lives, and what might an effective relationship between them be" (p. 6)?

Knobel's study reminds us, as does an important tradition of work in literacy theory and research, of the resources, both personal and community based, that children, adolescents, and adults bring to school. We think, for example, of Moll's work with Latino communities in the Southwest and his generative term *funds of knowledge*, used to describe the networked expertise woven through community practices (Moll, 1992; Moll & Diaz, 1987; Moll & Greenberg, 1990; see also Vasquez, 1993). The power of Moll's work for us is his convincing demonstration of how funds of knowledge can be used to bridge communities to classrooms by acknowledging the expertise of parents and community members. He has, for example, provided examples of lessons in which teachers have brought community members into the schoolroom to share their knowledge and know-how, and he has documented as well the positive effects of such activities on children's interest and investment in the curriculum.

Developing a culturally relevant pedagogy for teaching African American youth literary interpretation, Lee (1993) has also looked to cultural funds of knowledge, particularly language forms and discourse structures. In their most recent work, Lee and colleagues (Lee, 2000; Majors, 2000; Rivers, Hutchinson, & Dixon, 2000) have examined language practices across contexts, identifying participation structures of talk in the community, such as African American hair salons, and using these structures to inform ways of conducting classroom discussions about texts. This research shows that teachers can successfully engage students in high levels of reasoning about literary texts by drawing on their tacit knowledge about cultural forms out of school.

We think as well of Dyson's (1997, 1999, in press) long-term studies of early writing development in particular, the "resources" that children bring to their writing from their social worlds, including the linguistic and symbolic tools appropriated from popular culture. Dyson has argued for the permeability of the curriculum, where teachers imagine their classrooms in such a way as to continually welcome the diverse resources that children, of necessity, bring to their writing. While Dyson's research is situated physically within classroom walls, we think it noteworthy that her conceptual framework embraces children's out-of-school lives.

We see here two powerful, but distinct, ways to bridge home and school worlds. Moll and Lee literally go into homes, community centers, and other out-of-school contexts to learn about social and cultural resources; they then bring people and linguistic and cultural knowledge back into the classroom. Dyson, on the other hand, is continually alert to the ways in which children themselves bring their outside worlds into the classroom through their writing and the oral performances that encircle literacy events.

We admire work in the vein of Moll, Lee and colleagues, and Dyson, and we are captured by the portraits of classrooms, communities, and students that they give us. The question here is what such classrooms and the perspectives that undergird them can hold for students such as Jacques. Disaffected youth, adults, and even children are legion—those individuals and groups for whom alienation from school–based learning seems sadly confirmed. For them, perhaps, community-based opportunities are especially crucial for developing the desire we all share to become more fully human, to borrow Freire's (1970) still-inspirational words. Of course, the possibility of engaging in literacy activities in the community does not excuse school-based teachers or the rest of us from asking how out-of-school identities, social practices, and the literacies they recruit might be leveraged in the classroom. How might teachers incorporate students' out-of-school interests and predilections but also extend the range of the literacies with which they are conversant? And in what ways must our thinking about what constitutes curriculum and pedagogy be modified in order to appeal to students who don't handily fit the common mold? How, to ask the hardest question, do we keep youth involved in school when their adult lives seem to hold little promise of work or civic activity or personal fulfillment that draws strongly on school-based literacy?

Marquis, Delilah, and Samson: "You gotta pay."

Marquis (age 11), Delilah (age 10), and Samson (age 9) are at an inner-city community center when Ellen arrives, parking ticket in hand. A volunteer at the center and a friend of the children, she asks what to do with this ticket. Marquis asks where she found it, and Ellen answers, "On my windshield." "Oooo, you got a ticket for parking where you shouldn't have!" Delilah quickly chides, while Samson teases that she'll surely go to jail. Marquis states with the wisdom of his years, "She ain't going to jail for no ticket. She gonna pay somen." And then Marquis and Delilah set about problem-solving, analyzing the ticket and sorting through strategies for dealing with it.

Delilah suggests that Ellen will need to go downtown to pay it, but upon examining the ticket again, Samson figures out that it can be mailed and that the ticket itself, once folded over, will serve as an envelope. Marquis recommends simply putting it on someone else's car. "Yeah, on another Mazda," Delilah adds. But once the children deduce that Ellen's license number is recorded on the ticket, that plan seems less than ideal. "They got a copy of the ticket at the office, and if she don't pay, she'll go to jail," a sober child concludes. Marquis and Delilah have the final say: "You gotta pay." And they commiserate over the steep fine of $25. "You got it?" Delilah asks. The problem-solving moment ends with a story. Marquis tells how his little brother once gave him a ticket for parking his big wheel in front of the house, a ticket for $100. "Said I had to give it to him, too, or I was going to jail!" Everyone joins in the laughter.

And so we see a group of African American inner-city children turning a parking ticket this way and that, holding it up to the light, both literally and metaphorically. They draw on various literate and discursive strategies to find a way to obviate its influence—trying out scenarios, studying the artifact for information and directives, enumerating and questioning options. In other words, the children employ their developing language and reasoning skills to solve a material problem in their resource-scarce community. Their negotiation of a traffic ticket thus lays bare a host of literate and problem-solving practices and reveals as well the ways in which urban youth learn to hone their abilities to understand, function within, and circumvent the powers that be.

We are introduced to these children in Ellen Cushman's (1998) recent ethnography, *The Struggle and the Tools*, a book that documents and celebrates inner-city residents' "institutional" language—those oral and literate skills crucial for daily negotiations with gatekeeping institutions. Taking issue with critical scholars who too quickly resort to notions of hegemony and false consciousness when they theorize about the "underclass" or the "marginalized," Cushman takes as her project redefining critical consciousness. She demonstrates, and pays homage to, the ways in which the individuals she came to know as part of her research navigate the social structures that constrain them, both accommodating and resisting and even undermining such constraints through everyday language and literacy activities. In so doing, Cushman adopts what she calls an "activist methodology," one that lays bare her role as a participant in the research and the community (notice her presence in the vignette above) and that makes possible reciprocally beneficial relationships with the people from her study.

Cushman's study stands out for us first because of its insistence on acknowledging the communicative competence displayed by people in their everyday lives. She examines kids' conversations and finds, for example, not just chit-chat, but the use of a particular kind of strategic oral language to analyze that most common of local literacy artifacts, the dreaded parking ticket. Much of the work on out-of-school literacy has as its starting place a respect for and acknowledgment of people's abilities. As McDermott (1993) has noted, the stance that people are OK, that they are competent within their cultural milieu, is common within the field of anthropology—but expecting people to fail is more commonly an artifact of schooling.

Nowhere in the out-of-school research is an expectation for success more evident than in Heath's long-term work in a multitude of out-of-school youth organizations around the United States (e.g., Heath, 1994, 1996, 1998a, 1998b; Heath & McLaughlin, 1993). She has been especially impressed by young people's participation in arts-based organizations and offers this description of their important features:

> Within the organizations that host these arts programs, opportunities for young people to learn derive primarily from an ethos that actively considers them to be resources for themselves, their peers, families and communities. These programs thus engage the young in learning, both for themselves and for oth-

ers, through highly participatory projects that encompass listening, writing and reading, as well as mathematical, scientific and social skills and strategies. (Heath, 1998a, p. 2)

To be sure, one of the most important lessons to be gleaned from research on literacy and out-of-school contexts is the benefits that accrue from achieving competence. As Griffin and Cole (1987; see also Cole & Traupmann, 1981; McDermott, 1993) have discovered in their exemplary work with after-school programs, such competence becomes most apparent when we allow many starting points for learning and many paths to progress.

We wonder, as we admire Cushman's study and her activist stance: What we must do to cultivate such attitudes about children and adults' competence in formal classrooms? And having done so, how might teachers build on people's abilities as strategic language users in school? What, as a matter of fact, does "building on" entail? Terribly important, too, what special skills are required of teachers in order to nurture students whose critical consciousness as members of oppressed groups is finely honed (and rightly so)? Further, how can teachers and researchers learn about and participate in communities apart from school in a respectful and reciprocal manner?

The metaphor of a journey is often invoked as part of much research on out-of-school literacy, as researchers voyage into less familiar communities and cultures to retrieve collectibles for their scholarship and the classroom. Such studies have been valuable as ways of unveiling and foregrounding language and literacy practices that differ from those of the mainstream. But it is time, we think, to find a different metaphor and another reason for traveling, one that facilitates the sharing of projects with participants and that directs research toward the amelioration of problems that community members, along with researchers and teachers, find compelling. The work of Flower and colleagues in Pittsburgh (Flower, 1997, in preparation; Flower, Long, & Higgins, 2000; Peck, Flower, & Higgins, 1995; see also Chapter 5, this volume) and that of Engeström (1987, 1993, 1998) and colleagues in Finland stands out in this regard.

Mr. San: Of Mice and Managers

In a high-tech workplace in northern California's Silicon Valley, frontline workers, most of them recent immigrants, participate in numerous literacy-rich activities, activities that accompany their participation in "self-directed" work teams, their documentation of their own productivity and quality scores, and the oral presentation of problem-solving data. Literacy is everywhere in this factory, serving some 80 different functions and ranging from simple copying and decoding to marshaling reading and writing skills to argue certain points of view. Managers and supervisors have quite definite ideas about the purposes that literacy activities should serve. Yet the most carefully scripted plans of mice and managers do often go awry. Here is Mr. San, one of several frontline workers at this factory who has been directed to take his turn in front of supervisors and co-workers to practice the computation and reporting of quality and productivity numbers. He begins innocently enough:

> OK. (*puts transparency on the overhead projector*) Our team name is uh Turbo, Team number 31, and the area is First Mechanical and Handload. Shift day, and my coach is Engineer Kartano.

But it soon becomes apparent that Mr. San is about to seize the moment, having chosen not merely to participate in a practice exercise on oral reporting. Instead, he demonstrates that it is actually impossible to calculate productivity scores correctly because workers have been given incorrect "standard times." In a dramatic "voila!" moment, Mr. San unveils on the overhead projector a virtually unreadable chart, densely packed with numbers. Despite the fact that its details are obscured, the import of this chart is as clear as can be: Mr. San has managed to requisition a new set of standard times, or the times allotted for accomplishing the multitude of assembly tasks required throughout the workday:

> This is, now I just got this, that's why we are delayed in entering our data (*puts a new transparency up on the overhead projector*), here is the standard time. Wow! [*laughter*]. . . . They they're trying to modify the standard time because I complained all the datas that we got on the actual uh time that we finish one board doesn't count in the standard time.

The issue of speed at work is of course a theme that runs throughout the history of labor relations; how fast work gets done, or the "standard time" as it's called in Mr. San's factory, has been contested over and over again. In this most recent example of that long history, Mr. San appropriates a company meeting at which workers were expected just to practice, merely to get their feet wet, with public presentations of data by reading off their responses to pre-fab questions in rote fashion. Yet Mr. San chose not to be part of the dog-and-pony show, just as he had refused, even before this meeting took place, to complete elaborate graphs and charts and to provide a discursive rationale for his team's quality and productivity goals.

"How can we write goals," he had argued, "if our standard times are incorrect!" Pressing his point with an engineer, he eventually succeeded in having the company's time-study experts recalculate the standard times. Only after all of this did Mr. San consent to learn how to perform—and to encourage his team members to do so as well—the often burdensome, even daunting tasks of filling out multitudes of forms and completing the elaborate new documentation associated with productivity and quality measurements. In this case, it seems that Mr. San's willingness to participate in literacy-related activities was linked to the identity he was constructing for himself as a worker, an identity most aptly described as advocate for his team—"my people," as he liked to call them.

Hull (2000) provides our Silicon Valley vignette from her ethnographic examination of two companies in the circuit board assembly industry. She and her research team asked what kinds of workers the companies were looking to hire or to fashion, and what kinds of literacies the new forms of work, such as self-directed work teams, seemed to privilege. Frameworks drawn from the New Literacy Studies (e.g., Gee, 1996; Street, 1993) and sociocultural perspectives on writing (e.g., Freedman, Dyson, Flower, & Chafe, 1987) positioned Hull to link literacy and identity, focusing on how particular work identities can lead to acceptance or rejection of certain literacy practices. Constructing new work identities is not, of course, unproblematic. As Gee, Hull, and Lankshear (1996) illustrate in their analysis of the rhetoric of "fast capitalist" texts, the new work order calls on even frontline workers to invest themselves completely in their jobs, taking on the company's notions of the flexible, multiskilled problem-solver and worker cum manager. Yet doing so, and excelling at literate activities and developing a working identity that involves a sense of oneself as a proficient user of multiple semiotic systems, doesn't necessarily, or even often, lead to full-time work with benefits, let alone advancement. Such work makes urgent the need to rethink standard curricular fare for non-college-bound youth. But just as insistently, it asks us to acknowledge the contradictions that exist in even the most progressive high-performance work environments, where workers are directed to develop literate identities, but identities that are circumscribed. We are prompted, then, to ask: How should we think about school in relation to students' future work.

Other researchers who have examined the literacy demands of entry-level work include Gowen (1992), in her account of hospital workers; Darrah (1996), in his analysis of the electronics industry; and Hart-Landsberg and Reder (1997), in their look at auto-accessory manufacturers. However, the vast majority of studies have focused on the work and writing lives of college graduates who enter managerial or technical positions in which writing mediates work in quite visible and powerful ways. (For a review of the particular tradition of such work that draws on activity theory approaches, see Russell, 1997.) These studies help us look critically at how college writing courses, writing across the curriculum programs, and training in technical communication do and don't prepare students for professional lives in which the mastery of written genres is central. They also give us detailed understandings of the literacy requirements and literacy-related social practices of a variety of workplaces, often making the case that writing at school and at work are "worlds apart" (Dias, Freedman, Medway, & Paré, 1999). This body of research has provided, finally, compelling portraits of the struggles of competent writers engaged in high-stakes, real-world activity through which they become professional wordsmiths (Beaufort, 1999).

It of course makes intuitive sense for writing researchers to focus their attention on professionals in the work world for whom the production of written language is a prime activity. But such a gaze, when it does not also include entry-level workers at least in peripheral vision, can obscure the ways in which literacy has become part and parcel of most working lives. Even more importantly, if we ignore entry-level work, we will also ignore, if we are not vigilant, the ways in which literacy is implicated in the sustenance of traditional relations of power in the workplace, including career ladders and other means of advancement, making the gulf that separates occupational hierarchies too broad to span (Hull & Schultz, 2001).

There are other great divides that deserve the attention of researchers and educators if we are to rethink the school-to-work relationship and the roles of literacy within it. There is worry about a growing digital divide, one associated with schools (where access to technology and its meaningful use is unequal), with disparate technology and other resources, and also with workplaces in which low-income people of color are shut out of high-tech, well-paying jobs. How can teachers, researchers, and other educators join forces to bridge such divides? What models really have a chance of interrupting long-standing patterns of poverty and miseducation? Kalantzis and Cope (2000) argue persuasively for pluralism as an organizing concept for education in new times; similarly, they suggest that in imagining new work orders, we must work toward "productive diversity," whereby people are valued for their difference and expertise at work centers on the ability to engage and negotiate difference. Gee (2000) wonders whether new capitalist rhetoric and practice—flexibility, teamwork, communities of practice—can be reclaimed for more radical social and educational ends. For our own part, we see practical promise in new coalitions of community organizations, schools, and universities that are attempting to sponsor technology-rich after-school programs for children, job training for older youth and young adults, and technology access for the wider community (Hull, 2000).

Whatever our imaginings or our concrete efforts, we ignore at our students' peril the close connections that exist among economic change, the material conditions of people's lives, and literacy and literacy learning. Brandt (1999) warns us well:

> Downsizing, migrations, welfare cutbacks, commercial development, transportation, consolidation, or technological innovations do not merely form the background buzz of contemporary life. These changes, where they occur, can wipe out as well as create access to supports for literacy learning. They also can inflate or deflate the value of existing forms of literacy in the lives of students. Any of these changes can have implications for the status of literacy practices in school and for the ways students might interact with literacy lessons. (p. 391)

If we take Brandt's concerns seriously, we will move a historical awareness of the relationship among literacy, the economy, and work to center stage in our theorizing, and we will be especially interested in determining "what enhances or impedes literacy learning under conditions of change" (Brandt, 1999, p. 391).

Mary TallMountain: Creating "something true"

In the heart of San Francisco's Tenderloin, a down-and-out district associated mostly with drugs and crime, women file into the Herald, a residential hotel and meeting place for the Tenderloin Women Writers Workshop. Seated with pens and notebooks in their laps, they settle in to listen to Mary TallMountain. A Native American born close to the Arctic Circle in Alaska, Mary came to San Francisco in 1945 as a recent widow; she worked first as a legal secretary and later opened her own business as a stenographer. A bout with cancer without medical insurance left her bankrupt and homeless; it was then that she moved into a small room in the Tenderloin and began to write. Mary announces that she has finished a poem entitled "Soogha Dancing" (*soogha* being the Athabaskan word for "brother"). In Mary's poem her brother is honored by being asked to dance before his tribe. Here are the first, second, and last stanzas:

> *Soogha* eldest brother I never knew,
> The people gave you new clothes.
> In spring they honored men

Outstanding in Kaltag village.
At potlatch after giveaway
Those honored danced alone.

Your arms flying
Ermine parka whirling
Beaver hood like brown velvet
Lynx-trimmed mukluks
Furs trapped by your friends
The women stitched in winter.

. . .

You dance bright behind my eyes.
Soogha brother, I see you
In that spirit-given spring
Dancing for the people,
Arms open like furry wings.

The women in the workshop deeply appreciate this poem, and they are proud, too, of their own role in its creation:

Nikki: Oh, that was a wonderful last line.
Anita: I always liked that line.
Mary: All the help you gave me, you know, here. (*She leafs back through her papers.*) It's back here, all the different things you suggested.
Martha: It's a wonderful poem. And it's a pleasure, I think, for us to hear it after, you know, we critiqued it, to hear the suggestions in it.
Mary (*looking around the group*): You consider it finished, then, do you?
Clara: That turned out beautiful, Mary. That turned out beautiful.
Martha: Yeah, it's like you took some of the suggestions—other ones didn't work—and it turned into something true to you. (Heller, 1997, p. 4)

Thus Caroline Heller begins her book *Until We Are Strong Together: Women Writers in the Tenderloin*. This is an account of the power of literacy for members of an unlikely writing group who met weekly to share their experiences, poetry, and prose. Writing and conversing together served several important social, political, and educational functions for this group of "marginalized" women—among them, sharing life histories, raising political awareness, and building skills as writers through critique. The meetings also served as a point of integration for the emotional and the intellectual, the mind and the spirit. By providing a rich enactment of how literacy and community can intersect to nurture common needs, Heller builds from and extends Freirian and liberatory approaches to critical literacy.

Readers of Heller's work are sometimes surprised by the intensely literate activity of the Tenderloin women, noting that Heller found literacy where we might least expect it—in a distressed urban community facing the many problems that accompany poverty and neglect. Yet as our understanding of what counts as literacy has broadened, researchers from around the world have documented literacy practices in the lives of children and adults everywhere: taxi drivers in South Africa (Breier, Taetsane, & Sait, 1996); cattle auctioneers in Wales (Jones, 2000); scribes in Mexico City (Kalman, 1999); members of a youth basketball league (Mahiri, 1998); middle school girls with their teen 'zines in the North American Midwest (Finders, 1997); diary keepers and racing fans in Lancaster, England (Barton & Hamilton, 1998); and a 5-year-old Australian boy with his own Web site, "Alex's Scribbles—Koala Trouble" (Lankshear & Knobel, 1997). This work illustrates in glorious detail Geertz's observation long ago that "man's [sic] mental processes indeed take place at the scholar's desk or the football field, in the studio or lorry-driver's seat, on the platform, the chessboard, or the judge's bench" (quoted in Cole, Engeström, & Vasquez, 1997, p. 13). And it denotes as well the enlivened interest of current researchers from a range of fields in everyday practical activity (see Cole et al., 1997).

Evidence of the abundant, diverse forms of out-of-school literacy— crossing class, race, gender, culture, and nationality—certainly enrich our definitions of literacy. In an interesting way, juxtaposed to Heller's portraits, this work makes us think again of school-based, "academic" literacy and ask: What is or might be the value of essayist texts? The Tenderloin women described by Heller were empowered by what we usually consider traditional genres generally introduced in school—essays, poems, short stories, other fiction and imaginative writing. These longer texts contrast with the lists, forms, letters, and advertisements that make up everyday reading and writing. They also remind us of the permeability between in-school and out-of-school borders. In our efforts to document and validate the plethora of personal and local literacy practices, we don't want to abandon the opportunities that school could provide in developing valued forms of text-based expertise. But we might want to reexamine the way in which those opportunities are provided, taking care, with Heller (1997) and the Tenderloin Women Writers Workshop, not to "create false oppositions between the emotions and the intellect, the spirit and mind, the person and the community" (p. 160).

Others worry that, in honoring out-of-school capabilities, we also romanticize them. While readily noting that "children will adapt intelligently to their worlds" (p. 34), Damon (1990) acknowledges the tension between youth's perceptions of what about the world is useful to know and adults' understandings. Noting the tendency to valorize out-of-school skills and to put them on equal footing with schooled knowledge—perhaps, he speculates, in reaction to the long-standing tendency among academics to denigrate the nonacademic—he asserts:

> [I]t serves no useful purpose to imbue unschooled forms of knowledge with a sentimental gloss. Just as we should not lose sight of the remarkable adaptiveness of some unschooled abilities, we also must guard against expecting more from them than they can deliver. (p. 38)

These are strong words that run counter to the ideologies of much recent and useful literacy research. But perhaps they are a helpful reminder to give school-based literacies their due, and all children access to their power, while simultaneously honoring and building on everyday literacies (see Delpit, 1995).

At the end of her book, Heller (1997) asks how we might reconceive our relationships with the most marginalized. We ask, with her, how those who have "been excluded from the mainstream, or who have chosen to live and/or learn apart from it" (p. 160) can help us rethink in fundamental ways our theories and our work in formal classrooms.

Martha: "Yo no sabia que era bilingue."

A third-grade bilingual Latina, Martha likes to tell jokes and show her wit when she interacts with people she knows and trusts, such as friends at Las Redes. During this after-school program, children not only collaborate with each other and UCLA undergraduates as they play and master a variety of computer-related games and puzzles, they venture into cyberspace as well. A centerpiece of the children's activities is an e-mail exchange with a mysterious entity called "El Maga," whose identity and gender are objects of great speculation, but ultimately remain unknown. Children recount to El Maga their progress in completing the various computer games and related activities and report any difficulties they encounter. El Maga, for his or her part, is known to ask a lot of questions, as well as to initiate personal dialogues with individual children. The intent of these e-mail exchanges is to foster children's participation in and affiliation with Las Redes, socializing them, if you will, into the culture of an after-school activity system.

Martha begins her correspondence with El Maga by mentioning the sometimes frustrating experiences she has had playing a computer game that has as its central character a frog. Martha writes in one early message:

> dear El Maga, are are you? The pond was little bit harder. I couldn't understand the game and Christina [UCLA undergrad] helped me figure it out. In the end, I passed the first level and I was surprised. thanks for writing to me.

El Maga responds:

> Dear Martha,
> I am doing pretty good, thank you for asking!!! How are you?? I hope you still have that big smile!!! The pond was difficult to figure out, huh? That frog causes many of us problems. It has a mind of its own and sometimes it does not want to do what we program it to do. Que ranita [That mischievous little frog]. . . .
> El Maga

The next time Martha writes an e-mail message to El Maga, she does so in Spanish. She professes her surprise that El Maga is bilingual, presses El Maga for information on his or her gender, and reports her recent computer game activities. In so doing, Martha demonstrates certain Spanish literacy skills, such as knowledge about a formal register, and she also indicates, through her more familiar salutation and closing, that she is ready to establish a more intimate relationship with El Maga:

> Querido/a
> Yo no sabia que era bilingue. Usted es mujer or hombre? Haora juque boggle, y un rompe cabesas de batman, y Bertha nos ayudo armario.
> Adios, Martha

> [Dear
> I did not know that you were bilingual. Are you a man or a woman? Today I played boggle and a batman puzzle. And Bertha helped us put it together.
> Goodbye, Martha]

Soon Martha's correspondence with El Maga exhibits not only her proficiency in Spanish but also her "bilingual, bicultural, and biliterate knowledge and skills" (Gutiérrez, Baquedano-López, Alvarez, & Chiu, 1999, p. 91), including an interest in cross-cultural language play.

Over the next weeks, Martha continues to demonstrate, by means of her e-mail exchanges with El Maga, her fluency in both English and Spanish and a certain sophistication in her choices of language and register. Code-switching words and clauses, she also draws playfully on assumed shared cultural knowledge, alluding to the well-known Mexican American boxer Oscar de la Hoya as well as to elements of children's popular culture, such as cartoons. A happy, outgoing, playful child at Las Redes, Martha soon begins, in collaboration with the undergraduates and El Maga, to use an array of written language skills to represent these facets of herself in print as well as speech.

Martha's story comes from Gutiérrez, Baquedano-López, Alvarez, and Chiu (1999), who bring activity theory to bear on the study of children's language and literacy development. Their after-school club, Las Redes, operates out of an urban elementary school located near the Los Angeles International Airport and represents one instantiation of Cole's Fifth Dimension project (e.g., Cole, 1996; see also Chapter 6, this volume). Combining play and learning, Las Redes provides a context in which collaboration is the order of the day and in which the children and their undergraduate amigos/as from UCLA can mix languages, registers, and genres—or in Gutiérrez and colleagues' terms, engage in hybrid language and literacy practices (see Chapter 7, this volume). Gutiérrez and colleagues argue the importance of creating such learning contexts where hybridity can flourish, "particularly in a time when English-only, anti-immigrant, and anti-affirmative action sentiments influence, if not dominate, educational policy and practice" (p. 92).

We feature Gutiérrez and colleagues' work (see also Gutiérrez, Baquedano-López, & Tejeda, 1999; Gutiérrez, Baquedano-López, & Turner, 1997) to call attention to after-school programs that support children's and youth's intellectual and social development by providing supplementary instruction and, as in this and other instantiations of Cole's 5th Dimension project, constructing new, theoretically motivated learning environments or "activity systems." Such programs can serve a range of important functions, including helping us reimagine classrooms and students. As Gutiérrez and others have shown, children often interact and learn in very competent ways after school, despite poor records and reputations in traditional classrooms (Gutiérrez et al., 1997). And as Cole points out, after-school programs can reorganize learning such that typical student–teacher relationships and participant structures are turned on their heads. He writes: "This unusually heterogeneous distribution of knowledge and skill is a great resource for reordering everyday power relations, thereby creating interesting changes in the typical division of labor" (Cole, 1996, p. 298). He emphasizes as well the importance of choice—children participate voluntarily—but choice balanced by discipline and learning infused with play and imagination.

We agree with Cole (1996) and with Underwood, Welsh, Gauvain, and Duffy (2000) when they caution that early on such after-school programs must confront issues of sustainability. If after-school programs are to last, to become viable community institutions that exist past their founder's interest, then they must be accompanied by structural changes within both community institutions—such as YMCAs, Boys' and Girls' Clubs, and churches—and university partners.

A further tension that after-school programs must continually address is the extent to which they become school-like organizations—serving essentially as arms of classrooms that extend the schoolday, providing assistance with homework and safe spaces for youth after school—and the extent to which they define themselves apart from schools as alternative sites for learning (see Chapter 8, this volume). The push, we predict, will be toward the former, given the current availability of federal and local funding for after-school programs and given the tendency of textbook publishers and other vendors to provide standardized materials and prepackaged materials. The danger, of course, is that we will lose a currently available creative space for doing academics differently.

When researchers such as Dyson first began to document "unofficial" literacy practices in school—such as passing notes—there was worry that bringing these forms of writing into the official curriculum would take away the interest and delight students found in them. In a similar vein, there is sometimes concern about attempts to import new literacy practices that flourish in after-school programs and other after-school settings to school. This topic sometimes comes up in discussions of new technologies, such as multimedia composition, Web-based authoring, and chat rooms and other sites for identity construction and playful writing, as documented by Lankshear and Knobel (1997). The concern is that, if school appropriates these potentially subversive forms, there is the chance that they will be domesticated and lose their vigor, appeal, and edge. On the other hand, an important opportunity to address the digital divide comes with preparing teachers to think differently about what counts as literacy and with equipping schools with technology, making opportunities to engage with new technologies available to more students. We need examples, then, of the integration of new media and Internet use into schools in ways that allow youth culture and its varied literacies to flourish alongside, as well as to influence, academic genres.

Denise: "This world is a world of fear and hate. That is what led me to be a writer."

Denise attends a multi-racial, comprehensive high school set in an urban West Coast community, one caught in the cross-currents of long-standing, systemic problems of poverty, crime, and malaise. As her classmates sit together and write their arguments for a constitutional convention, arguing loudly with each other and alternatively focusing on the task at hand, Denise is off to the side working on her homework and staring into space. She has refused to participate in this exciting set of activities that draw in even the most reluctant students. In fact, she has made clear her decision not to engage in any public performances, and even accepted an "F" as a consequence for this strongly held view.

At home Denise writes poetry about her grandmother and a play for a favorite middle school teacher. The play, titled "Gangsta Lean" after a rap popular at that time, is based on actual events in her own life—the shooting death of her cousin in a drug-related incident at a dice game. One day Denise shows the script to her drama teacher who produces it in the only drama class in the school. Yet Denise keeps her distance from this performance in its initial stages and only reluctantly steps forward to receive flowers at the evening performance of the play.

After the performance of her play, Denise seems to link her writing of poetry and plays at home to her identity as a writer at school. After her teachers point out that she can use her play as her senior project, she reluctantly begins work on this step toward graduation. On an audio-tape that accompanied this final project of her high school career, she speaks these words which describe the role of writing in her life:

> Growing up in [our city.] Me, my mother and my brothers. It wasn't easy. It's not easy. And it ain't going to be easy. Every time I walk home from school, I don't feel safe. Not at all. I start to think of my family and all the friends I have seen killed, that have been killed. And I also think about the one that might be killed. When a car goes past me, my neck shrugs as if I am going to be shot. It's a terrible, terrible feeling. . . . This world is a world of fear and hate. That is what led me to be a writer . . .
>
> While writing I don't feel nothing. . . . All I think about is writing. If I don't write, all I think about is the deaths in the world today. So to keep my mind off of that, I write. It's not easy to be a writer. You have to have your mind set on being a writer. . . . When writing a play popped into my mind, all I thought about was the painful things that I see in the world today. . . . So, I started to write.

And I couldn't stop. It felt like I was being trapped. I was being held captive. And believe me, I know what that feels like. (Senior project tape, June 1994)

Denise's out-of-school speaking and writing is a stunning reminder of her daily experience. Her teachers found a way for her to bring this writing into the school curriculum on her own terms. While she attended school, Denise continued to resist the official school curriculum and continued to write at home. Once she graduated, she stopped writing all together.

Katherine Schultz introduces us to Denise and a few of her classmates in her study of writing in the lives of urban adolescents (Schultz, in press). She describes the writing that seemed to flourish outside of school from students who were reluctant writers inside their classrooms. Student writing took many forms: primarily they wrote poems, letters, and journals, although some of them wrote plays and a variety of fiction and non-fiction prose. For the most part, they did not share their writing with their peers. Schultz describes the ways that youths like Denise tentatively constructed literate identities while in school by writing at home, and how, once they graduated, they seemed to stop writing. She poses the question: How can we construct pedagogy and curriculum that support students to construct and hold on to enduring literate identities and to become powerful speakers, readers, and writers while they are in school and beyond?

Schultz's study on personal out-of-school writing is unusual in being longitudinal: she stayed in touch with the young people for several years after they graduated from high school, documenting their writing across home and school contexts rather than focusing on one context or the other. We suggest that it would be useful to explore what it is about being in school, even if students are reluctantly biding time in classrooms, that allows them to find these alternative spaces to write. We recognize that for all of us, writing may be more or less important at various times in our lives; for a virtual non-writer in early adulthood, the written word may become central later on. This leads us to ask: How are time and space organized in adolescents' lives while they are in school in such a way as to allow them to develop identities as writers? Is the personal writing students engage in connected to a particular time in their lives? If so, will these students hold on to the knowledge that writing was important to them at one time and return to it later on? How can educators reconceptualize classroom practices to account for the writing students engage in outside of school, and how can practitioners teach in such a way that adolescents acquire and hold onto literate identities past their time in classrooms?

More broadly, how can we conceptualize education, and literacy within it, as a system of second chances, one that allows multiple entry points across the life span, and that provides support for individuals who wish or need to return to a focus on writing or literacy after a time away? "The notion of a second chance," wrote Dan Inbar, "is derived from the basic belief that everyone has the right to attempt success and mobility, and the right to try again, to choose a different way, and that failures should not be regarded as final" (1990, p. 1). We might think of literacy the very same way.

Conclusion

When researchers have looked at out-of-school literacy, they have done so with several goals in mind, including a desire to decouple the effects of literacy from the effects of schooling. They have asked questions such as: What are the cognitive consequences of literacy separate from the mediating impact of formal schooling? How are our conceptions of literacy constrained by one version of literacy, that is, schooled literacy? Researchers have also sought to develop the notion of literacy as multiple, asking questions such as: How do language and literacy practices in homes and communities differ from those valued in school? What new forms of and technologies for literacy exist out of school?

An early goal in research on out-of-school literacy was to account for school failure and out-of-school success through questions such as: What are the resources that children and youth from diverse backgrounds, cultures, and socioeconomic groups bring to the classroom? What are the differences among contexts, conceptions of knowledge, and performance for successful learners out of school and unsuccessful learners in school? In addition, researchers hoped to identify additional support mechanisms for children, youth, and adults. They wondered, for example: What institutions in addition to our beleaguered schools can support learning? How can out-of-school learning environments serve as stimuli for rethinking schools and classrooms?

Researchers have looked to out-of school settings to push notions of learning and development. They have posed questions such as: What understandings of mature versions of social practices can be found in out-of-school settings that we can connect to child or adult learning? How might we document the intersection of literacy with social identity or study the connection of ways of reading and writing to ways of talking, acting, interacting, valuing, and being in the world? How might we cultivate a long and broad view of learning, one that focuses on "human lives seen as trajectories through multiple social practices in various social institutions" (Gee et al., 1996, p. 4)?

What has been accomplished through the body of research we have reviewed in this chapter is more than impressive. Yet despite dazzling theoretical advances in how we conceive of literacy, despite provocative research on out-of-school literacies in an array of interesting settings, a depressing fact remains: We still have not succeeded in improving the educational experiences and life chances of the vast majority of children, adolescents, and adults. Indeed, the gap between those deemed literate and those labeled poor readers and writers and performers at academic tasks has widened and widened and widened some more. To make this situation sadder still, the educational pendulum in the United States, Australia, and Great Britain has taken a big swing to the right of late, in effect halting and reversing many of the conceptual and practical steps forward that have been made in conceptualizing and teaching reading and writing. Taylor offers this portrait: "In the UK children sit each day and do their phonics, and in the USA there are cities in which every child in a particular grade is supposed to be working on the same page, in the same way, at the same time, on any given day" (2000, p. xiii). What counts as appropriate literacy in school is being narrowed and narrowed and narrowed still more.

Countless school-based educators teach their hearts out and do so with intelligence and energy and commitment, working their magic in their classrooms day in, day out. Indeed, many of the current educational reforms that we and others believe take us backward, not forward, are handed down to teachers for implementation, not debate or consideration. Thus the unflattering portraits of schools and teachers and academic literacy that sometimes accompany the literature on out-of-school learning are, we believe, overly harsh. We wince when we read the sweeping claims—in-school learning is top-down with teachers doing most of the thinking; schooled literacy is based on a universal model that reduces other literacies to deficits; schools are hostile, demeaning places where young people aren't heard nor their interests considered. Out of school, these accounts sometimes go on to claim, learning is participatory and democratic, literacies are multiple and satisfying, and programs so appeal to children and young people that participants have to be turned away. It must be more complicated than that. In a discussion of the last decade's impressive body of research on "situated" learning, some of which we reviewed earlier, Rose (1999) gives this work its due, noting its worth to both theory-building and educational practice. But he also observes that the sometimes stated, sometimes implied critique of traditional schooling that is a part of this work "tends to be quickly executed, a single-hued portrait of mainstream classrooms that has the unintended effect of stripping instruction from its setting" (p. 155). We share his concern.

The fulfillment of the promise of equity through education is in important ways at the heart of each of the theoretical positions we reviewed earlier and the raison d'être, at least implicitly, for much of the research on out-of-school literacy and learning. And it is also the goal of progressive educators everywhere. Given the vast gulfs that separate, there is no better time for literacy theorists and researchers, now practiced in detailing the successful literate practices that occur out of school, to put their energies toward investigating potential relationships, collaborations, and helpful divisions of labor between schools and formal classrooms and the informal learning that flourishes in a range of settings.

Note

1. Most of our vignettes are written in the ethnographic present. We are aware of the dangers of representing people as static, and their situations as perpetual, but have chosen to write in present tense in an effort to make our vignettes more engaging.

References

Barton, D., & Hamilton, M. (1998). *Local literacies: Reading and writing in one community.* London: Routledge.

Beaufort, A. (1999). *Writing in the real world: Making the transition from school to work.* New York: Teachers College Press.

Brandt, D. (1999). Literacy learning and economic change. *Harvard Educational Review, 69*(4), 373–394.

Breier, M., Taetsane, M., & Sait, L. (1996). Taking literacy for a ride—Reading and writing in the taxi industry. In M. Prinsloo & M. Breier (Eds.), *The social uses of literacy: Theory and practice in contemporary South Africa* (pp. 213–233). Cape Town, South Africa: Sached Books.

Cole, M. (1996). *Cultural psychology: A once and future discipline.* Cambridge, MA: Harvard University Press.

Cole, M., Engeström, Y., & Vasquez, O. (1997). Introduction. In M. Cole, Y. Engeström, & O. Vasquez (Eds.), *Mind, culture, and activity: Seminal papers from the Laboratory of Comparative Human Cognition* (pp. 1–21). Cambridge, UK: Cambridge University Press.

Cole, M., & Traupmann, I. (1981). Comparative cognitive research: Learning from a learning disabled child. In W. A. Collins (Ed.), *Aspects of the development of competence (Minnesota Symposia on child psychology,* Vol. 14) (pp. 125–154). Hillsdale, NJ: Erlbaum.

Cushman, E. (1998). *The struggle and the tools: Oral and literate strategies in an inner city community.* Albany: State University of New York Press.

Damon, W. (1990). Reconciling the literacies of generations. *Daedalus, 119*(2), 33–53.

Darrah, C. (1996). *Learning and work: An exploration in industrial ethnography.* New York: Garland.

Delpit, L. (1995). *Other people's children: Cultural conflict in the classroom.* New York: Free Press.

Dias, P., Freedman, A., Medway, P., & Paré, A. (1999). *Worlds apart: Acting and writing in academic and workplace contexts.* Mahwah, NJ: Erlbaum.

Dyson, A. H. (1997). *Writing superheroes: Contemporary childhood, popular culture, and classroom literacy.* New York: Teachers College Press.

Dyson, A. H. (1999). Coach Bombay's kids learn to write: Children's appropriation of media material for school literacy. *Research in the Teaching of English, 33*(4), 367–402.

Dyson, A. H. (in press). The stolen lipstick of overhead song: Composing voices in child song, verse, and written text. In M. Nystrand & J. Duffy (Eds.), *Towards a rhetoric of everyday life.* Madison: University of Wisconsin Press.

Engeström, Y. (1987). *Learning by expanding: An activity-theoretical approach to developmental research.* Helsinki: Orienta-Konsulit.

Engeström, Y. (1993). *The working health center project: Materializing zones of proximal development in a network of organizational learning.* Paper presented at the 10th annual Work Now and in the Future Conference, Portland, OR.

Engeström, Y. (1998, April). *Distinguishing individual action and collective activity in the study of organizational literacy.* Paper presented at the annual meeting of the American Educational Research Association, San Diego.

Finders, M. J. (1997). *Just girls: Hidden literacies and life in junior high.* New York: Teachers College Press.

Flower, L. (1997). Partners in inquiry: A logic for community outreach. In L. Adler-Kassner, R. Crooks, & A. Watters (Eds.), *Writing the community: Concepts and models for service-learning in composition* (pp. 95–117). Washington, DC: American Association of Higher Education.

Flower, L. (in preparation). Talking across difference: An activity analysis of situated knowledge, conflict, and construction. In C. Bazerman & D. R. Russell (Eds.), *Activity and interactivity: A collection of research and theory.*

Flower, L., Long, E., & Higgins, L. (2000). *Learning to rival: The practice of intercultural inquiry.* Hillsdale, NJ: Erlbaum.

Freedman, S. W., Dyson, A. H., Flower, L., & Chafe, W. (1987). *Research in writing: Past, present, and future* (Tech. Rep. No. 1). Berkeley and Pittsburgh: University of California, Berkeley and Carnegie Mellon University, Center for the Study of Writing.

Freire, P. (1970). *Pedagogy of the oppressed.* New York: Seabury.

Gee, J. P. (1996). *Social linguistics and literacies: Ideology in discourses* (2nd ed.). London: Falmer.

Gee, J. P. (2000). New people in new worlds: Networks, the new capitalism and schools. In B. Cope & M. Kalantzis (Eds.), *Multiliteracies: Literacy learning and the design of social futures* (pp. 43–68). London: Routledge.

Gee, J. P., Hull, G., & Lankshear, C. (1996). *The new work order: Behind the language of the new capitalism.* Boulder: Westview.

Gowen, S. (1992). *The politics of workplace literacy: A case study.* New York: Teachers College Press.

Green, J., & Harker, C. (Eds.). (1988). *Multiple perspective analyses of classroom discourse.* Norwood, NJ: Ablex.

Griffin, P., & Cole, M. (1987). New technologies, basic skills, and the underside of education. In J. A. Langer (Ed.), *Language, literacy and culture: Issues of society and schooling* (pp. 199–231). Norwood, NJ: Ablex.

Gutiérrez, K., Baquedano-López, P., Alvarez, H. H., & Chiu, M. M. (1999). Building a culture of collaboration through hybrid language practices. *Theory into Practice, 38*(2), 87–93.

Gutiérrez, K., Baquedano-López, P., & Tejeda, C. (1999). Rethinking diversity: Hybridity and hybrid language practices in the third space. *Mind, Culture, and Activity, 6*(4), 286–303.

Gutiérrez, K., Baquedano-López, P., & Turner, M. G. (1997). Putting language back into language arts: When the radical middle meets the third space. *Language Arts, 74*(5), 368–378.

Hart-Landsberg, S., & Reder, S. (1997). Teamwork and literacy: Teaching and learning at Hardy Industries. In G. Hull (Ed.), *Changing work, changing workers: Critical perspectives on language, literacy, and skills* (pp. 359–382). Albany: State University of New York Press.

Heath, S. B. (1994). The project of learning from the inner-city youth perspective. In F. A. Villarruel & R. M. Lerner (Eds.), *Promoting community-based programs for socialization and learning* (New Directions for Child Development, No. 63) (pp. 25–34). San Francisco: Jossey-Bass.

Heath, S. B. (1996). Ruling places: Adaptation in development by inner-city youth. In R. Jessor, A. Colby, & R. A. Shweder (Eds.), *Ethnography and human development: Context and meaning in social inquiry* (pp. 225–251). Chicago: University of Chicago Press.

Heath, S. B. (1998a). Living the arts through language plus learning: A report on community-based youth organizations. *Americans for the Arts Monographs, 2*(7), 1–19.

Heath, S. B. (1998b). Working through language. In S. M. Hoyle & C. T. Adger (Eds.), *Kids talk: Strategic language use in later childhood* (pp. 217–240). New York: Oxford University Press.

Heath, S. B., & McLaughlin, M. W. (1993). *Identity and inner-city youth: Beyond ethnicity and gender.* New York: Teachers College Press.

Heller, C. E. (1997). *Until we are strong together: Women writers in the Tenderloin.* New York: Teachers College Press.

Hull, G. (2000). Critical literacy at work. *Journal of Adolescent and Adult Literacy, 43*(1), 648–652.

Hull, G., & Schultz, K. (2001). *Literacy at work: Moving up in an entry level job.* Unpublished manuscript.

Inbar, D. E. (1990). Introduction: The legitimation of a second chance. In D. E. Inbar (Ed.), *Second chance in education* (pp. 1–15). London: Falmer Press.

Jones, K. (2000). Becoming just another alphanumeric code: Farmers' encounters with the literacy and discourse practices of agricultural bureaucracy at the livestock auction. In D. Barton, M. Hamilton, & R. Ivanic (Eds.), *Situated literacies: Reading and writing in context* (pp. 70-90). London: Routledge.

Kalantzis, M., & Cope, B. (2000). Changing the role of schools. In B. Cope & M. Kalantzis (Eds.), *Multiliteracies: Literacy learning and the design of social futures* (pp. 121-148). London: Routledge.

Kalman, J. (1999). *Writing on the plaza: Mediated literacy practice among scribes and clients in Mexico City*. Cresskill, NJ: Hampton.

Knobel, M. (1999). *Everyday literacies: Students, discourse, and social practice*. New York: Peter Lang.

Lankshear, C., & Knobel, M. (1997). Different worlds? Technology-mediated classroom learning and students' social practices with new technologies in home and community settings. In C. Lankshear, *Changing literacies* (pp. 164-187). Buckingham, UK: Open University Press.

Lee, C. D. (1993). *Signifying as a scaffold for literary interpretation: The pedagogical implications of an African American discourse genre*. Urbana, IL: National Council of Teachers of English.

Lee, C. D. (2000, April). *The cultural modeling project's multimedia records of practice: Analyzing guided participation across time*. Paper presented at the annual meeting of the American Educational Research Association, New Orleans.

Mahiri, J. (1998). *Shooting for excellence: African American and youth culture in new century schools*. Urbana, IL: National Council of Teachers of English.

Majors, Y. (2000, April). *"Talk that talk": Discourse norms transversing school and community*. Paper presented at the annual meeting of the American Educational Research Association, New Orleans.

McDermott, R. (1993). The acquisition of a child by a learning disability. In S. Chaiklin & J. Lave (Eds.), *Understanding practice: Perspectives on activity and context* (pp. 269-305). New York: Cambridge University Press.

Moll, L. C. (1992). Bilingual classroom studies and community analysis: Some recent trends. *Educational Researcher, 21*(3), 20-24.

Moll, L. C., & Diaz, S. (1987). Change as the goal of educational research. *Anthropology & Education Quarterly, 18*, 300-311.

Moll, L. C., & Greenberg, J. B. (1990). Creating zones of possibilities: Combining social context for instruction. In L. C. Moll (Ed.), *Vygotsky and education: Instructional implications and applications of sociohistorical psychology* (pp. 319-348). Cambridge, UK: Cambridge University Press.

Peck, W. C., Flower, L., & Higgins, L. (1995). Community literacy. *College Composition and Communication, 46*, 199-222.

Rivers, A., Hutchinson, K., & Dixon, K. (2000, April). Participatory appropriation in a cultural modeling classroom. Paper presented at the annual meeting of the American Educational Research Association, New Orleans.

Rose, M. (1999). "Our hands will know": The development of tactile diagnostic skill—Teaching, learning, and situated cognition in a physical therapy program. *Anthropology & Education Quarterly, 30*(2), 133-160.

Russell, D. R. (1997). Writing and genre in higher education and workplaces: A review of studies that use cultural-historical activity theory. *Mind, culture, and activity: An international journal, 4*(4), 224–237.

Schultz, K. (in press). Looking across space and time: Reconceptualizing literacy learning in and out of school. *Research in the Teaching of English*.

Street, B. V. (Ed.). (1993). *Cross-cultural approaches to literacy*. New York: Cambridge University Press.

Taylor, D. (2000). Foreword. In D. Barton, M. Hamilton, & R. Ivanic (Eds.), *Situated literacies: Reading and writing in context* (pp. xi–xv). London: Routledge.

Underwood, C., Welsh, M., Gauvain, M., & Duffy, S. (2000). Learning at the edges: Challenges to the sustainability of service learning in higher education. *Language and Learning Across the Disciplines, 4*(3), 7–26.

Vasquez, O. A. (1993). A look at language as resource: Lessons from La Clase Mágica. In B. Arias & U. Casanova (Eds.), *Bilingual education: Politics, research, and practice* (pp. 119–224). Chicago: National Society for the Study of Education.

Wagner, D. A., Messick, B. M., & Spratt, J. (1986). Studying literacy in Morocco. In B. B. Shieffelin & P. Gilmore (Eds.), *The acquisition of literacy: Ethnographic perspectives* (pp. 233–260). Norwood, NJ: Ablex.

Part II

LITERACY AT HOME AND IN THE COMMUNITY

3

Literate at Home but Not at School

A Cambodian Girl's Journey from Playwright to Struggling Writer

ELLEN SKILTON-SYLVESTER

> Through my writing I found myself again after a long time of being lost. I learned who I was in the past, who I was then, and who I wanted to be in the future. There I finally found freedom in writing. I flew in the sky with my pencil and notebook. (Ngo, 1994)

In more than 3 years of participant observation in home and school contexts with seven young Cambodian girls in Philadelphia, it became quite clear that there was a big separation between school literacy and home literacy in the lives of these girls.[1] At home, it was possible to imagine many of them "flying in the sky with their pencils and notebooks," but at school, this image was much more difficult to visualize. For the girls in my study, across home and school contexts, there were differences in written genres, differences in the social and academic prestige of writing, differences in the functions of writing, and incredible differences in volume and quality of written texts. Their experiences with writing took place within a social, academic, and cultural context in which writing often had negative connotations.

At the school these girls attended, being good at literacy had quite negative peer-group consequences. In describing why she had a hard time relating to the academically oriented members of her class, one middle school student described them disdainfully in terms of their literacy practices. She explained, "They're always reading books. All the time. If I see them and try to talk to them, they can't even talk because they're reading some book" (fieldnotes, 4/4/94). This student devoured magazines and romances outside of school but made a point not to become a "school-oriented reader." Another Cambodian teenager explained what makes someone popular in this way: "Smart people are not popular." When I asked who is popular, she said, "class officers . . . people who get in trouble. Bad people" (interview, 5/23/94).

The peer culture at this school was complemented by an academic culture in which true engagement in the work of school was rare. Much of the work students were asked to do was quite disconnected from their interests and lived experiences. In many situations, I saw students focused on filling in blanks on worksheets, copying already written texts that they could not comprehend, getting better grades for copying the summaries of books from the back cover than for writing their own, and being evaluated based on whether or not they had finished an assignment but not on how they had finished it or what they had written on the page (Skilton-Sylvester, 1997). In those cases where literacy activities at school overlapped with the interests and experiences of students (e.g., journals, pictures, autobiographies), they were often seen as peripheral to the "real work of school."

Because the families of the girls in my study are refugees, we also need to consider the role that literacy has typically played in rural Cambodia and how this influences family literacy practices in the United States. Aside from monks, many Cambodians, women especially, have had little formal schooling and have little knowledge of the Khmer or the English script. Several of the Cambodian women I know in Philadelphia find it both physically and cognitively challenging to write on a page. In a study of women in Cambodia, Ledgerwood (1990) highlights the emphasis on oral performance throughout Cambodia's history, even when there were written texts available. Ledgerwood also discusses the suspicion many had of those who were highly literate. This historical stance toward those who are literate was reinforced by the genocide of Pol Pot's regime in which being literate was a reason for being killed.

In spite of the social, academic, and cultural reasons for a young Cambodian woman to turn her back on reading and writing if given a choice, several of the girls I worked with most closely enjoyed an active writing life at home that was nearly invisible at school. One girl in particular, Nan, who was in third, fourth, and fifth grade during the 3-year fieldwork period, had been held back once and struggled with academic literacy throughout the time I knew her. However, she was a prolific writer outside of school and had explored several genres: plays, fictional and nonfictional stories, captioned pictures, letters.

In order to understand Nan's experiences with writing, one must be careful not to construct artificial dualisms about her ethnolinguistic background or her writing. First, it is not accurate or helpful to conceive of Cambodians in the United States as bicultural. Ledgerwood, Ebihara, and Mortland (1994) explain why the refugee experience of Cambodians in the United States makes understanding culture much more complex than simple notions of biculturalism:

> One needs to abandon a view of Khmer refugees as biculturals . . . and exchange it for a perspective that sees war, flight, camp life and resettlement as a series of distinctive cultural experiences that have far-reaching impact on refugees. . . . Americans trying to understand Khmer refugees in the United States explain behavior they do not understand by saying "That is Cambodian." It may be, but it has been influenced by the intervening experiences and by the particularities of the experience of being newcomers in a strange environment (pp. 18–19, 20).

All the parents of the Cambodian girls I knew had spent a few years in refugee camps, as had the oldest children. Nan, the focal child in this chapter, was born in the United States, but her parents' experiences of refugee camp life deeply colored her sense of what it means to be Cambodian.

While it is tempting to see Nan's struggles primarily as a mismatch between her home and school practices, it is also true that her own very particular subjectivities—her ways of being in the social worlds of home and school—played a powerful role in framing her literacy practices in both contexts. Heller (1999) has recently shown how students with similar cultural and linguistic backgrounds can respond variously to the linguistic, academic, and social demands of schooling; they meet the overt expectations of the school while at the same time finding ways to meet their own needs as well. In reviewing the ethnographic literature on how student subjectivity is related to school experiences, Levinson (1998) highlights the ways in which it is limiting to think of students' selves as being imported into the school context:

> *Student subjectivity, while formed in important ways outside the school, also comes to be (re) formed within the space of the school itself.* Contingencies of school and student culture play a significant role in this outcome, and the eventual form that subjectivity takes depends on processes of cultural production and affiliation not entirely predictable from the patterns of enculturation outside the school. (Levinson, 1998, p. 267; emphasis added).

In fact, this debate is quite similar to that sketched earlier on how limiting it is to think of Cambodians in America as merely living out their intact Cambodianness—brought with them across miles and miles of ocean—in a new context. In much the same way, Nan did not arrive in school with a predetermined set of practices that she imported into the school context. Instead, she came to school with a set of resources that continued to expand and be reshaped as she negotiated with particular teachers and particular peers to, in Dyson's (1993) words, use writing to do "social work." Learning to write in school is a complicated process that involves negotiating the expectations and evaluations of multiple "imaginative universes," which do not always make their values explicit (Dyson, 1993, p. 17).

Nan was able to do significant "social work" through her writing outside of school, I want to argue, but had a hard time accomplishing the social work of school through her writing. Other researchers have discussed the distinction between the school and non-school writing done by students both in and out of school (Camitta, 1993; Dyson, 1993; Finders, 1996). In her study of junior high school girls, Finders (1996) describes the two literate systems at work in these girls' lives. On the one hand, students engaged in "sanctioned literacies" that teachers were aware of and supported. And on the other, students also engaged in a "literate underlife" that allowed them to break with the official conventions of the sanctioned literacies and to express more controversial opinions. I believe that understanding Nan's literate underlife is valuable in part because it allows us as educators to imagine how the knowledge of writing she does in fact have could serve as a bridge to engaging in other more sanctioned literacies.

What can we learn from out-of-school literacy practices that could help us reshape what happens in schools around literacy? Is it possible that the kind of investment Nan demonstrated in her out-of-school writing could be fostered in her in-school writing as well? If students believe that the best return on their investment comes from their peers, and if their peers see literacy as an unpopular activity, how can we convince them that reading and writing in school are worth their energy and attention?

Context, Participants, Methods

Nan's school and home were located just blocks from a major university. Although predominantly African American, the neighborhood included a concentration of Cambodian families not far from the elementary school Nan attended. Nan, her two younger sisters, her older brother, and her parents lived in a one-bedroom apartment not far from the elementary school. Her parents had come from rural Cambodia and struggled to find economic stability in the urban landscape in Philadelphia. Nan's family was on public assistance, and her parents also did seasonal work picking berries at different times of the year. Unlike her cousins' parents (who lived in the same building), neither of Nan's parents spoke English and both had had very little schooling in Cambodia. Nan's apartment was always a welcoming, warm, and comfortable place for me to be, but it was clear that her family was struggling to make ends meet, with few of the resources needed to succeed economically in urban Philadelphia.

The data presented in this chapter are part of a larger ethnographic study (Skilton-Sylvester, 1997) documenting the identities, literacies, and educational policies that are part of the lives of several Cambodian women and girls in Philadelphia. The fieldwork on which this chapter is based consisted of weekly tutoring sessions over a 3-year period with Nan and her cousins in either of their apartments (located in the same building on different floors). These sessions focused primarily on homework structured around the particular needs of individual girls in any given week. But as we built relationships, they extended to weekend trips to the museum, to my apartment, or to local parks. The girls often gave me drawings, paintings, and writings as parting gifts, especially Nan. And at the end of our tutoring sessions, they also often performed skits, dances, ice-skating competitions, and lip-syncing in the living room. As themes emerged from the data, I interviewed the girls about their points of view concerning particular findings or issues.

Fieldwork also included regular visits to the neighborhood elementary school. I had visited the English for Speakers of Other Languages (ESOL) classrooms in this school regularly for a year before I met these particular girls as part of another research project. These regular visits to the school continued during the early phases of my work with Nan, her sisters, and her cousins. During the second year of tutoring the girls, I spent several months visiting each of their ESOL classrooms and each of their grade-level classrooms. In addition, I interviewed each girl's ESOL and grade-level teachers.

I focus on Nan in this chapter because there are such dramatic differences between her in-school and out-of-school writing identities and products. Although the girls were from similar cultural, linguistic, and socioeconomic backgrounds, their school trajectories were not so similar. Nan's younger sister and her cousin both now attend an academic program at a local high school. Nan, however, is on the nonacademic track and still struggles to get to class and to not give up on school altogether (personal communication, 2/2/00). Nan interests me greatly both because the resources she brought to school were often invisible or devalued and because I can imagine other possibilities when I see her out-of-school writing. In the right classroom, her enthusiasm for making meaning through print, pictures, and performance could have been a resource to build on in learning to use writing as a tool to do the social work of school.

Taller than her sisters, brother, and cousins, with shoulder-length dark hair, Nan spent a lot of time imagining that being white and American would be better than being Asian and Cambodian American. She also spent a lot of time imagining a glamorous future for herself, possibly in Hollywood. Perhaps more than any of the other girls, she devoted much energy to managing her relationships with her peers.

Nan viewed her academic limitations as linked to her "Cambodianness," as demonstrated by the choices she made in finding an American name. Although other girls had likewise chosen American names, Nan seemed to tie her ability to choose the right American name to her success at school. In fifth grade,[2] she began writing "Mandy" before her Cambodian name on all her homework sheets. Just before she did this, I noticed what a difficult time Nan was having in copying down her homework. When I later realized that she had copied all her homework very, very neatly for several days, I asked her what had changed. She replied, "I changed my name to Mandy. Now I can copy my homework." Later I noticed that Nan had adopted still another name, Stacey, a choice she again connected to her academic identity: "When I was Mandy, I was too lazy, so I changed it to Stacey" (fieldnotes, 2/1/95). I would argue that at some level, Nan sensed that she did not have the resources she needed to succeed in school but that if she could somehow be someone else, she might be able to flourish.

Nan's Out-of-School Writing

The prolific nature of Nan's out-of-school writing always amazed me, as did the way she alternately used such writing to tackle tough subjects and create fantasies. The variety in her writing and the joy with which she produced it were also startling—in part because her school experiences were so challenging. Her ESOL teacher remarked, "I don't think Nan will ever test out of ESOL" and went on to talk about the difficulty Nan faced because she "writes in circles" (fieldnotes, 5/10/94). Her fourth-grade teacher expressed similar doubts: "She's lacking in a lot of the basics in reading and writing skills. . . . She's going to go into fifth grade. My concern is a lot of them are going to go into fifth grade and they're not really ready. . . . Nan wouldn't be able to do the fifth-grade math" (taped interview, 6/2/94).

Meanwhile, outside of school Nan appeared unable to stop writing. I collected more examples of out-of-school writing from Nan than from the other six focal girls in the larger study combined. During our tutoring sessions at her family's apartment, Nan regularly wrote something to give to me when she had finished her homework. In fact, many times I had to encourage her not to rush through her schoolwork in order to finish it quickly and be able then to write a story. During the fieldwork period, she gave me 25 pieces of writing. This out-of-school writing spans several genres: pictures without words (2), pictures with captions (5), multipage fictional stories with pictures (4), stories/reports about real events with pictures (6), letters to me (6), a questionnaire (1), a play (1), and one picture that combines several genres: a picture with a memo to me including a few sentences about the weather (this format was characteristic of much of the daily writing done at her school).

Nan's Strengths

When I compared Nan's in-school and out-of-school literacy practices, one of the first things I noticed was how her oral, visual, and creative focus was often at odds with what mattered most in the school writing she encountered. Whereas at home her strengths as a speaker, an artist, and a storyteller were assets, at school such strengths did not help her master the powerful discourse in which the written word is more valued than speech, words are more important than pictures, and accuracy often matters more than meaning.

Orality and Performance

When Nan wrote at home, it was first and foremost an enjoyable experience. She was totally engaged with the process and could not wait to "perform" what she had written for an audience. To her, writing was meant to be read orally for an audience. There were often many mistakes in her writing, and she usually had some trouble reading what she had written. It was when her written work was performed orally that it really came to life, as she paraphrased the words on the page. She consistently strayed from the text of the story, even though she held the story in front of her. And she often crafted a much more complicated story as she "read" during the performance. This practice of reading texts orally fits with a tradition in Cambodia whereby performance is an essential aspect of reading (Ledgerwood, 1990, p. 72).

For the women and girls in my study, orality and literacy were connected. Even in English, a Cambodian practice of viewing performance as part of reading crossed generations, socioeconomic classes, and levels of English (see Thierry, 1978). An emphasis on oral performance could cer-

tainly be found by looking at the reading goals of adult Cambodians in Philadelphia. Many discussed their desire to learn better pronunciation as they
discussed their reading skills, and most read out loud even if they were
reading alone. The tendency to see speech and performance as part and
parcel of literacy fits well within what has been written about Khmer literacy practices in Cambodia (Ledgerwood, 1990; Thierry, 1978). Interestingly, although most Cambodian children in Philadelphia are not learning
to read and write in Khmer, they continue a tradition of performance and
oral reading in the context of their English literacy.

An emphasis on orality, while not present in the grade-level classrooms
of the Cambodian girls in my study, complements a historical and current
emphasis on spoken language in ESOL classrooms in the United States. The
well-known audiolingual method does not foreground reading and writing,
especially at the lower levels. Observational and interview data that I collected from elementary and middle schools similarly revealed an emphasis
on oral language in ESOL. This focus was a common source of tension between grade-level teachers and their ESOL colleagues, since reading and
writing are key components of academic work outside the ESOL classroom
(Skilton-Sylvester, 1997).

In fact, reading and writing were key concerns in the development of
a "New Instructional Model" for Asian ESOL students; this mandated curriculum resulted from a class action suit filed against the school district: *Y.S.
v. School District of Philadelphia*.[3] As the new program was developed,
there was consensus that ESOL needed to focus on more than just oral
English if the program was going to prepare students to succeed in their
grade-level classes. It is particularly important that there be an emphasis on
reading and writing in ESOL when bilingual students, such as the Cambodian girls in this study, are often fluent *speakers* of English by the time they
reached second grade.

My findings show the congruence between an oral/performance orientation of Cambodian students at home and the emphasis on oral language
in the ESOL classroom. Such a continuity can make for a good match between home and school practices in relation to ESOL. This was particularly
noticeable for Nan, who attended an ESOL class that regularly required students to read aloud from their journals (Skilton-Sylvester, 1997). In this setting, Nan was able to use her oral strengths in ways that were connected
to her out-of-school writing practices. This congruence often makes it possible for Cambodian students such as Nan to be more engaged in their work
in their ESOL classrooms than in their "regular" classrooms. However, for
children and young adults, success in the grade-level classroom (especially
in the upper grades) depends more and more on so-called decontextualized
literacy skills that do not include an oral component. What is missing, then,

is a bridge between the "comfort zone" represented by oral language use and the different demands outside of home and ESOL contexts.

Visual Images

In looking at Nan's writing, it is clear that visual images overshadow the words on the page in most of her texts. Quite a talented young artist, she took great pride in her drawing abilities. When asked what she wanted to do when she grew up, she explained why she wanted to be an artist: "Because I like to draw and I draw good. When I come and paint at your house, I'll make something pretty." After her cousin's comment that she wanted to be a lawyer because she could make a lot of money, Nan added to her earlier response, saying: "I want to be a cartoonist and work at Disney World and make a lot of money at Disney World and Hawaii and everywhere" (fieldnotes, 5/14/94).

In *Before Writing*, Kress (1997) explores the semiotic systems that children have at their disposal before they become writers. One key system of signs is pictures, and Kress makes a compelling point that, in this regard, children are in step with the world at large. As he suggests, words are literally being pushed off the page in current newspapers and textbooks where visual images are prominent. According to Kress, while we discuss with panic the ways in which children are oriented to television and video, we ignore the fact that modes of communication are increasingly visual. In teaching children about writing, we tend to see pictures as superfluous; they are there to complement the writing but are often not "counted" in school contexts as a part of making meaning. Kress believes that we think of pictures as expressions of children's feelings but not as ways that they communicate their interest. Of the 25 pieces of Nan's writing that I analyzed for this chapter, just 4 have no picture/graphic image accompanying the text: 3 letters and 1 play. In all the others, pictures are a key, if not the main part, of what Nan created. (See, for example, Figure 3.1, a picture she drew of my husband and me.) Kress discusses how difficult it is for children to go from a semiotic system in which form and function are closely matched to a writing system in which symbols themselves are quite distant from what is meant. As he explains, "For children who learn alphabetic writing, the path is from drawing images to the drawing of sound, a path which takes them across a chasm which not all manage to negotiate, a shift from spatial display to sequences in time" (Kress, 1997, p. 137).

Nan's orientation to visual images is common among children her age, but her orientation to drawings and pictures also coincides with Cambodian practices in the United States that value visual images over written texts in the transmission of culture. Many scholars have discussed the importance

FIGURE 3.1: Nan's Use of Pictures and Text to Convey Meaning

of television and video for Cambodian families in the United States (Hardman, 1994; Hornberger, 1996; Smith, 1994). Television has become a key method for finding out about American culture, and video has become a way of remaining connected to the home culture through Chinese videos dubbed in Khmer. In Cambodian homes, it is videos, photographs of family members, and posters of scenes from Cambodia—not books or magazines—that allow Cambodians in Philadelphia to remain connected to their homeland.

Creating a Message

Watching Nan compose something for school was quite a different experience from watching her compose something for her own purposes. Her difficulties with spelling and grammar in English never seemed to get in her way when she was writing a story or a letter for her own purposes. Her focus on creating a message and her ability to use oral language and pictures to supplement her meaning made it possible for her to write without being particularly focused on whether the form of her message fit the spelling and grammatical conventions expected at school. There were times when this orientation didn't work for the reader, but it worked for Nan as an out-of-school writer. For example, one of her earliest stories, entitled "The Store is Come Tonight," is quite difficult to follow, even with pictures:

> One day the man owner a stor he said to the stor! stor! stor! give me a moeny. So his pocker is a picture of a stor so the man is a number of a stor. So his mother say are you are Right day! his mother say, you must put it in your pocker. So the man mother Leater go to the New big store and owner of the store Right Now. The End.

Even given the benefit of knowing Nan personally and being able to examine the accompanying pictures, it was hard for me to decipher this story. It has something to do with a man getting some money and buying a big new store, but many of the details are lost. As in much of her writing, in this piece Nan did a better job putting her personal thoughts and ideas on paper than communicating them to a reader. One of the interesting aspects of this story is the way that Nan gets the spelling of *store* right in some cases but not in others. This isn't, then, an instance of not knowing how to spell the word, but one in which getting the form right is not what matters most.

In her out-of-school writing, Nan was able to compose much clearer stories as time went on when she controlled the topic and the genre. One of her most polished writings (and also one of the last I collected) is a play entitled "Daytime":

> *Lindsey*: Oh, it seem sad that my sister's had forgot about my birthday. Oh will. (Lindsey walks out of the room).
> *Lemming*: I didn't not want Lindsey to think we're not thinking about her birthday party
> *Karen*: Oh, it's OK Lemming don't worry she will know soon (put her hand on Lemming shoulder).
> *Banky*: Ha, want me to tell her (sitting on Manny's lap)
> *Lemming, Karen*: big mouth
> *Manny*: Ha don't say that to he she is just an tiny little sweet girl.
> *Karen, Lemming*: but
> *Manny*: no but (Linda—stuck her tongue at them)
> *Manny*: go to sleep
> *Banky*: did you buy everything

Manny: Oh no, we can because we have no money
Banky: Ha we have no moeny But we could make a card for her

One of the things that is most interesting about her mastery of this genre is that it is a written version of oral speech. In merging her oral strengths with writing, Nan produced a piece of writing that contains the most standardized language of any of her texts. The play is also the only piece of writing besides three letters that does not have a picture to accompany it. In writing down speech, it seems that Nan did not need visual "data" to represent her ideas; rather, the genre itself helped her to compensate for some of her difficulties with capitalization and punctuation because it is clear who is speaking each line. Although she replaces *will* for *well* in the first line, the only other spelling error is *moeny* for *money* in the last line.

Kress (1997) distinguishes between the representation of a message—what an author wants to say or mean—and the communication of a message—how an author gets that meaning across—as two central aspects of writing and other forms of communication. My analysis of Nan's out-of-school writing suggests that she emphasized representing the message using both words and pictures. She was often so absorbed in creating her text that its representation took precedence over communication. In addition, her ability to communicate to the reader/listener outside of school was not based primarily on the form of the words she used in her text. She relied on pictures and oral explanation to supplement the written word. Outside of school, she often performed her texts; this "performance" also occurred in her ESOL classroom, where she regularly read from her journal, but rarely in other school contexts. Dyson (1993) suggests that privileging communication over performance is common in academic writing in which "the composer is never a performer, only a communicator" (p. 16). In her academic writing, where form mattered more and where she often could not supplement her words with pictures or embellish the text with oral performances, Nan struggled more with both representing and communicating her message.

It is also important to note that power relationships at home were quite different from those Nan experienced at school. At home she had significant prestige as the most fluent writer of English and the kind of power that comes when immigrant and refugee children speak more English than their parents (Auerbach, 1989; McKay & Weinstein-Shr, 1993). At school, as a nonnative (and struggling) writer of English and an elementary student, she had vastly less power. These shifts in prestige and power relations influenced Nan's ease with composing. As Kress (1997) explains, "Participants who have greater power are able to force other participants into greater efforts of interpretation. They have a different notion of 'transparency' than other participants who have less power and have to make every effort to produce messages which truly require minimal efforts of interpretation" (p. 14).

Transparency of message was something Nan actively struggled with in her school writing, as demonstrated when she was asked to write a report about a black explorer named Matthew Henson. As she wrote, Nan referred to photocopies of several encyclopedia pages about him (of which a few portions were missing) and struggled to make sense of what she had read. She also wrestled with what to write if she weren't going to copy directly from the published text. When Nan wrote stories for her own purposes, she rarely worried about spelling and easily constructed new texts. In contrast, as she worked on this assignment, spelling and accuracy became very important as she realized that this writing would be judged by how well it followed spelling rules and how much it was connected to the actual facts of Matthew Henson's life (fieldnotes, 12/14/94). The first draft of her report reads as follows:

> Mattrew was born in 1837. he was an exporter he was black he was lucky because ~~it help him~~ every people thought he was their family. he explorer greenland North pol. Mattrew helped Aruther parory He was ~~Story~~ that people would Story ~~and~~ gave up and he dies in 1855.

After talking about her text for a while, we worked on revising it together. The final version of her story ended up like this:

> Matthew was born in 1837. He was an explorer. Matthew helped Admiral Peary. Admiral Peary was a very famous explorer who discovered the North Pole. Matthew was black. He was lucky because the Eskimo people thought he was their family. He explored Greenland and the North Pole. He was strong. Other people would give up, but he didn't. He died in 1855.

In this genre, Nan's strengths were not readily available as resources. There was no link to oral speech or to visual images that would help her construct her message. As in much academic writing, she had only words to use as tools for conveying her message. Especially because of her positioning as a student and as a nonnative speaker of English, she needed to make her message as transparent and accurate as possible for the reader. All the meaning needed to be contained in the words she wrote. As a result, this assignment was a real challenge for her because she simultaneously had to focus on accuracy, representation, and communication without the oral and visual tools that assisted her in out-of-school writing.

Nan's Written Meaning-Making

In analyzing Nan's out-of-school writing, three questions are important in understanding the texts themselves: What is she writing? To whom is she writing? And why is she writing? Sociolinguistic studies of written language have tended to focus on the form of the writing, its context, the functions it serves, and the roles and statuses of the writer(s) and audience. (For a review of this literature, see McKay, 1996.) Only recently have sociolinguists concerned themselves with the content of writing (Hornberger & Skilton-Sylvester, 2000). Here I examine not only the form of Nan's writing but the topics that she chose to write about as well.

Understanding the audiences Nan wrote for is especially important, since so much of school writing is done solely for the teacher to read. Notions of audience are quite connected to issues of purpose and function. In Camitta's (1993) study of out-of-school writing at a Philadelphia high school, she found that audience and purpose intersected in significant ways for adolescents:

> Personal and creative writing is a motion toward intimacy, and . . . its exchange weaves the strands of friendship and understanding. . . . For adolescents, writing is personal and social, an act of invention in which everyday actions are shaped and influenced by the content and by the symbolic value of written texts (p. 243).

As I show in the analysis that follows, the genre/content, purpose/function, and audience of Nan's out-of-school writing were quite different from those of her school writing. In part, this analysis can explain why she was such an engaged writer at home and such a disengaged writer at school.

Genre

Although Nan's out-of-school writing included several different genres, she was most comfortable with narrative stories and letters to people she knew. Even the accounts that she wrote about real events had a storylike quality to them. Most of her fictional and nonfictional writing began with "One day . . . " For example, two nonfiction stories about me started: "One day is a girl name Miss Ellen." Here's the shorter version of this story:

> One day is a Girl name Msr. ELLEN
> Who like to teach a student
> her name is <u>ELLEN</u>
> She like to teach a lettle student

Another nonfictional story that started this way recounted how Nan's friend had thrown away the disposable camera she had taken to school. This story begins "One day I give my camera to my freind." All of her fictional stories (except the play) also began in this same way; for example: "One day it was a cloud and it was so cold." Nan's fictional and nonfictional stories as well as her single-page and multipage stories shared this storytelling mode. Her multipage stories were different in that each concluded with "The End." In all of the other fictional and nonfictional writing, the only other story that ended this way was the one about the camera. These beginnings and endings show, I think, that she had mastered aspects of the story genre and preferred it over other kinds of writing. More than half of her writing used these "story-oriented" conventions. The emphasis on narrative in her out-of-school writing illustrates the somewhat narrow set of conventions that she was comfortable working within. Clearly, as a student she needed to master other genres. What is unfortunate is that her rhetorical knowledge of storytelling was not made visible in ways that would allow her to make comparisons to alternate ways of making meaning in the classroom.

The other genre that Nan used most often was the letter. She wrote six letters to me during the fieldwork period, several around the time of my wedding. For example:

Dear Mrs, Mr, Ellen and Paul

Have a very good time I wish
you and Paul have a baby so we
can see what he or her looks like

We wish	Fr, Bnom * Rem
he or her	Family
well be	To you and and
pretty and	Mr. Paul
cute	

In this letter, Nan showed that she knew some of the conventions for writing a letter, such as starting with "Dear" and ending with some kind of closing. She didn't use a typical convention for letters, but rather the kind of headings often found in memos or on gifts. She ended with a section that shows whom the note is from and whom it is to. Although she still struggled with punctuation (there is none in this writing sample), she did capitalize appropriately, making it easier to distinguish the boundaries between ideas.

About a year later, Nan sent me a letter in the mail which shows that she had figured out several other letter-writing conventions:

Dear Mrs. Ellen

How are you! Thanks for the letters you sent to us. Did you know I have got a crush on a boy name Tommy he's cute and he's in 7th grade he's my typ but he have a girlfriend I got a crush on him since's he frist came to this school went he didn't have a girlFriend yet. please write back what should I do.

Love. Tiff

ask know ask <————AKA

Nan

P.S. wish you a nice time
  my friend knew I like him thy say they'll hook
  me up with him
  wish you like my letter

In this later letter, Nan demonstrated that she had learned about closing personal letters and that she could also append a "P.S." for additional thoughts. She used more punctuation, and she had also learned a common preteenage convention of putting "AKA" after her name to include both a nickname and her more formal name. Although she used this convention correctly, she incorrectly indicated that it stands for "ask know ask" rather than "also known as." In this case, Nan had learned the form but did not completely understand the meaning.

Certain features of the school genres she regularly produced can be found in the writing she did outside of class. I first noticed this practice in the writing of Nan's younger sister, Chamran. After a huge struggle with reading and writing in first and second grade, one day Chamran asked me if she could write a story. This was a monumental event because she had never asked to write something for fun. When I gave Chamran a piece of paper, she wrote her name in the top right corner of the page and then put "Spelling" as a title centered at the top of the page and numbered from one to ten down the left-hand side. In her first piece of out-of-school writing, she had decided to compose a spelling test. This was the genre that she felt most comfortable with and the only kind of "story" she knew how to write. In contrast, Nan always embraced story writing, and there were few traces of typical school genres in her writing. The one exception was a picture at the top of which she had written "Today is Monday, January

18, 1993. It is a cold and sunny." This type of note consisting of the date and a short sentence about the weather was typically written on the chalkboard in the ESOL classes at her school.

Content

Before looking at particular themes in Nan's out-of-school writing, I would like to draw attention to one general feature of its content—the fact that in most of the texts I analyzed, women and girls are the main characters. The only exceptions in the writing she gave me are the "store opening" story, which had a man as its main character and the drawing of me with my husband (see Figure 3.1). At one point during the fieldwork period, Nan told me that she had added a boy character to a story she was writing about a girl who encountered some bees. When she rewrote the story to include the boy, she changed the title to reflect this change. Interestingly, although the female character had a name, she did not name this boy. When I asked her why she had made the decision to add a boy to her story, Nan explained: "My friend told me it is better if there's a boy, too."

This example shows that Nan talked about her writing with her friends and sometimes took their advice about the content of what she was composing. It also shows that when writing for her own purposes, the content of her writing was typically connected to her own interests and experiences as a girl. Although the topic of her writing was not always herself, it was the starting point for much if not all of what she wrote. This is yet another way in which the school writing Nan did differed from the writing she did on her own, for she was often not able to include herself or her experiences in her school writing (Skilton-Sylvester, 1997).

In Nan's out-of-school writing, there was a dual emphasis on fantasy and reality. Her thematic focus ranged from (1) seemingly mundane topics (such a story about her mother cooking, a story about seeing a bird in a tree, and a letter telling me that she had drawn a lot of pictures); to (2) fantasy topics (such as one about dressing in glamorous dresses and dancing, several about participating in my wedding, and a few that take place in nonurban settings quite unlike her neighborhood—settings with trees, birds, flowers, and single-family homes with chimneys); to (3) topics about difficult realities (including one about a fictional family living in poverty and another about a girl who cannot go to school because she is pregnant).

An example of the first set of topics about seemingly mundane realities is a text about her mother cooking. It included a picture of an overhead light and a table set with plates, forks, knives, and spoons. The text reads, "My mom is making a fried. But is good to eat." Even in this apparently straightforward story, one can see the ways that Nan situated herself, not just as a reporter of what she saw, but a creator of written realities. She wrote this text as if she were writing a description of something that she had witnessed, but she also transformed the message in ways that vary from reality. Nan's family did not own a table; they typically ate sitting on the floor. They also ate using chopsticks, not forks, knives, and spoons. Even in this seemingly straightforward story, Nan created a reality with her message; she didn't merely transcribe it. The insertion of a table, chairs, and silverware fit with Nan's interest in the lives of the families she saw on TV and of other Americans. She regularly interviewed me about my family's practices and asked if we ate the way that people do on television. Her choice also fit with her ambivalence about being Cambodian:

> *Nan*: I don't want to be Asian American. I want to be just American.
> *Me*: Why?
> *Nan*: Cause it's better.
> *Me*: Why is it better?
> *Nan*: It just is. (fieldnotes, 2/5/95)

In her pictures and stories, she sometimes had the power to "Americanize" her family in ways that did not fit her lived reality.

Nan's ability to create new realities was even more present in the writings that clearly included fantasy content. In these stories, she created the content completely, rather than basing it partially on her own lived experience. The same is true of her later drawings (see Figure 3.2). In these stories and pictures, the figures were typically women who are dressed in long, elaborate gowns. Another example can be seen in the story called "The Pretter Girls" ("The Pretty Girls"): "One day it was six pretter girls and They all dances pretter like a pretter women that has a picture for me. Some of the pretter girls were asleep now." This particular story and drawing had six girls, all in full-length gowns with one lying down and sleeping at the bottom of the page; in many others Nan created similar situations in which women are described as pretty and are dressed quite formally and extravagantly. Her interest in stories about formal occasions became more intense before my own wedding; Nan spent a long time talking about what I would wear and how pretty I would look.[4]

The final set of themes have to do with fictional stories written about difficult realities; they are not about Nan but instead address issues that are relevant to her life. In addition to challenges similar to those facing other girls in school, the Cambodian girls in my study often had significant family responsibilities that outweighed those of their brothers or their non-Cambodian classmates, strict rules about interacting with the opposite sex, and

FIGURE 3.2: Nan's Two Sisters and Her Cousin in a Fantasy Drawing

uncertainty about their language abilities or limited experience with participation patterns found in the classroom (Skilton-Sylvester, 1997).

In addition, the girls often worried about getting pregnant early, a fear closely linked to concerns about not finishing school and a potential version of their futures. When I visited college campuses with Nan's older cousin Ty, her mother kept lecturing her about how important it was not to get pregnant if she were allowed to live on campus (Skilton-Sylvester, 1997). On a similar topic, in fourth grade Nan wrote the following story entitled "The girl that can not got out of School":

> One day she went home with not tell the teacher. The teacher cannot found her. The girl went up the sky and down the dry and then she got home early. But she forgot to go to school. The teacher was very happy that she did not go to school. The girl said "Oh no." In the next morning, she did not go home. Her mother was very sad because she did not go home. The girl's mom give her a wedding. The girl cry today. The girl is a mommy and the girl's mother is a grand-

mother and she have a baby. The girl cannot go to school because she had a baby. The End.

While the title seems to suggest that the girl cannot get out of going to school (i.e., she has to go to school), the story ends by stating that she can't go to school. This might be just an inadvertent mix-up, but I think it may also point to ambivalence about school, which is supposed to be a place where people want to be but often is not. It is also interesting (and disturbing) that the teacher in the story is happy when the girl doesn't come to school. Although this story line may not have been directly applicable to Nan's experience with school, there were certainly times for all the girls in this study when they did not feel good about going to school, often because of peer relationships and negative connotations associated with being in ESOL. For example, Nan's youngest sister Chamran once asked me when I would come to her class to visit again "because sometimes I don't have any friends." She went on to explain that her friend "took" her other friend by saying that Chamran wasn't good at ESOL (fieldnotes, 6/2/94). At other times, discomfort with school had more to do with academic struggles. Nan's older cousin Saporn talked about her difficulty in school this way: "I'm doing so bad in school. I've never been this scared. I study and study and I fail, but my other friends, they didn't even study and they know how to do it. It just doesn't make any difference. I study and it does nothing" (fieldnotes, 2/22/95).

Most of the pictures that Nan drew for "The girl that can not got out of School" illustrate directly what was happening in each segment of the plot, except in the first section when the girl left school early, and there are a few rhyming words that don't seem to make sense: "the girl went up the sky and down to the dry." The picture in Figure 3.3 shows a car near the school with what looks like a young man in it; in this context these words seem to allude to what she is doing with him. Since most Cambodian girls Nan's age don't seem to know too much about pregnancy, it makes some sense that whatever she is doing with this boy is in almost indecipherable terms. (One of her cousins who is the same age was surprised that I didn't have a baby when I got home from my week-long honeymoon.)

It is also noteworthy that the girl in the story sees the boy under the guise of school. This fits with my understanding of the uses of an "education" label in increasing freedom and mobility for young women. If an event is seen as a school event (i.e., going to the library, meeting a tutor), girls and young women can often do things they wouldn't ordinarily be able to do (dancing with a boy, wearing a sleeveless dress). As Kulig (1994) states, "There are many opportunities for freedom here for these young women

FIGURE 3.3: First Page of "The girl that can not got out of school"

The girl that can not got out of School

One day she want Home with
not tell the teacher. the teacher
can not found her the girls went up
the Sky and Down to the Dry and then
she got Home early

because they attend school where they can meet and spend time with young men without parental supervision" (p. 139).

This story says a lot, I think, about the fear girls have about not living up to their parents' goals for their future. The fears expressed by Nan about getting pregnant as a teenager are an example of this. However, it is important not to see their fears simply in terms of the disruption of having a baby as a teenager. Nan's story also seems to express well both the ambivalence these girls often have about school and a sense that they do not always feel wanted when they are there. In a more general way, this story illustrates the fact that going or not going to school is often a gendered process; that is, that processes that influence girls (i.e., pregnancy, needing to take care of siblings, rules about interactions with the opposite sex, marriage) can be in conflict with being a student.

Clearly, in the content of her writing, Nan did not focus primarily on the specifics of her own everyday reality. Instead, she transformed those realities, dreamed of other realities, and worked out fears about current and/or future realities. Although her own life was typically the starting point, she often created her stories at the intersection of fact and fiction. My analysis of the reading and writing that these students did in school indicates that outside of the ESOL classroom, there were few opportunities to write with their own lives (or the lives of other Asian Americans) as a starting point. The writing that these girls did in school focused much more on fact than on fiction, making Nan's stories sometimes seem like false representations of the facts, rather than her own "trying on" of different possibilities.

Audience/Function

Unlike much of Nan's school writing, for which the teacher was the only audience and the purpose of writing was often "to finish the assignment for a grade," Nan's out-of-school writing had multiple audiences and served multiple functions. I was surprised to see how much copying students were required to do in their school writing, especially in the early grades. I was also somewhat surprised to hear Saporn, Nan's cousin, say that students got higher grades when they copied something from the book than when they wrote something themselves (fieldnotes, 5/30/94). Saporn's copying during middle school could be framed as plagiarism, but it could also be seen as a product of many years of school training in which copying was the main genre of school-based writing. In fact, in first grade, almost all Chamran's homework had to do with copying. From this perspective, Saporn used the training that she received in elementary school, despite the fact that the rules for writing had changed. She had developed few skills for meeting the writing expectations of middle school and high school.

The notion that it matters more to put something on the page than to write something good or original was echoed many times in the comments of these school-aged girls. As Saporn explained, "Sometimes when I copy what I write, I don't even know what it means anymore" (fieldnotes, 2/25/94). Not knowing what things mean seemed to hamper other aspects of writing for some of the girls. Ty, for example, thought that not knowing the meaning made it hard for her to spell words. She questioned, "They asked me about the spelling of the words, but if I don't know what they mean, how can I know how to spell them?" (fieldnotes, 6/2/95).

In contrast to the school writing Nan had to do, her out-of-school writing had multiple audiences and multiple functions. For example, letter/note-writing was something that Nan (and the other girls) did a lot and not just with me. They regularly used letters to repair and maintain relationships, write to members of the opposite sex, and keep in touch with friends (Skilton-Sylvester, 1997). In fact, when Nan sent me the letter about her crush on a boy, she also included a copy of the note that had been passed back and forth between her and her friend about this boy. In the note, parts were crossed out as new messages were exchanged:

> ~~Whatever you name Tommy~~
> ~~Why you ask me if I like him~~
> Because I'm gonna hook you up with him
> No I got a boy already
> Who?
> My friend brother in Maine name Timmy

This strategy of maintaining relationships through writing was particularly appealing to these girls in part because it was difficult for many of their parents to read what they had written. Neither of Nan's parents could read in English, so a note was a safe way for her to communicate even about things that her parents might not want her to talk about (i.e., a crush on a boy). So, in addition to there being a real audience, the value of communicating in this way was also connected to a "nonaudience"—knowing, that is, that one's parents could not read what was written.

Although Nan often focused more on creating and representing her message than on being sure it was communicated as she intended, it is clear that her out-of-school writing was always done to be shared with someone. In some cases, it was performed; in others, it was passed along to show her interest in a topic or to show that she cared about the receiver. In our tutoring sessions, she gave me pieces of her writing as gifts when I left, as something of value that she had created. Another example of this practice can be seen from the story line of her play "Daytime," when disappointed girls cannot buy a birthday present for their sister: "We have no money but we can make a card for her." Here is the foundation of the audiences and purposes Nan imagines as she writes. Although she struggled in school and did not have much money, Nan was able through her pencil and paper to give those around her a creation that was part of herself. In this way, writing was a limitless resource for connecting with others outside of school.

Investment

Understanding Nan's experiences with writing requires thinking about her investment (Norton Peirce, 1995) in using and learning about writing. This notion acknowledges that power relationships and other particulars of the context can shape identities and language practices at any given point in time. Norton Peirce's (1995) term *investment* is connected to the idea that those who are learning a new language need to believe that they have the "right to speak," that what they say will be heard and responded to with interest, respect, and action. Drawing on Bourdieu's (1977) work, she suggests that we cannot assume that listeners always grant those who are speaking (or writing) English as a second language the "right to speak."

I believe that Nan's experiences with writing in home and school contexts can be understood in terms of investment, identity, and the right to speak. In thinking about Nan's experiences with school writing, it would be easy to conclude that she was just not motivated, that she simply had little interest in print. What her out-of-school writing shows is that she could be incredibly invested in using and learning about the written word when she was granted the right to write and knew that there were those who really wanted to listen to her thoughts, experiences, and ideas. At school, when she was framed as a "struggling writer" and where the purposes of writing were not primarily to "do social work," she was often unable to reveal her literacy strengths. In her ESOL classroom, however, where she was given the opportunity to "perform" parts of her journal for her classmates, she was able to demonstrate some of her literacy strengths within the school context. At home, where she was framed as storyteller and playwright, she wrote with great enthusiasm and creativity. We have often failed in schools because we tell students we want them to speak/compose their thoughts on paper, yet we constrain their "right to speak" by making our responses primarily evaluative. As teachers, we are often not a real audience, and so it is difficult for students to invest in the work we are asking them to do. Nan's engagement in the writing of her ESOL classroom shows, however, that when purpose and audience are meaningfully constructed, she was able to claim the right to write within the classroom context.

Implications for Teachers and Schools

Both Norton Peirce (1995) and Cummins (1997) point to the important role that teachers can play in shaping the identities students have at school. In discussing what makes it possible for language-minority students to succeed, one of the key elements Cummins (1997) stresses is "the identity options that are being opened up or closed off for students" (p. 425) in the school context. Similarly, Norton Peirce (1995) discusses this changing subjectivity of students in different contexts and concludes that because identities can be shaped by those who listen to students and read their texts, educational intervention can really have an impact. Norton Peirce (1995) suggests:

> Motivation is not a fixed personality trait but must be understood with refer-
> ence to social relations of power that create the possibilities for language learn-
> ers to speak. . . . It is their investment in the target language that will lead
> [learners] to speak. . . . The lived experiences and social identities of language
> learners need to be incorporated into the formal second language curriculum
> (p. 26).

My study has shown, however, that if students' lives only enter the school walls through writing that is on the periphery of how students are ulti-mately evaluated, we have not created the bridge needed to make the out-of-school strengths of a student such as Nan visible when she is tackling academic literacy. It is also important, as Zamel (1993) has pointed out, that we not merely prepare students for the academic world that already exists, but that we work to make that academic world take the realities of writing in a second language into consideration in evaluation.

Nan's writing also highlights the importance of visual and oral dis-course in the ways she augmented the meaning-making she does with let-ters and words. Bridges need to be built between these multisensory mes-sages and the ways that school writing is often judged and interpreted based on the messages that the words themselves convey. Kress (1997) suggests, "As texts draw more and more overtly on visual means of communication, the skills and knowledge of visual design and display will need to be fos-tered as a central part of any literacy curriculum" (p. 58).

If schools are to compete with peer groups for the investment of stu-dents, it needs to be clear to students that they have something to gain by learning school writing conventions. This "return on investment" needs to be more than a good grade. We need to show the doors that open up if one can write "transparent" messages as part of academic discourse. Even more, we need to show that there is an immediate return on students' investment in school writing, that this writing is being written for real audi-ences and real purposes beyond evaluation.

In Nan's writing, there was just one time that a school writing genre visibly appeared in her out-of-school writing (that is, when she placed a date at the top of a page and described the weather). Her genres of choice—fictional stories with pictures and letters—were not typical genres she was asked to write in school. The genres that she liked best had an emphasis on creative storytelling and personal connections, two features often not present in school writing. The one place where school and out-of-school genres intersected was in the journal that she kept in ESOL class that she was often able to read out loud to her classmates. The journal captured both the creativity and the emphasis on relationships that are central characteristics of the genres she most often picked, and it included a performance element that also highlighted her strengths. Unfortunately, journal-writing was not a type of genre that had much importance at school, so this link was not a powerful enough bridge between her home and school writing practices. Also, in other classes I observed, journals were not linked to performance but were primarily used as communication tools to discuss ideas and thoughts with an audience that included the teacher, but not necessarily other students.

During Nan's fourth-grade year, I spent a significant period of time in her grade-level classroom. Her teacher, Mrs. Jackson, explained that she was at a second-grade reading level and that the school had recently adopted a textbook series that meant that all students in a particular grade read the same text at the same time. This was quite difficult for Nan, who got the most out of the lessons when the stories were read out loud or listened to on tape. It appears that her comfort in speaking in the classroom could also have been used as a bridge. Mrs. Jackson explained, "Well, the Cambodian girls are very quiet, very timid. . . . Nan on the other hand is very vocal. I mean, whether she has the right or wrong answer or has any idea what you were talking about, she'll . . . offer an answer to a question" (taped interview, 6/2/94). Even so, much of the "language work" that went on in her fourth-grade classroom was "over her head." On one of the days that I observed the class, while much of the class read a story, Nan worked in a small group of students focusing on phonics exercises from a workbook not associated with the main text (fieldnotes, 5/22/94).

When Mrs. Jackson spoke about writing instruction in her classroom, she first mentioned the lesson that she thought was most successful that year. It was an exercise the children did after reading a story that contained a lot of similes; most of the students then successfully created similes of their own. As Mrs. Jackson goes on to discuss what her goals were for writing instruction, one can sense how much she wanted writing to be fun for her students:

> One thing I work on from the very beginning is just building sentences. . . . I work on creative writing and my feeling is writing is just something the kids should do. We go through all the writing pro-

cess. I go through all the steps—brainstorming, the rough copy, the editing, the final copy. It takes maybe a whole week to do one story. And my goal is not so much to get a finished piece of work that is grammatically correct, punctuation and all. My goal is to get a story that shows some imagination and shows that the child was able to go through those steps, was able to . . . get their ideas down. . . . I will grade them, but I don't put the marks all over the paper. *So my goal is that by the end of the year, they've had an enjoyable experience writing.* . . . We read autobiographies in the book and then from that we just took off and wrote an autobiography. (taped interview, 6/2/94, emphasis added)

The writing Nan most often did in her fourth-grade classroom clustered around three types: (1) writing based on readings done in class, (2) creative writing in which students showed their ability to go through the writing process, and (3) workbook exercises that included individual words or the construction of sentences.

There are several ways in which Nan's strengths from her out-of-school writing could have been evident here—the emphasis on meaning-making in creative writing (rather than on correctness) and the writing of autobiographies were both potential pathways for Nan to participate in school writing. However, the emphasis in the creative writing process was on communication for the teacher who would be grading the writing and not on performance or relationship-building through the writing. Also, pictures were not a part of the meaning-making she did for these creative writing activities. In addition, because the readings were often inaccessible to Nan, the writing of autobiographies or the writing of similes might have been difficult to even begin to understand.

It is not difficult to imagine that the classroom context could be one in which oral and visual meaning-making exist alongside written communication, where both teachers and students are an authentic audience for the written work of others in the classroom, and where the purposes for writing are connected to multiple real reasons why class members would want to communicate with each other. And in fact, in some of the many classrooms I visited, this very kind of writing instruction did occur. If Nan had been in such an environment, her abilities as a playwright might have been a springboard for doing the social work of school through writing.

Aside from the ways that writing instruction occurred in the classroom, two other factors might have made Nan's writing trajectory quite different. First, if she had learned to read and write in her native Khmer, there is reason to believe (Garcia, 1999, in press; Snow, Burns, & Griffin, 1998) that she might not have fallen so far behind her native-English-speaking peers in her ability to understand and create texts in English. Like Nan, all her sisters and cousins struggled with the technical skills of reading and writing in the early grades, and this continued to make them fall farther and farther behind their peers. Much of Nan's writing, although expressive, creative, and interesting, did not meet the expectations of school personnel for what children of her age should be able to accomplish with print.

Nan's in-school writing was also influenced by her perception of herself within the school context. As I mentioned above, student subjectivities are "(re)formed within the space of the school itself" (Levinson, 1998, p. 267). Nan was a part of a peer culture in which being literate was not the pathway to popularity. Part of why Nan's out-of-school writing was more visible than her in-school writing may have had to do with the fact that mastering "sanctioned literacies" was seen as the key to unpopularity. Her desire to win popularity, however, was also connected to the fact that she saw herself losing at the academic game. As we saw earlier, Nan believed that adopting an American name was a good way to achieve better academic results. At some level, when she was not in her ESOL classroom, she had given up on herself as someone who could do "sanctioned literacy" and so it is not surprising that her "literate underlife" was so much more vibrant than what she did at school.

Nan did find some success in her ESOL classroom, where she was able to use her multimodal resources to perform literate acts in the classroom, where many of the students had similar reading and writing difficulties, and where her linguistic and cultural differences were "normal." However, the reading and writing she did in ESOL was not the kind of reading and writing she was expected to do outside it. The engagement she experienced with writing out-of-school shows that she saw the potential power of the written medium to convey meaning and build relationships—to "do social work" with writing. Nan's out-of-school literacy resources—and those of many nonmainstream students in U.S. schools—can be a foundation for school literacy if we are able to read the words and the worlds that children bring with them to school and help them to engage in new and related words and worlds as they use writing to do the social work of school. There are many things to learn by looking at Nan's out-of-school writing in relation to her in-school writing. It is abundantly clear that we, as teachers, have as much to learn from Nan as she from us.

Notes

1. The research reported in this chapter was made possible in part by a grant from the Spencer Foundation. The data presented, the statements made, and the views expressed are solely the responsibility of the author.

2. Most of the girls did not choose American names until high school.

3. *Y.S. v. School District of Philadelphia* was a class-action suit filed in 1985 on behalf of Asian students in Philadelphia. The resulting court mandate included restructuring curriculum, placement, and staffing in schools with a significant number of Asian students.

4. She was, in fact, somewhat disappointed by how informal my wedding was, which did not fit with how (fueled by television) she imagined such an event. At one point she told me, "You have to have a pink cake like they did on *Full House*" (one of her favorite television shows).

References

Auerbach, E. R. (1989). Toward a socio-contextual approach to family literacy. *Harvard Educational Review, 59*(2), 165–181.

Bourdieu, P. (1977). The economics of linguistic exchanges. *Social Science Information, 16,* 645–668.

Camitta, M. (1993). Vernacular writing: Varieties of literacy among Philadelphia high school students. In B. Street (Ed.), *Cross-cultural approaches to literacy* (pp. 228–246). Cambridge, UK: Cambridge University Press.

Cummins, J. (1997). Minority status and schooling in Canada. *Anthropology & Education Quarterly, 28*(3),411–430.

Dyson, A. H. (1993). *Social worlds of children learning to write in an urban primary school.* New York: Teachers College Press.

Finders, M. J. (1996). "Just girls": Literacy and allegiance in junior high school. *Written Communication, 13*(1), 93–129.

Garcia, G. E. (1999). Bilingual children's reading: An overview of recent research. *ERIC/CLL Newsbulletin.* ERIC Clearinghouse on Language and Linguistics, Center for Applied Linguistics.

Garcia, G. E. (in press). Bilingual children's reading. In M. Kamil, P. Mosenthal, P. D. Pearson, & R. Barr (Eds.), *Handbook of reading research* (Vol. 3). New York: Longman.

Hardman, J. (1994). *Language and literacy development in a Cambodian community in Philadelphia.* Unpublished doctoral dissertation, University of Pennsylvania, Graduate School of Education, Philadelphia.

Heller, M. (1999). *Linguistic minorities and modernity: A sociolinguistic ethnography.* New York: Longman.

Hornberger, N. H. (1996). Mother-tongue literacy in the Cambodian community of Philadelphia. *International Journal of the Sociology of Language, 119,* 69–86.

Hornberger, N. H., & Skilton-Sylvester, E. (2000). Revisiting the continua of biliteracy: International and critical perspectives. *Language and Education: An International Journal, 14*(2), 96–122.

Kress, G. (1997). *Before writing: Rethinking the paths to literacy.* New York: Routledge.

Kulig, J. C. (1994). Old traditions in a new world: Changing gender relations among Cambodian refugees. In L. A. Camino & R. M. Krulfield (Eds.), *Reconstructing lives, recapturing meaning: Refugee identity, gender and culture change* (pp. 129–146). Basel, Switzerland: Gordon and Breach Science Publishers, S.A.

Ledgerwood, J. (1990). *Changing Khmer conceptions of gender: Women, stories and the social order.* Unpublished doctoral dissertation. Departments of Anthropology and the Southeast Asia Program, Cornell University, Ithaca, NY.

Ledgerwood, J., Ebihara, M. M., & Mortland, C. A. (1994). Introduction. In M. Ebihara, C. Mortland, & J. Ledgerwood (Eds.), *Cambodian culture since 1975: Homeland and exile* (pp. 1–26). Ithaca, NY: Cornell University Press.

Levinson, B. A. (1998). Student culture and the contradictions of equality at a Mexican secondary school. *Anthropology and Education Quarterly, 29*(3), 267–296.

McKay, S. L. (1996). Literacy and literacies. In S. L. McKay & N. H. Hornberger (Eds.), *Sociolinguistics and language teaching* (pp. 421–445). Cambridge, UK: Cambridge University Press.

McKay, S. L., & Weinstein-Shr, G. (1993). English literacy in the United States: National policies, personal consequences. *TESOL Quarterly, 27*(3), 32–52.

Ngo, H. (1994, March). *From learner to teacher: Language minority teachers speak out.* Paper presented at the 28th annual convention of Teachers of English to Speakers of Other Languages, Baltimore.

Norton Peirce, B. (1995). Social identity, investment, and language learning. *TESOL Quarterly, 29*(1), 9–31.

Skilton-Sylvester, E. (1997). *Inside, outside and in-between: Identities, literacies and educational policies in the lives of Cambodian women and girls in Philadelphia.* Unpublished doctoral dissertation, University of Pennsylvania, Philadelphia.

Smith, F. (1994). Cultural consumption: Cambodian peasant refugees and television in the "first world." In M. Ebihara, C. Mortland, & J. Ledgerwood (Eds.), *Cambodian culture since 1975: Homeland and exile* (pp. 141–160). Ithaca, NY: Cornell University Press.

Snow, C. E., Burns, M. S., & Griffin, P. (Eds.). (1998). *Preventing reading difficulties in young children.* Washington, DC: National Academy Press.

Thierry, S. (1978). *Etude d'un corpus de contes Cambodgiens traditionnels.* Unpublished master's thesis, University of Paris, Paris, France.

Zamel, V. (1993). Questioning academic discourse. *College ESL, 3*, 28–39.

VERDA DELP RESPONDS

> These tensions are not markers of unruly children but of complex
> children, who are differentiating, organizing, and reorganizing
> their symbolic and cultural resources and their ever widening so-
> cial and ideological worlds. (Dyson, 1999)

In looking at Nan's school and out-of-school writing practices from a teacher's perspective—one that embraces an array of intertwined literacy practices and that recognizes the dissonance that exists when students take on
and learn to use newly developing skills—I have come to see that Nan
purposively struggles to practice the writing skills she has appropriated in
school in both of these settings. Her affect and the strategies she uses reflect
her awareness and understanding of the conditions and constraints that exist and the resources that are available to her in each of the contexts. Moreover, Nan's written texts provide nuanced evidence—much like a docu-
mentary—of the writing skills she has yet to acquire.

At school, Nan's affect—that of a "struggling" writer—reflects her dili-
gence and commitment to her learning. Her behavior indicates that she
works hard to complete her assignments within the confines of the classroom *structure*. She receives help from her tutor when she revises her
written texts, which demonstrates how she calls upon and uses resources
that support her practice—in this case, gaining help with form and correctness, an appropriate endeavor in this particular context.

Notwithstanding these strengths, Nan's written texts illustrate her profound need to acquire more language—language that will hopefully become
an internalized resource and will enable her to express her ideas in writing
more effectively and completely. For this reason, I believe that Nan should
be steeped in language models—models that reflect an array of genres and
represent a legion of patterns and structures of written text. These models
need to be available resources (in the form of written text) for Nan whenever she writes. Concomitantly, and perhaps most importantly, Nan must
be given many, many opportunities to practice her writing—occasions

when she can consult these written models while she tries out her newly developing skills.

At home, where her affect is that of an "engaged" writer, Nan also works hard to portray her ideas in writing and takes advantage of the resources that are available to her. Drawing on what Skilton-Sylvester refers to as "strengths" and "cultural" preferences, Nan augments her written texts with the resources at hand—in this case, embellishing her writing with oral language and visual imagery to communicate fully and correctly the meaning of her text to her audience.

Nonetheless, while acknowledging Nan's preferred literacy practices, I believe that her writing, even in this setting, reflects identical implications as her school writing—the acquisition of an abundance of language. Rather than interpreting her augmenting strategies as purely cultural-linguistic practices, I think they may also be seen as guideposts that mark Nan's need—and perhaps desire—to appropriate the lexical equivalents of these aural and symbolic representations of written language.

Rather than merely adding narrative and letter-writing genres to the classroom curriculum as Skilton-Sylvester proposes—which would, nonetheless, call for the use of skills that Nan does not yet possess—I would argue that teachers need to provide for their students an abundance of models of written texts that represent many genres, language patterns, structures, and writing strategies. Referring to written resources of these models when they write, students must be given innumerable opportunities to practice their developing skills of writing in classroom settings where their struggles to appropriate these literacies are understood and honored.

Reference

Dyson, A. H. (1999). Coach Bombay's kids learn to write: Children's appropriation of media material for school literacy. *Research in the Teaching of English,* *33*(4), 367–402.

MARCI RESNICK RESPONDS

Skilton-Sylvester poses early on in her chapter the question: What can we learn from out-of-school practices that could help us reshape what happens in schools around literacy? An accompanying question for me is: What are the many ways in which teachers can know their students—their strengths, challenges, and interests—in order to inform classroom literacy practices? The implications from this chapter, not just for teachers but for school structures and policies, are many.

Let me first share the lens through which I read this chapter. I am not an ESL teacher. In many ways this is appropriate, since most often it is teachers with no ESL background who are working for large portions of each school day with second-language learners. I have been an elementary school teacher for 20 years and director of a literacy-based teacher network working with hundreds of urban K-12 schoolteachers for the past 5 years. So it is with these experiences that I respond.

There are three themes that run through this chapter that have captured my attention. The first centers on knowing a student's culture and understanding what this means about literacy practices. There is a growing recognition of the importance of familiarizing students with a variety of cultures and cultural experiences. Yet this does not necessarily translate into an intentional building of bridges by the classroom teacher or school administrations' instructional leaders among cultures, families, and schools. For example, when Skilton-Sylvester writes about Nan's strengths as a storyteller, this obviously has classroom implications. Considering the wonderful stories in Nan's head, we can imagine the audiotaping, dramatizing, and transcribing of her stories. These very stories could be the resources used to help Nan become a successful writer. They would certainly hold a greater potential for impacting Nan's writing than traditional textbooks. Her drawings could be her story maps or her "rehearsal" for writing. She could easily be invited into what is known as the "literary club" with the strengths she brings.

I know I found it very powerful to read this chapter and couldn't help but imagine what I would do as a teacher to support Nan as a learner. But

I also couldn't help but wonder how much of this story and world history Nan's teachers knew. How were they supported and encouraged in finding out? Where and who were their supports in discussing Nan and who she was as well as the instructional practices that would move her writing forward? With large classrooms, full teaching schedules, enormous amounts of paperwork, and increased number of mandated meetings, how do we insure that the important details of a child are paid attention to, not just the broad landscape where everything seems to blend and be one?

I recently read an article about students' being asked how their teachers could best help them with their writing (Zaragoza & Vaughn, 1995). An overwhelming number reported that the single most *unhelpful* practice that the teacher employs is to tell them what to write. The second theme I want to discuss and which was embedded throughout this chapter is evidence of the need for schools and classrooms to allow for students to make choices and decisions about their own writing. Skilton-Sylvester discusses the differences in Nan's in-school and out-of-school writing, when the content of Nan's writing connects to her interests and experiences and when she controls the topic and genre. One could easily draw the conclusion that teachers, therefore, should just let students decide. Yet I have spent endless hours as a teacher and a mother listening to children unlike Nan say that they have nothing to write. So the implication is not just to let students decide but to help children learn where ideas might come from so they have a rich body of experience from which to choose. Books, classmates' stories, authors' memoirs, and the keeping of a record, journal, or notebook that reflects what is important to the students (such as the use of a Writer's Notebook) are all explicit ways we can help students discover what they want to say and how to say it.

Finally, the chapter discusses how some of the students copied or plagiarized their work in school but not out of school, when they had a clear purpose and authentic audience for their work. This was a reminder for me to give careful thought to the writing assignments and invitations I create for students. I have recently been working with groups of teachers in looking at the relationship between teacher assignments and student work. It has been quite an eye opener when, collectively, we critically look at teacher assignments and what they are actually asking students to do. This also speaks to the need for teachers to look collectively at student work. The multiple perspectives of colleagues might have identified the distinctions between copying and attempting an analysis of one's own. Providing time and space for teachers to work together in serious ways to examine their own practices and the work of their students is an important step in ensuring that this happens.

Hopefully, Nan's story will be an entry point for teachers to discuss, share, and learn about Nan's out-of-school writing experiences and the lessons they hold for educators about in-school instructional practices.

Reference

Zaragoza, N., & Vaughn, S. (1995). Children teach us to teach writing. *The Reading Teacher, 49*(1), 42–47.

4

Writing on the Margins

The Spiritual and Autobiographical Discourse of Two *Mexicanas* in Chicago

JUAN C. GUERRA and MARCIA FARR

Literacy researchers increasingly are aware of the variety and richness of literacy practices carried out by all kinds of people in the different settings of their lives. This awareness stands in stark contrast to the "conventional wisdom" that assumes, in the midst of another national "literacy crisis," that millions of people can't read or write. While we ourselves would argue for more support of adult literacy programs for those who are not literate, as well as for those who want to expand their current literacy abilities, we regret the public rhetoric that, sometimes in an effort to increase such support, decries rampant illiteracy, which is then assumed of entire groups of people who would be clients in such programs. Our long-term ethnographic research in the Mexican community of Chicago, in contrast, has impressed on us the creativity, resourcefulness, and substantial capacities that ordinary people demonstrate in their everyday uses of written language. In spite of the fact that this is no doubt true of any community, denigrating stereotypes of minority communities lead us to "prove competence," that is, to prove what should already be assumed as a given.

Thus our research has as its overall goal the documentation and description of the communicative competence (Hymes, 1974) of one social network of families in this community. Since it is a bilingual and biliterate community, this description involves a sociolinguistic repertoire in both Spanish and English. Such a repertoire, however, entails more than grammatical competence in Spanish and/or English; it includes as well knowing how to use one or both of these languages appropriately in various contexts. As many people who have studied a foreign language only in school could attest, knowing the rules of grammar does not ensure communicating effectively with native speakers of that language. One also needs to know, for example, how to be polite, how to offer sympathy, how to ask for help. These pragmatic aspects of language use are cultural, and so our research involves the cultural as well as the linguistic, the oral as well as the written.

Such language abilities are central to education. As noted by Cazden (1988), language is not only the object of instruction in formal schooling, it is also the medium of instruction. This means that, whenever classrooms include individuals (students and/or teachers) from different cultural backgrounds, the potential for miscommunication increases. This is even the case when the students are fluent in the same language as the instructor and the textbooks, for miscommunication can arise from differences in styles of using language, either oral or written. Bilingual individuals, in fact, often transfer styles of speaking from their native to their second languages (Gumperz 1982a, 1982b; Scollon & Scollon, 1981, 1995), and even native speakers of a language vary greatly in styles of language use that they prefer and/or are accustomed to (e.g., Kochman, 1981; Morgan, 1994; Smitherman, 1977, 2000).

We are particularly concerned with the potential for such cross-cultural misunderstandings in college composition classroom for two reasons. First, the successful completion of required composition courses is essential for graduation, and it recently has been shown to be the single most important factor in retaining undergraduates at the University of Illinois at Chicago (UIC) until graduation (Bulanda, 1994). Second, the centrality of language in the educational process is especially foregrounded in composition courses; instructors realize that they have comparatively little time to prepare their students to write academic prose successfully enough to survive not only the sequence of composition courses but also other courses in the university. That is, learning to write in a particular register of language, what various researchers have termed "essayist literacy" in English, is the most important goal of composition courses. As one young woman from a family in the social network who attended UIC said to one of us during her first semester, "Oh, Marcia, my *life* is writing now!"

What kind of writing does this young woman have to produce to successfully complete her university classes? What expectations do her instructors hold as they read her essays? What implicit models are these instructors using as they evaluate these essays? What, in other words, is "essayist literacy"? Although there certainly are discipline-specific characteristics of this language register, there are also general characteristics pertaining to most academic writing that can be described. Various scholars have provided descriptions of aspects of essayist literacy, and these descriptions converge in important ways (Farr, 1993). Some, including Olson (1977), Ong (1982), Goody and Watt (1968), and Scollon and Scollon (1981), have referred to the "autonomous" or decontextualized quality of this kind of language (though generally written, essayist literacy can be expressed orally, too). These descriptions include as well assumptions of readers and writers as rational, idealized minds that either generate or comprehend the autonomous, decontextualized language under discussion. Scollon and Scollon (1981) and Walters (1990) add another characteristic: the foregrounding and importance of a particular kind of logical order within the text; that is, sentences must have an order that often is explicitly signaled—for example, with the use of "transition" words and phrases such as *moreover* or *however*. Elbow (1991) adds that essayist literacy relies on the specifying of reasons and evidence, rather than only feelings and opinions.

Recently some scholars have critiqued the restrictions of academic literacy. For example, Anzaldúa (1987) has decried the "language shame" of Chicano/as, in reference to both their dialectal Spanish and their often "mixed" English. Others have stressed the importance of writing in other genres, such as autobiography (e.g., hooks, 1989). In response to these and other works, some loosening of the strictures of essayist literacy, especially in English Department composition courses, has occurred in the past decade or so. In some university composition courses, other genres are emphasized, particularly narrative genres. Outside of English Departments, however, most instructors continue to expect traditional essayist conventions and genres, usually argumentative ones (Lunsford & Ruszkiewicz, 1998), albeit with discipline-specific features (Feldman, 1996). And it has been argued that *not* to teach the conventions and genres that meet these expectations is ultimately disenfranchising for students who come to the university without full control of essayist literacy (Delpit, 1995; Farr, 1993; Graff, 1999; Guerra, 1997). Our own position is that students should be prepared to handle the demands of essayist literacy in order to succeed in college and beyond, but that such teaching should be accompanied by an attitude of full respect for the oral and literate genres—as well as the dialects and languages common in their homes and communities—that students bring with them to the classroom.

Those students who don't learn, or aren't taught, to control essayist literacy conventions and genres must struggle to survive academically, regardless of their native intelligence or their linguistic skills in other genres, registers, and/or languages. And here is the crucial point: Teaching this "new" register is much more effective when the instructor understands the "variant" styles that occur in the initial (and sometimes later) compositions of students from homes and communities in which this academic register is not common. Yet extremely little is known about these "variant" styles of language from the variety of communities from which many contemporary university students come. Ethnographic and sociolinguistic research on these ways of using language can play a crucial role in the improvement of composition instruction. Minimally, it is important for instructors to understand that essayist literacy itself—what we teach when we teach "writing"—is not "naturally" logical or superior as a way of using language but, in contrast, has its own cultural and historical context. Maximally, however, it is better for instructors to understand and respect the communicative competence of their students' communities, aspects of which undoubtedly emerge in their writing, as they do in their speaking.

Our primary goal in this chapter, then, is to examine two genres of the "variant" writing of two women who reside in and are part of a social network that we have been working with for more than 10 years in Pilsen and Little Village, the largest and most densely populated Mexican-origin neighborhood in Chicago. Before we discuss the ways in which these two *mexicanas* establish rhetorical personas grounded in their lived experiences, we will first briefly describe the process we went through to establish a presence in the community and to identify the focal members of a social network we could enter to gather ethnographic data.

Identifying and Establishing a Relationship with Research Participants

While most people are aware of the fact that Mexican-origin people live in large numbers throughout the southwestern United States, few realize that Chicago has the second-largest *mexicano* population in the United States and the fourth-largest combined *mexicano*/Mexican American population behind Los Angeles, San Antonio, and Houston (Garza, 1994). The history of *mexicanos* in Chicago has its origins in the recruitment and "contracting" of 206 *mexicano* railroad track laborers in 1916 in the midst of a period of prosperity and industrial expansion in this country (Año Nuevo Kerr, 1976). Since then, three major waves of immigration from Mexico and migration from the southwestern United States, especially Texas, have resulted in a population of more than 350,000 Mexican-origin people in the city of Chicago (Garza, 1994). Almost one-third of this population currently resides in Pilsen and Little Village, the two contiguous and most concentrated Mexican-origin neighborhoods in the city. Mexican music pours out of record and tape stores, street vendors sell *elotes* (roasted ears of corn) and other fresh and frozen Mexican foods, signs for most business establishments are in Spanish, a number of *tortillerias* turn out thousands of *tortillas* daily, and grocery stores sell an abundance of Mexican food, both fresh and canned. In short, the cultural and linguistic ambience of these neighborhoods is so "Mexican" that a stroll along 18th or 26th Streets, two primary commercial avenues, can convince the stroller that he or she is in Mexico.

When we began our ethnographic work in August 1988, we optimistically planned to identify and work with three different social networks that would represent the major groups in the Pilsen/Little Village community: *mexicanos* (immigrants raised in Mexico), Mexican Americans raised in Chicago (who generally prefer the terms *Mexican* or *Mexican American* to *Chicano*), and Mexican Americans raised in Texas (who often refer to themselves as *tejanos*). Eventually, we decided to limit our work to a *mexicano* social network and identified a married couple who agreed to participate in our research project.

Jaime and Rocío Durán arrived in Chicago as undocumented immigrants in 1970 from two *ranchos* (small rural communities of small landowners) located about 120 miles from each other in the states of Guanajuato and Michoacán, respectively, in western Mexico. They, like many other Mexican migrants to Chicago, identify as *rancheros* (tough, independent "ranch" people), a subgroup of the larger Mexican society (Farr, in preparation). Once they met and married in Chicago, Jaime and Rocío joined the two extended families each had living in the Chicago metropolitan area and formed a large and complex social network. In the course of our work, we visited and worked with the 10 families that Jaime and Rocío's family interacted with the most. Of the adults in these families, only two had obtained more than a sixth-grade education; most had fewer than 3 years of schooling or no formal education whatsoever. Almost all adults in the social network, both male and female, worked full time as dishwashers or cooks in restaurants, as laborers in meat-processing or -distribution plants, or as railroad workers or window washers. While many of their younger children had been born in Chicago, most of their older children had been born in Mexico. Among the children, very few had graduated from high school, and only six—including four from one family—have thus far gone on to college. Several of the younger children who are currently in high school, however, have indicated an interest in pursuing a college degree.

Most of the data that we collected during the first 2 years of our work with members of Jaime and Rocío's social network involved reading and oral language use. We have reported on many of these findings in earlier publications (Farr, 1993, 1994a, 1994b, 1994c, 1998, 2000; Farr & Guerra, 1995; Guerra, 1996, 1998). Aside from the homework that the children in the household did every night, the lists and notes the adults and children wrote in the course of the day, and the letters they wrote to members of their families in Mexico (but which they did not share with us at the time), we witnessed few instances in the course of our first 2 years of research of individuals engaging in writing extended pieces of discourse. The lack of extended writing, however, was not a reflection of their inability to engage in it but the result of the limited occasions that their daily lives present them with to take pen or pencil to paper for the purpose of writing more than a few words on a list or a note.

Over the past 8 years, as our individual research projects have taken us in different directions, each of us has developed an increasing interest in the kinds of writing members of the social network do or are capable of doing. While one of us (Farr, 2000) has developed an interest in the kinds of literacy practices that take place in the religious domain, the other (Guerra, 1996, 1998) has developed an interest in two very different genres of writing: personal letters written between members of the social network residing in Chicago and one of their *ranchos* in Mexico, and personal narratives written by a group of young women that reflect various aspects of their lives in Mexico and the United States. For the purposes of this chapter, we examine a number of spiritual letters that Doña Josefina wrote to God and several pieces of autobiographical writing by María Guadalupe, one of Doña Josefina's nieces.[1]

The Spiritual Writing of Doña Josefina

Doña Josefina, in her late 50s, is the oldest sibling in a family of nine who began to migrate to Chicago in 1964, the last year of the U.S. Bracero Program in which manual laborers were recruited from Mexico to work in the United States. Of the nine siblings, four of the five brothers now live in San Jacinto, their *rancho* of origin, three of them after having worked in Chicago for varying numbers of years, and one brother lives in Chicago, as do all four of the sisters. Doña Josefina was born and raised in San Jacinto, where she attended school only through the second grade; after that she was needed to help with family chores, even though other residents of the *rancho* have commented on how "good" she was in school. That she is quite intelligent is apparent in her speaking, since she uses analogies and "critical thinking" to discuss various topics, including the treatment of Mexicans in the United States (Farr, 2000). Moreover, her school-oriented identity is revealed in the fact that her oral language more closely approximates "Standard Mexican Spanish" than does the language of some (but not all) of her sisters and brothers. Like Standard American English, Standard Mexican Spanish is taught in schools and is considered more "correct" than the rural dialect that many from or in the *rancho* speak.

The family network is strong and tightly woven, maintained by continual visits of members on each side of the border to the other side. The family (here *la familia*, meaning the extended, not nuclear, family) attends a Catholic church on 18th Street in Chicago, in the heart of Pilsen, in recent decades the traditional "port of entry" neighborhood for Mexican immigrants. While many in the family have moved to "better neighborhoods" (in their own words) by buying houses farther south and west of Pilsen, several, including Doña Josefina, have remained in Pilsen, and most still attend the same church on 18th Street, especially for special events such as baptisms, *quinceañeras* (religious and social celebrations when girls turn 15), and other special occasions.

This church tends to be less "activist" in orientation (in social and political terms) than some other churches in the neighborhood, and the priests are more tolerant of charismatic activities by church members, who use the church building for meetings. The charismatic renovation is an evangelistic, "Protestant-like" pentecostal movement within Catholicism that stresses self-expression and direct communication with God through the scriptures and prayer, rather than solely through the church hierarchy. Some Catholic priests oppose this movement within their churches for various reasons. Those who are Freirean-inspired "liberation" theologians criticize the movement for distracting church members from working together to more radically affect social and political change in their communities. Others object because it is so uncharacteristic of traditional Catholicism and the priestly authority that goes with it. The emphasis on direct communication with God differs radically from traditional (pre–Vatican II) Catholic practices in which literate priests interpreted scripture for the laity, who, in most isolated Mexican *ranchos* until the 1950s, were relatively unschooled. Catholic charismatics, however, like members of similar Protestant movements, emphasize personal interpretation of the Bible and believe in direct appeals to God, through prayer, to be filled with the Holy Spirit. Contemporary Catholic churches, of course, also vest the church hierarchy with authority, and Doña Josefina notes how this hierarchy provides one with someone to turn to for help, although some priests are not as accepting of charismatics as are others. She has had, then, to strike a delicate balance between respecting the church hierarchy as authoritative and claiming that authority for herself, through her reading, writing, and reflection. In addition to the reading of scripture and a variety of other published religious books, she writes prayers in advance of her weekly prayer circle that often take the form of letters addressed to God, Jesus, or the Holy Spirit.

Charismatic activities, then, are experienced as empowering for the participants. Since religion is a domain in which females have the most authority in these families, these activities can be viewed as liberatory from a gendered perspective (Juárez Cerdi, 1997). In charismatic prayer circles, being filled with the Holy Spirit gives one power: One prays to be filled with the Holy Spirit, which brings peace to one's soul and empowers one to heal others through the laying on of hands. This power is experienced and perceived as so forceful as to be frightening, and even dangerous, but it is also perceived as being effective.

Because the renovation allots a central role to self-expression through language, charismatics are more frequently involved in literacy activities than traditional church members. For example, in western Mexico, charismatic women form groups that teach nonliterates how to read and write (Juárez Cerdi, 1997). The women in this social network who are active in the renovation (and not all are, as some view it — including some priests — "crazy") attend prayer circle on Tuesday nights and Bible study on Thursday nights, as well as other events and meetings, including an occasional book fair where they can purchase books and videos. Once Doña Josefina commented that she was reading a book she had bought at such a fair that told the story of a young girl and her family who were hiding in an attic "during the revolution of Hitler," presumably a Spanish-language edition of *The Diary of Anne Frank*.

For the Tuesday night prayer circle (*Circulo de Oración*), Doña Josefina writes short prayers that are read and responded to with a short comment by the leader of the prayer circle. At the bottom of each page on which she has written a prayer, the leader writes a response, such as *Cristo te ama* (Christ loves you), *Viva Jesús* (Long live Jesus), *Maria, eres de Dios* (Maria [her first name], you are of God), and even *Aleluya* (Halleluja), with its Protestant, pentecostal connotations. It is interesting to note the parallel between these written comments and those that teachers write on student essays in school. Even though these comments do not seem to evaluate the prayers, as school essays are evaluated, the process of reading and then writing a response on the paper is evocative of formal education, since teachers and prayer circle leaders enact a similar role with regard to the writing. Moreover, Doña Josefina refers to this practice as "evaluating" the prayers, using the verb *calificar*, which is used in Mexico to refer to the grading of schoolwork.

What form do the prayers take? The following is an example that is relatively typical of the set of prayers that were shared with me. (For a view of the original handwritten prayer, see Figure 4.1.) Here is a literal transcription and a slightly edited English translation[2]:

Padre Yavé	Father Yahweh
te pido que redames [derrames]	I ask that you pour
tus gracias el dia del	your grace the day of the
vautismo en el Espirit	baptism in the Holy

FIGURE 4.1: A Prayer by Doña Josefina

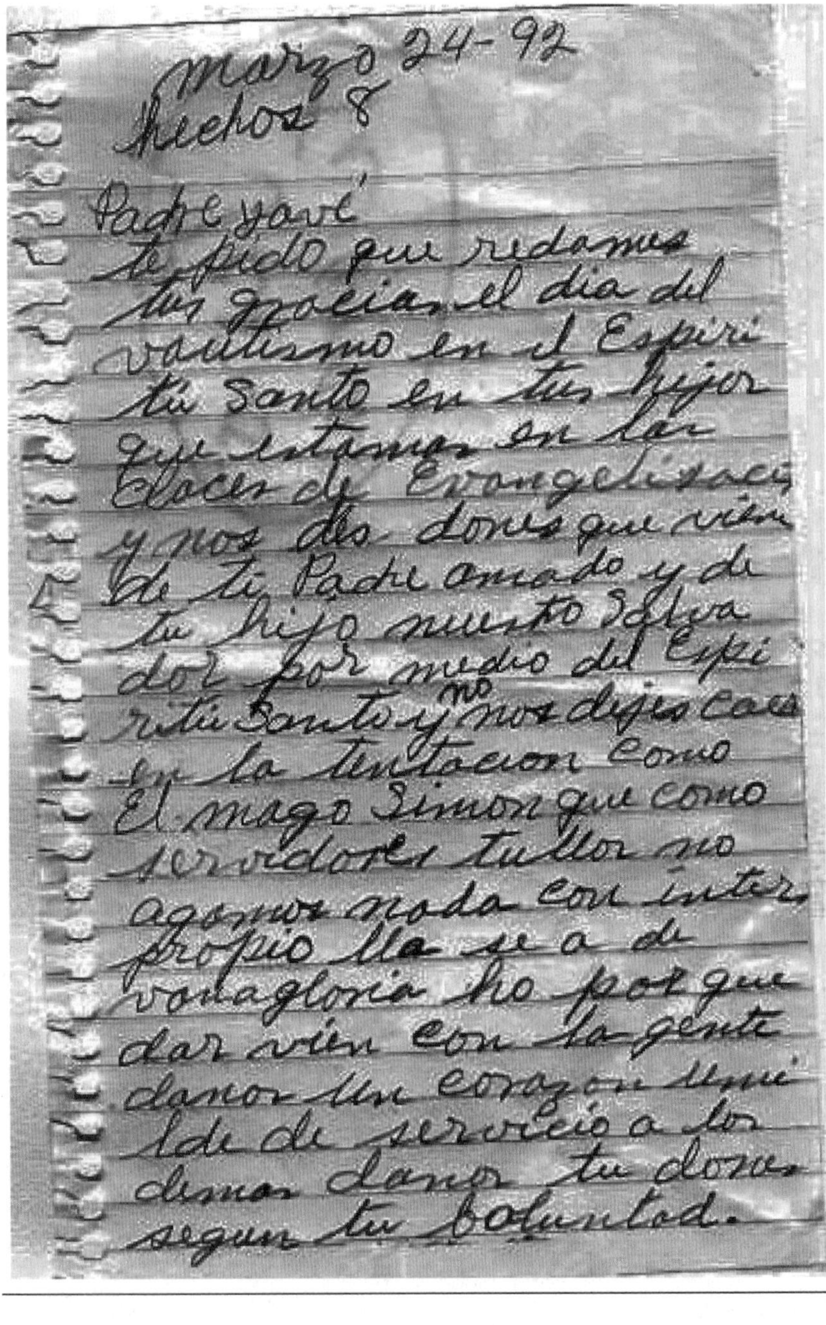

ú Santo en tus hijos	Spirit over your children
que estamos en las	who are in the
claces de Evangelisación	classes of evangelization
y nos des dones que viene	and may you give us gifts that come
ti Padre amado y de	from you beloved Father and from
tu hijo nuestro Salva	your son our Savior
dor por medio del Espi	by means of the Holy
ritu Santo y no nos dejes	Spirit and may you not
caer	let us fall
en la tentacion como	into temptation as
El mago Simon que como	the magician Simon did that as
servidores tullos [tuyos] no	your servants
[L]agamos nada con inter[e]s	we do nothing with self-
propio Lla [ya] se a [sea] de	interest whether it be
vanagloria ho [o] por que	vanity or to look
dar [quedar] vien con la gente	good in other people's eyes
danos un corazon umi	give us a humble heart
lde de servicio a los	of service to
demas danos tu dones	others give us your gifts
segun tu boluntad.	according to your will.
Maria J. Rodriguez	Maria J. Rodriguez

Some of the letters are addressed to God, others are addressed to Jesus, and one is addressed to the Holy Spirit. Many of them begin with thanks: *Gracias Espiritu Santo* . . . (Thank you, Holy Spirit . . .), *Sr. Jesus te doy gracias* . . . (Señor Jesus, I give you thanks . . .), *papá gracias por* . . . (Papa, thank you for . . .). Thanks are given for the love that God or Jesus has sent to her; for the strength to endure sickness and familial problems; for the teachings of Jesus, God's only son; and even for permitting her to read the Gospel. Other letters ask for things: for God to send the Holy Spirit to her; that there be much love among her children, among her brothers and sisters, and among the parishioners of the church; and for the Holy Spirit to come so that they don't fall into temptations.

All the prayers end with Doña Josefina's full signature, although many also include, just before the signature, an appositional phrase such as *tu hermana* (your sister), *tu hija* (your daughter), or *tu servidora* (your servant), depending on the addressee. She is "your sister" or "your servant" in letters to Jesus and "your daughter" in letters to God or the Holy Spirit. All these identities, and the fact that she uses *tu* rather than *usted*, index a personal, intimate relationship with God. Although the use of *tu* rather than the usually more respectful and socially distant *usted* is conventionally used when addressing God (although He is also referred to as El Señor) in this community, self-references as "your sister" or "your daughter" are not. These self-identities may reflect the charismatic emphasis on personal and direct communication with God. Yet they may hint at something else as well. Inasmuch as having *dones* (gifts sent by God) is empowering, since it allows one to help and guide others spiritually, being such an active servant of God places one closer to Him as well, reducing not only distance but also power differentials, however slightly. *Dones* make one special and augments one's powers here on earth, however humbly one enacts these powers. Women with *dones* are seriously respected by many in these families, and even those who are skeptical leave open the possibility that such spiritual powers might be "true" (*de verdad*) and could even be dangerous.

Thus these letters to God function to affirm and augment Doña Josefina's sense of power within her family and community. They, and her other charismatic practices, reassure her that she is not alone, but connected to others and to God and receiving their support. This enables her to deal better with personal and familial problems, such as her own diabetes, her husband's drinking, and the gang pressures on her son. She has explained that she sometimes composes a prayer (orally) while doing household chores, such as cooking, and that she uses her spiritual reading, either of the Bible or of other books, to cope during moments of particular stress. Moreover, I have observed Doña Josefina follow the priest during a *quinceañera* mass, shaking the hands of and blessing each of the attendants. She clearly felt no ambivalence about assuming a priest's role, which illustrates her sense of spiritual, and worldly, power. Given her other comments about the rights of women, this can be interpreted as an illustration of her "grassroots" feminism.

How do her letters, as a community literacy practice, relate to school writing? As has been noted, prayer circle members enact roles similar to those of students and teacher in school: The leader reads, evaluates, and responds to the prayers that the others write and turn in to him or her each week. Perhaps because these meetings are seen as sources of knowledge, as places of learning and growth, the participants create a school-like structure for them. The letters themselves, however, are quite different from most school writing. First, they employ many phrases characteristic of religious, rather than academic, discourse: *Mi muy adorado Jesús* (my much adored Jesus), *tus servidores* (your servants), *las tentaciónes de la carne* (the temptations of the flesh), and so forth. Such phrases index the religious context of this writing and are reminiscent of the kinds of phrases in student writing that index the academic context in which they are written.

A second, and more important, way in which these letters are different from most school writing lies in their striking tone of confidence and authority. There is a clear personal voice in the letters that many teachers of writing despair of ever finding in student papers. Some of the "voice" in these letters is institutional, of course, especially in those portions that use many more or less "stock" religious phrases. But much of the writing is original: Specific requests are made for specific occasions or reasons and sometimes include personal references to her own sickness and family problems. One letter even uses an agricultural (and biblical) metaphor, referring to herself as a *rama tuya* (your branch) and asking Jesus to "clean" her as one cleans and cuts a tree so that the tree will bear better fruit:

Marzo-10-92	March-10-92
Juan 15	John 15
mi muy adorado Jesus	my much adored Jesus
te escrivo esta carta	I write you this letter
para darte gracias	to thank you
por tu mansage [mensaje] de	for your message of
amor nos mandas	love you send us
y nos ordenas amarnos	and you order us to love
los unos a los otros	each other
como tu nos [h]as ama	as you have loved
do danos al espiritu	us give us the Holy
Santo para asi poder	Spirit and in this way be able
amar a mis hijos a	to love my children
mi esposo a mi fami	my husband my whole
lia entera tan ven [también]	family as well
te pido que como ra-	I ask you that as your branch
ma tuya mi lipes [me limpies]	clean me
y cortes todo lo que	and cut all that
no da vein [bien] fruto	does not bear fruit well
para que asi limpias	so that in this way you clean
de fruto y fruto	fruit and good
vueno es todo aura [ahora]	fruit that's all for now
[h]asta maña [mañana]	until tomorrow
tu hermana	your sister
Maria J. Rodriguez	Maria J. Rodriguez

Related to the strong personal voice in these letters is their fluency. The language seems to flow easily, even though the small $5'' \times 8''$ spiral-bound paper on which they are written allows little space per line, and phrases, even words (with or without a hyphen), sometimes are left dangling at the end of one line to be finished on the next. Yet despite these and other surface errors, the language is rich, persuasive, and confident.

The surface errors in the letters (primarily misspellings) are a reflection of Doña Josefina's limited formal schooling. The letter *v* is frequently written for *b*, since these are pronounced similarly in Spanish. Likewise, *y* and *ll* are sometimes substituted for each other, since they, too, are pronounced similarly. Thus many, though not all, misspellings result from how words are pronounced orally. Occasionally syllables in words are reversed (e.g., *redames* for *derrames*), but this, too, can be attributed to how these words are pronounced orally, since these reversals are characteristic of some rural dialect speakers in Mexico. Such surface errors, however, can be improved upon through instruction, and had Doña Josefina been able to continue her formal education, she would doubtless have made fewer of these errors in her letters. What is more difficult to teach, however, is voice, and this she clearly has already found, as it is abundantly evident in her writing here. The confident voice that speaks with such authority in these letters developed in a particular context, one in which she was encouraged and supported in her self-expression. Unfortunately, much writing instruction in school does not do this, and even well-meaning teachers, energetically trying to teach "structure" and "correctness," unwittingly undermine students' developing voices (Ybarra, 1997).

A final contrast between these letters and academic writing has to do with the critical analytic stance taught in school. This stance is plainly absent in much religious discourse, including these letters to God. Because of the context, then, and the function of these letters, such critical reasoning would be inappropriate here. It is important to note, however, that Doña Josefina uses this kind of reasoning in oral language, in other contexts. In one conversation with me, she pointed out that the historical situation of the Hebrews in Egypt was quite similar to the contemporary situation of Mexicans in the United States:

> Porque él, él [Moises] era hebreo, y los egipcios no querían la raza hebrea porque los hebreos estaban multiplicándose rápidamente. Tenían miedo que les quitaran el, el poder. Es lo mismo que en Estados Unidos está pasando. . . . Si uno analiza las cosas es lo mismo. Estados Unidos tiene miedo que los hispanos gánemos [*sic*] este país, destrúyamos [*sic*] su, su, su raza. Porque la raza de, de, del mero mero es an—anglosajón, es poca. Pero este país está—está mezclado con muchas razas. Y la que más ha crecido es la raza morena y la raza hispana. Entonces, ellos tienen miedo que nosotros al—a lo largo de la historia, quite—los destrónemos, los, los quítemos [*sic*]

del poder, me entiendes? Eso mismo tenía—ese mismo—esa misma historia pasó en Egipto.³

(Because he, he was Hebrew and the Egyptians didn't like the Hebrew race because the Hebrews were growing rapidly. They were afraid that they would take the the power. It's the same thing that is going on in the United States. . . . If one analyzes things, it is the same. The United States is scared that the Hispanics will win this country, we will destroy their, their, their race. Because the race of, of, of the real is an—Anglo-Saxon, is few. But this country is—is mixed with many races. And those that have grown the most are the black race and the Hispanic race. So, they are afraid that we, in, in the long run of history, and, we dethrone them, we take power from them, do you understand me? That was the same thing—that very thing—the same story happened in Egypt.)

Thus Doña Josefina makes an analogy between two different historical contexts, critically analyzing the politics within them. It should be clear, then, that if this kind of reasoning is not displayed in particular pieces of writing, either in classrooms or elsewhere, we cannot assume that the writer does not know how to reason in this way. The reason, instead, may lie in the context. This argues for exploring the contexts in which we teach writing, looking for reasons that the literacy abilities displayed in community practices are so lacking in school writing.

The Autobiographical Writing of María Guadalupe

Malú (María Guadalupe's preferred nickname) is the oldest of four children born in the United States to Olga Ramírez, one of Doña Josefina's younger sisters. Although Malú and her parents lived in a northside neighborhood in Chicago for several years after her parents first arrived from Mexico in the early 1970s, the family moved into the Pilsen community more than 10 years ago and currently lives down the street from Doña Josefina's home. Like many of her cousins, Malú attended parochial and public schools in Chicago and in San Jacinto, her family's *rancho* in Mexico. The difficulties created by this experience are highlighted by her self-representation in the title of one of her personal narratives as someone "Caught Between Two Cultures," between the very different social and linguistic worlds of Mexico and the United States. As the oldest sibling in her family, Malú bears the burden of setting an example for her two younger brothers and sister. Moreover, as one of the first members of the social network to graduate from high school and go to college, Malú is also responsible for serving as an example for the other young members of the social network who aspire to receive an advanced formal education and to enjoy the economic opportunities that such an accomplishment is likely to bring.[4]

When I first met her, Malú had just returned from Mexico, where she had spent the equivalent of her middle school years. Never one to attract attention to herself, Malú often sat or stood on the periphery of the activities and conversations taking place in the homes where I would see her. Even when I would visit her family in the course of my regular cycle of visits to the homes of various families in the social network, Malú would sit quietly or go into her bedroom while I was engaged in conversation with her parents or was helping her siblings with their homework. The breakthrough in our relationship came when I visited her home one evening while she was working on a writing assignment for one of her classes during her first year at UIC. Because she was having trouble getting started, her mother encouraged her to tell me about the assignment and to get some help from me. After we talked about it and brainstormed together for a few minutes, Malú developed a better sense of the options at her disposal and proceeded to generate some text on her own. Later that evening, I reviewed what she had written and, as a friend of the family rather than her teacher, offered advice about some of the things she could do to expand and improve her piece of writing.

While I had learned about the personal letters that adult members of the group often wrote to one another (see Guerra, 1998), I had not yet successfully solicited examples from any of them. I had often seen them reading letters they had received from members of the group living in Mexico and had even delivered or brought back stacks of letters during several trips that I had taken between Chicago and their *ranchos*, but early on the personal nature of their letters discouraged me from asking them for copies. In an effort to collect and develop a cache of personal letters, I attempted to establish correspondence with several of the teenagers in the social network. When that effort failed, I decided to shift gears and elicit autobiographical narratives from several of them. Because they were younger, better educated, and, I thought, less self-conscious about their writing, I was certain that a group of about ten young people with whom I had developed a firm and positive relationship would jump at the opportunity. As it turned out, only three young women in their late teens agreed to do some writing for me, and more than a year passed between the time I first asked them to write and the time they started giving me samples of their work. Malú was one of these three young women.

Over the course of a 21-month period between August 1994 and April 1996, Malú gave me a series of six narratives. Unlike her aunt, Doña Josefina, who wrote her letters in a context not directly related to school, Malú

wrote a total of six autobiographical narratives that were influenced to varying degrees by school-oriented expectations. The first three narratives were
based on my request that she write about aspects of her life that she found
interesting and that she thought would appeal to a general audience. These
three samples were first-draft attempts written in Spanish, English, and a
combination of the two languages. The last three pieces were written in
response to assignments given to her in three different composition classes
at the university: one in Spanish and two in English. Unlike the pieces that
she had written for me, these three were revised several times. While the
final draft of the first narrative she wrote for one of her college teachers
was handwritten, the last two were typed. And although the essays she
wrote for her teachers dealt with much the same subject matter as the three
she wrote for me, they were different in terms of the extent to which she
constructed a narrative or expository text; her overall style, especially in
terms of technical correctness and language choice; and the manner in
which she elected to frame or organize her ideas.

One of the most salient features of the three personal narratives that
Malú wrote for me is the increasing length and complexity of the texts,
especially in terms of the number of different topics she elects to address
in each and their movement from a narrative to an expository perspective.
While her first piece of writing is only 533 and her second 832 words in
length, her third explodes to 1,278 words. Along with this willingness to
extend the range of words is a related interest in complicating her writing
by addressing more than one topic as she seemingly becomes more comfortable with the task and finds more interesting issues to address in the
course of her self-reflections. Malú also complicates matters further by using
English exclusively in the first piece and Spanish in the second (except for
an English word that she borrows at one point), then shifting back and
forth from Spanish to English to Spanish in her third narrative. In the first
two pieces, Malú appears to shift from one language to another on the basis
of how closely the topic she is addressing is related to school (English) or
home life (Spanish). The third piece of writing, however, totally disrupts
this convention when Malú's decision to shift is more stylistic than topical.

Malú's first personal narrative, which she wrote in English, is a chronological representation of a transformation that she undergoes during her
first day in kindergarten. It begins with her getting ready for class, is followed by a description of a series of experiences there, and ends with her
acknowledgment that she became "well adjusted to going to school." The
kinds of vivid details that Malú uses throughout the piece ("my mother
bought [me] a new school bag, with pencils, crayons and paper" and "my
aunt [helped] me put on a brown and black checked dress with a white
blouse") help contextualize the experience for her readers. They are imme-

diately made aware of the self-conscious circumstances in which Malú is beginning her schooling. Because her mother, like her father, has to work to support the family, Malú is taken to school by an aunt in the company of her cousins. Her description of the clothes she wore that day and the location of the school itself clearly indicate that she will be attending a parochial school. Moreover, Malú's use of such phrases as "I can still recall" and "I remember" let the reader know that she is actively and explicitly recalling a past event. While there are a few minor problems with punctuation, grammar, and spelling, they are never enough to disrupt the reader's ability to interpret Malú's representation of the moment.

In one very important way, Malú's second narrative mirrors the first. In place of the rite of passage that she experienced in the course of adjusting to school, the second piece begins with a focus on the process that her parents went through in their search for the first home they would ever own in the United States and ends, unexpectedly, with how Malú's new babysitter, *la señora* Eloisa, overcame her illiteracy. Despite the shift in topics, Malú remains faithful to the narrative of transformation that informs her first piece. The second narrative again begins with an unstable set of circumstances; this time, however, it is her parents who are full of *dudas* (doubts) because *en ese tiempo no tenian papeles y pensaban que eso les fuera a affectar* (at that time they didn't have papers and they thought that was going to affect [their ability to purchase a home]).[5] Reminiscent of the language that Esperanza uses in Sandra Cisneros's (1984) *The House on Mango Street*, Malú recalls *aver llegado a una casa pequeña* (having arrived at a small house). While Cisneros's Esperanza laments the home that her parents end up buying in Chicago, Malú reports a different take on the same experience:

> Entramos a la sala y de ayi nos enseñaron las recamaras, la cocina, y
> el bano. La casa es sensilla pero lo que ami me emoc[i]ono fue
> cuando nos enseñaron la yarda. Era una yarda tambien de espacio re-
> ducido pero a mi se me hacia como algo muy grande, tenia una silla
> meseda [mecedora] en el lado izquierdo, un gardin en frente y a tras
> y en el lado derecho enfrente del garage habia una casita. La casita
> era supuestamente de perro, pero era grande, tenia su puerta, shelfs
> y una ventana. Y me quede encantada con la casa [de] perro más
> [que] con la casita.

> (We entered the living room and from there they showed us the bed-
> rooms, the kitchen, and the bathroom. The house is simple but what
> moved me was when they showed us the yard. It was also a fairly

small yard but to me it seemed like something very big, it had a rock-
ing chair on the left side, a garden in front and back and on the
right hand side in front of the garage there was a little house. The little house was apparently a dog house, but it was big, had its own
door, shelves and a window. And I remained more enchanted with
the dog house [than] with the little house.)

Malú's second narrative proceeds to describe how they then moved
their few belongings into their new house once her parents purchased it.
Unexpectedly, Malú then shifts the focus of her story away from the house
to *la señora* Eloisa, the new baby-sitter responsible for taking her to her
new school. Malú ends the piece with a digression that emerges as a consequence of something her baby-sitter elected to do "on her own":

> De la Señora Eloisa no me puedo quejar por que siempre fue muy
> buena conmigo. La Señora Eloisa es una persona que admiro, quiero
> y respeto mucho porque cuando yo la conoci ella ya era grande de
> edad y no sabia leer ni escribir. Ahora a veces cuando vamos a la
> casa [de ella] y la veo la [h]e visto leyendo la Biblia, ella solita fue a
> clase de ana[l]fabetizmo y la enseñaron a leer y escribir.

> (I can't complain about Mrs. Eloisa because she was always very
> good to me. Mrs. Eloisa is a person that I admire, love and respect a
> lot because when I met her she was already an older person and
> didn't know how to read or write. Now when we sometimes go to
> her house and I see her I have seen her reading the Bible, she on
> her own went to literacy classes and they taught her to read and
> write.)

Unlike the first narrative, this second one conflates two story lines and con-
sequently ends in a different place from where it began. Interestingly, the
first story line ends with her acknowledging that because she was "*una
persona que le gusta la soledad*" (a person who enjoys solitude), "*yo creo
que por eso no resenti mucho nuestra mudanza*" (I think that's why I
didn't resent our move very much). Because there is no conflict for her
here, there is no moral lesson to be learned or taught and no transformation
to be experienced. The shift at this point to how *la señora* Eloisa became
her baby-sitter and, over the years, managed to overcome her illiteracy,
grants Malú the opportunity to conclude her narrative with a tale of transformation, a commonplace that begins to emerge in her writing as an important way to bring a narrative to closure.

Malú's final piece of autobiographical writing is not only longer and more complicated, both in its use of two languages and of two different story lines; it also includes a series of transformative experiences that she undergoes as a consequence of the support that she gets from her parents and her peers. Unlike the first two pieces of writing, each of which began with a phrase that signals the beginning of a chronological narrative—"I can still recall" and *"Durante este tiempo"* (During this time)—the first sentence of Malú's third piece signals a blending of narrative and expository writing and thinking. Its first sentence sets the stage in very stark and dramatic terms:

> Las razones por las que decidi ir al collegio son muchas pero las principales son para mejor[ar] la vida economica de mis padres y mia, para encontrar un trabajo que me sea grato desempeñar y para dejar la ignorancia.

> (The reasons I decided to go to college are many but the principal ones are to improve the economic life of my parents and myself, to find a job that will be a pleasure to perform and to leave ignorance behind.)

While the sentence is clearly imitative of the kinds of thesis statements that students are often taught to compose, especially for five-paragraph essays that will include an introduction, three supporting points, and a conclusion, what follows it partially disrupts the constraints implied by this convention as Malú not only moves back and forth between and among the three points but, as she did in the second piece, shifts to a new topic about a third of the way through the autobiographical piece. The shift in topic is casually announced by a sentence that explains why she has managed to go to college and survive: *"Yo siempre [h]e dicho que lo que yo logre sera para ellos [mis padres] porque siempre me [h]an brindado su apoyo y confianza"* (I've always said that what I have attained is for them [my parents] because they have always offered me their support and trust). Thereafter, Malú discusses in great detail the ways in which her father, her mother, and a group of young women with whom she attended high school and now attends college have made and continue to make it possible for her to continue her education. The back-and-forth shift in languages also demonstrates her ability to engage in one of the stylistic variations that Gloria Anzaldúa (1987) promulgates in *Borderlands/La Frontera* but that is still rarely encouraged in English-dominant, university writing classrooms. Again, her text—which she concludes with the following sentence—highlights the potential for transformative change:

"Realmente uno nunca sabe lo que puede pasar, a lo mejor ni si-
quiera me graduo del collegio pero siquier[a] tuve la satisfaccion de
aver tratado y no quedarme con duda"

(In reality, one never knows what might happen, maybe I won't
even get to graduate from college but at least I had the satisfaction
of trying and not wondering what might have been.)

The autobiographical pieces that she wrote for her university classes,
especially the last two, highlight some of the differences between the kind
of writing Malú is likely to do at home and in a classroom setting. Some of
the most obvious differences emerge from the mere fact that what she
wrote at home for me went only through a single draft, whereas what she
wrote for her classes was revised several times with input from her friends,
classmates, and teachers. As a consequence, her personal essays for class
contain fewer surface errors and are typed, self-consciously divided into a
series of paragraphs (the three pieces she wrote for me consisted of continuous text with no indentations), and given formal titles. Both of them also
begin and end with clearly delineated introductions and conclusions and
present a series of related supporting ideas in the middle sections. Finally,
instead of demonstrating an actual or potential transformation, the essays
end with Malú caught in a stalemate, paralyzed by the conflicting options
that she faces. For example, the essay for her Spanish class, titled "*¿Español
o Inglés?*", concludes with the following two sentences:

"Mi problema es no dominar correctamente los dos lenguajes al nivel
que debo. Ni modo, me tendré que conformar con hablar el español
y el inglés a medias"

(My problem is not being able to deal correctly with the two languages at the level that I am supposed to. No matter, I will have to
be satisfied with speaking Spanish and English as best I can.)

On the other hand, the essay for her English class, titled "Caught Between Two Cultures," ends with the following two sentences: "I just happen to be always caught in the middle. Between a Mexican family's expectations and wanting to enjoy some American freedom."
The two major differences between the writing that she did for me
and the writing that she did for her college teachers reflect her tendency
to highlight a sense of transformation and to engage in digressive thinking
in the former, something which seems toned down or nearly absent in the

latter. While the number of narratives are inadequate to suggest that the variant forms of writing that she feels comfortable exploring in her out-of-school writing are typical of her writing, much less the writing of *mexicanas* in her social network, the contrasting tendencies that she exhibits in the two kinds of writing suggest that divergent thinking and its representation in writing is not necessarily a lack of organizational control on her part but a reflection of her desire to allow the narratives that she wrote the opportunity to disrupt the sometimes formulaic organizational structure that we as writing teachers often demand of our students in classroom writing. As such, it should alert us to the importance of context and the variations in style that inform the writing of individuals like Malú who live and write both at home and in school. We need to be careful not to assume that digressive or divergent thinking and writing are somehow a reflection of a writer's inability to think rationally or to marshal a set of ideas into some predetermined order. It may well be another way of constructing a narrative text that eventually morphs into an expository one. At the very least, it should encourage us to think twice about the extent to which we need to revise our expectations about the kinds of writing experiences students bring into the classroom and the kinds of writing that we expect them to undertake in that context.

How Home and Community Writing Can Inform School Writing

As writing teachers in a university setting, each with more than 20 years of experience, we have struggled with the difficult task of helping students from diverse backgrounds learn how to write within the "essayist literacy" tradition. Caught between having students value and make use of the personally and culturally based language registers and styles they bring into the classroom and introducing them to the demands of a more autonomous, academic register and style that requires them to reposition themselves in unfamiliar ways, we have had to reconsider our expectations and the pedagogical strategies we use in the writing classroom. Clearly, there are no easy answers. Still, instead of trapping ourselves in the assumption that we have to *either* respect our students' multivoiced approaches to writing *or* demand that our students simply surrender to the expectations of academic discourse, we realize that we must do both. Teachers are more likely to succeed in teaching academic writing if they make an effort to understand and value the variant styles of language manifested in the kinds of writing that people do in the communities from which more and more university students are coming.

No doubt two of the main reasons why researchers have generally ignored the rich possibilities inherent in examining writing done in minority communities are (1) that we have focused our research on their oral language use or have restricted our research to the kind of writing they do in school-based settings, and (2) that instances of extended writing are less visible and take much longer to encounter, especially when the search is being undertaken by scholars who, because of their social and educational status, are more likely to intimidate individuals who often tell us they can't write. In our case, for example, we limited our focus during the early years of our research to reading and oral language use because they were the more visible acts in which members of the social network engaged. Moreover, when we did ask them for letters at the outset of our research and they hesitated, we became concerned that they would hold back in other ways and so we ceased to continue exploring those particular facets of their language use. Fortunately, we decided to continue our research long enough so that members of the social network began to think of us less as language researchers engaged in academic-oriented critical analysis and more as family friends interested in learning about certain linguistic and discursive aspects of their lives. In short, patience and trust eventually opened up new research possibilities for us.

The writing we examine in this chapter is but one small peek into the vast and still largely unexplored area of writing in home and community settings. What it reveals, though, suggests that members of these communities regularly use various genres of extended written discourse. Given occasion and purpose, the two women whose writing we have reviewed generated texts that communicate their personal views and experiences, and their spiritual hopes and identities. Despite the fact that some of their writing contains the kinds of grammatical and orthographic features that signal a lack of familiarity with standard conventions, the rhetorical stance implicit in their writing is often very powerful and self-assured. There is also a clear familiarity on their part with the cadence of rich and meaningful language that is aesthetically pleasing.

More specifically, however, what kinds of insights does the out-of-school writing of women like Doña Josefina and Malú provide college composition teachers who are increasingly encountering students from similar communities in their classrooms? Demographic projections, after all, suggest that by the year 2050, one of every four residents of the United States is likely to be of Latino origin (Suárez-Orozco, 1998). Obviously, our analysis of the writing of two women cannot provide the basis for establishing a set of pedagogical strategies that will respond to the needs of college-bound members of this community. Without question, scholars need to continue and expand their work on the literacy practices of Latinos and Latinas if we are ever going to develop understandings that will adequately inform the work that writing teachers need to do. Still, we believe that it is possible to speculate about some issues that directly address the development of curriculum and pedagogy in writing classrooms.

To begin with, we can no longer ignore the communicative competencies that students bring into the classroom. Despite the fact that over the years an array of scholars have urged us as writing teachers to take into consideration the discursive and rhetorical practices students bring with them, too many of us are still hamstrung by our assumed responsibility to focus narrowly on issues of grammar, mechanics, spelling, and organization. This is not to suggest that underrepresented students do not need help in developing their skills in these areas. As a matter of fact, in the course of our research, many of the members of the social network with whom we discussed writing acknowledged that these were areas that seriously concerned them. While some of us may be prone to argue that they held this belief because those among them who had received formal schooling had been told over and over again that they didn't know how to write because they had not yet developed these skills, our interviews with them suggest that they are well aware of the crucial role that the etiquette of writing plays in influencing what others think of them as writers and human beings. At the same time, we cannot ignore their ability to manipulate language in sophisticated ways and, especially, their awareness of how rhetoric plays itself out in the genres in which they choose to write. It goes without saying that we need to give them an opportunity to demonstrate what they already know so that we can help them build new skills on that foundation. This is an idea as old as the teaching of writing itself; unfortunately, many of us continue to ignore it now as much as teachers have done in the past.

Once we have a better sense of what our students bring to our classrooms, we need to be prepared to use a more comprehensive array of pedagogical strategies that will address the varied writing needs of such students. Unfortunately, far too often, we as writing teachers claim allegiance to a particular pedagogical theory and develop blind spots about the potential inherent in alternative theories. This is not to say that the answer is to develop an eclectic approach to the teaching of writing so pragmatic in its goal that student needs alone inform practice or to dismiss theory as an annoying burden imposed by scholars who have nothing better to do with their time. We prefer an approach that acknowledges the contingent nature of the teaching of writing itself. The option we advocate is one that plays itself out in the tension between an eclectic and mono-ideological stance. Because it doesn't recommend that two contradictory positions must be held simultaneously, it does not propose a synthesis. If anything, it recommends a symbiosis of sorts, a process wherein one commits to a particular pedagogical stance but periodically pulls back and questions it. Such questioning, however, does not always result in a fundamental change, as it does with those who consistently choose to be self-critical. Instead, it acknowledges the importance of accepting the fact that one can be ideological without becoming an ideologue. To put it in slightly different terms, we must be prepared to support what Leki (1997) calls "a pedagogy that views writing instruction as the effort to make all students, not just non-English speaking students, aware of the options and choices appropriate in a variety of text types and writing contexts" (p. 244).

An examination of the kinds of writing that Doña Josefina and Malú do in out-of-school contexts raises another critical issue for us: As writing teachers, we must continue to develop a more flexible notion of what we conceive of as academic writing. While we have focused on the importance of variant styles of writing, our analysis implicitly touches on questions about how the concepts of discourse community and genre emerge as critical concerns in our discussion about the relationship between writing done at home or the community and in school. For several years now, such scholars as Bizzell (1982), Bruffee (1984), Bartholomae (1985), Harris (1989), and Spellmeyer (1993) have debated the existence of discourse communities and the extent to which the concept has given us any useful insights in understanding the experiences of underrepresented students as they make their way from their home communities to academic communities that demand a different set of discursive practices. For the most part, the argument has focused on whether students indeed experience a discontinuity between the two discourse communities. At this point, Lu's (1992) argument that students do not experience an initiation into a discourse community but must instead learn the art of "repositioning" themselves rhetorically has seemingly won the day. Although we would agree on the importance of such repositioning, we still argue that many students are also faced with the task of learning new discourse practices, from the level of language to the level of rhetoric. That they are often not "initiated" into such practices is an important shortcoming of contemporary composition courses.

Finally, in light of the fact that Doña Josefina and Malú are not only writing in contexts very different from those students face in school, but in genres that are in some ways different from those students are likely to encounter in writing classrooms, we need to consider whether or not it is possible to disrupt the genres of school writing and destabilize them in ways that will allow for more varied approaches to writing in the classroom. Miller (1996), for example, attempts to disrupt the assumed hard boundaries between genres, especially between what we as writing teachers often think of as personal writing represented in narrative form and academic writing represented in academic form, by arguing that we must "take down the cordon separating the public and the private and . . . recognize that all intellectual projects are always, inevitably, also autobiographies" (p. 285). Moreover, Miller contends, we must "expand our notion of the rhetorical project to include the ongoing work of learning how to make oneself heard in a variety of contexts" (p. 282). Bawarshi (2000) complicates this position further by helping us better understand how the kind of writing that Doña Josefina and Malú do out of school can inform the kind of writing that we expect from our students in school. In Bawarshi's view, we need to take into consideration "the role that genre plays in the constitution not only of texts, but of their contexts, including the identities of those who write them and those who are represented within them" (p. 335). While all this suggests that individuals such as Doña Josefina and Malú who eventually show up in our classrooms must learn to write in the contexts of the genres that are preferred in college classrooms, it also means that we as teachers are sorely lacking in our knowledge about the texts, contexts, identities, and acts of representation that they may be engaging in when they write in genres that are preferred outside of school. Clearly, there is much for both of us—students and teachers—to learn about writing and, especially, about one another. The writing done by individuals such as Doña Josefina and Malú in out-of-school contexts is certainly a good place for us to initiate this process for the benefit of all involved—teachers, students, and the communities from which they come.

Notes

1. In the two sections that follow, we shift to the first-person singular because the material we discuss was gathered as part of two separate research projects. Farr collected and analyzes Doña Josefina's letters to God, while Guerra collected and analyzes María Guadalupe's autobiographical writing.

2. In transcribing these letters, Farr has left misspellings and other surface errors as originally written; in cases in which the meaning may not be clear, she has included the intended standard Spanish word in brackets. Words split between lines in the original (because Doña Josefina ran out of space on the 5″ × 8″ inch spiral notebook pages on which she wrote the prayers) are transcribed in the same way; the English translation tries to parallel this. In translating the letters, Farr has edited only the spelling.

3. Words followed by [*sic*] are pronounced with an intonation characteristic of some rural dialect speakers in Mexico. In the Standard Spanish pronunciation of these words, the second to last syllable, rather than the third to last, is stressed. Here I have transcribed Doña Josefina's words as she spoke them.

4. Malú graduated with a bachelor's degree from UIC in December 1999. Meanwhile, her younger sister, Linda, entered the freshman class at UIC in August 1999.

5. In transcribing these autobiographical narratives, Guerra has left misspellings and other surface errors as originally written. He has included a missing word or letter or the standard word in brackets only in cases in which the meaning may not be clear to a Spanish reader. In translating the narratives, Guerra has edited only the spelling of words.

References

Año Nuevo Kerr, L. (1976). *The Chicano experience in Chicago: 1920-1970.* Unpublished doctoral dissertation, University of Illinois, Chicago.

Anzaldúa, G. (1987). *Borderlands/La Frontera: The new mestiza.* San Francisco: Aunt Lute Books.

Bartholomae, D. (1985). Inventing the university. In M. Rose (Ed.), *When a writer can't write: Studies in writer's block and other composing process problems* (pp. 134-165). New York: Guilford.

Bawarshi, A. (2000). The genre function. *College English, 62*(3), 335-360.

Bizzell, P. (1982). Cognition, convention, and certainty: What we need to know about writing. *Pre/Text, 3,* 213-243.

Bruffee, K. (1984). Collaborative learning and the "conversation of mankind." *College English, 46,* 635-652.

Bulanda, B. (1994, February). [Internal memo to Wanat, John]. Chicago: University of Illinois at Chicago.

Cazden, C. (1988). *Classroom discourse: The language of teaching and learning.* Portsmouth, NH: Heinemann.

Cisneros, S. (1984). *The house on Mango Street.* New York: Vintage.

Delpit, L. (1995). *Other people's children: Cultural conflict in the classroom.* New York: The New Press.

Elbow, P. (1991). Reflections on academic discourse: How it relates to freshmen and colleagues. *College English, 53*(2), 135-156.

Farr, M. (1993). Essayist literacy and other verbal performances. *Written Communication, 10*(1), 4-38.

Farr, M. (1994a). Echando relajo: Verbal art and gender among *mexicanas* in Chicago. In M. Bucholtz, A. C. Liang, L. A. Sutton, & C. Hines (Eds.), *Cultural performances: Proceedings of the third women and language conference* (pp. 168-186). Berkeley: University of California Press.

Farr, M. (1994b). Biliteracy in the home: Practices among *mexicano* families in Chicago. In D. Spener (Ed.), *Adult biliteracy in the United States* (pp. 89-110). McHenry, IL, and Washington, DC: Delta Systems and Center for Applied Linguistics.

Farr, M. (1994c). *En los dos idiomas*: Literacy practices among *mexicano* families in Chicago. In B. Moss (Ed.), *Literacy across communities* (pp. 9-47). Cresskill, NJ: Hampton.

Farr, M. (1998). El relajo como microfiesta. In H. Pérez (Ed.), *Mexico en fiesta* (pp. 457-470). Zamora, Michoacán, Mexico: El Colegio de Michoacán.

Farr, M. (2000). Literacy and religion: Reading, writing, and gender among Mexican women in Chicago. In P. Griffin, J. K. Peyton, W. Wolfram, & R. Fasold (Eds.), *Language in action: New studies of language in society* (pp. 139-154). Cresskill, NJ: Hampton.

Farr, M. (in preparation). *Rancheros* in Chicagoacán: Ways of speaking and identity in a transnational community.

Farr, M., & Guerra, J. C. (1995). Literacy in the community: A study of *mexicano* families in Chicago. *Discourse Processes, 19*(1), 7-19.

Feldman, A. (1996). *Writing and learning in the disciplines.* New York: HarperCollins.

Garza, M. M. (1994, August 19). Mexico's election: Campaign trail this year makes a stop in Chicago. *Chicago Tribune,* pp. 1, 20.

Goody, J., & Watt, I. (1968). The consequences of literacy. In J. Goody (Ed.), *Literacy in traditional societies* (pp. 27-68). Cambridge, UK: Cambridge University Press.

Graff, G. (1999). Opinion: Hiding it from the kids (with apologies to Simon and Garfinkel). *College English, 62*(2), 242-254.

Guerra, J. C. (1996). "It is as if my story repeats itself": Life, language, and literacy in a Chicago *comunidad. Education and Urban Society, 29*(1), 35-53.

Guerra, J. C. (1997). The place of intercultural literacy in the writing classroom. In C. Severino, J. C. Guerra, & J. E. Butler (Eds.), *Writing in multicultural settings* (pp. 248-260). New York: Modern Language Association.

Guerra, J. C. (1998). *Close to home: Oral and literate practices in a transnational Mexicano community.* New York: Teachers College Press.

Gumperz, J. (1982a). *Discourse strategies.* Cambridge, UK: Cambridge University Press.

Gumperz, J. (Ed.). (1982b). *Language and social identity.* Cambridge, UK: Cambridge University Press.

Harris, J. (1989). The idea of community in the study of writing. *College Composition and Communication, 40,* 11-22.

hooks, b. (1989). *Talking back: Thinking feminist, thinking black.* Boston: South End Press.

Hymes, D. (1974). *Foundations in sociolinguistics: An ethnographic approach.* Philadelphia: University of Pennsylvania Press.

Juárez Cerdi, E. (1997). *Mi reino sí es de este mundo.* Zamora, Michoacán, Mexico: El Colegio de Michoacán.

Kochman, T. (1981). *Black and white: Styles in conflict.* Chicago: University of Chicago Press.

Leki, I. (1997). Cross-talk: ESL issues and contrastive rhetoric. In C. Severino, J. C. Guerra, & J. E. Butler (Eds.), *Writing in multicultural settings* (pp. 234-244). New York: Modern Language Association.

Lu, M.-Z. (1992). Conflict and struggle: The enemies or preconditions of basic writing? *College English, 54,* 887-913.

Lunsford, A., & Ruszkiewicz, J. (Eds.). (1998). *Everything's an argument.* New York: Bedford.

Miller, R. (1996). The nervous system. *College English, 58,* 265–287.

Morgan, M. (1994). The African-American speech community: Reality and sociolinguists. In M. Morgan (Ed.), *Language and the social construction of identity in creole situations* (pp. 121–148). Los Angeles: UCLA, Center for Afro-American Studies.

Olson, D. R. (1977). From utterance to text: The bias of language in speech and writing. *Harvard Educational Review, 74,* 257–281.

Ong, W. (1982). *Orality and literacy: The technologizing of the word.* London: Methuen.

Scollon, R., & Scollon, S. B. (1981). *Narrative, literacy, and face in interethnic communication.* Norword, NJ: Ablex.

Scollon, R., & Scollon, S. B. (1995). *Intercultural communication: A discourse approach.* Cambridge, MA: Blackwell.

Smitherman, G. (1977). *Talkin' and testifyin': The language of black America.* New York: Houghton Mifflin.

Smitherman, G. (2000). *Talkin that talk: Language, culture, and education in African America.* New York: Routledge.

Spellmeyer, K. (1993). *Common ground: Dialogue, understanding, and the teaching of composition.* Englewood Cliffs, NJ: Prentice Hall.

Suárez-Orozco, M. (Ed.). (1998). *Crossings: Mexican immigration in interdisciplinary perspectives.* Cambridge, MA: Harvard University Press.

Walters, K. (1990). Language, logic, and literacy. In A. A. Lunsford, H. Moglen, & J. Slevin (Eds.), *The right to literacy* (pp. 173–188). New York: Modern Language Association.

Ybarra, R. (1997). *Communication conflict between Latino students and Anglo-mainstream instructors: An ethnographic study of a composition classroom.* Unpublished doctoral dissertation, University of Illinois, Chicago.

JULIA MENARD-WARWICK RESPONDS

In this thought-provoking chapter, I see the authors struggling to achieve twin purposes: to "prove the [literacy] competence" of the Chicago *mexicano* community and to suggest ways to enhance the teaching of college writing to minority students. Having taught ESL writing for a number of years, I fully support their mission to improve composition classes by "tak[ing] into consideration the discursive and rhetorical practices that students bring with them." However, Guerra and Farr do not provide much practical guidance on how teachers can bring this consideration into their classroom routine. Moreover, the writing practices analyzed in this paper do not, to me, "suggest that members of th[is] communit[y] regularly use various genres of extended written discourse," as the authors contend. Nevertheless, I think that college writing teachers can find much to learn from the textual evidence presented here.

Certainly, Doña Josefina's "letters to God" do illustrate "the creativity, resourcefulness, and substantial capacities that ordinary people [bring to] their everyday uses of written language." As Farr states, charismatic prayer circles allow women with minimal formal education to "claim authority . . . through reading, writing and reflection." The confidence that Doña Josefina has in her relationship with God gives her writing "fluency and a strong personal voice," while her intensive reading of the Bible offers tools to critically analyze contemporary society. Although college composition instructors are unlikely to be presented with documents that bear much resemblance to the prayers that Farr describes, her account of Doña Josefina offers a potent reminder that seemingly unlikely people can read critically and write with authority. Moreover, Doña Josefina's "rich, persuasive" texts suggest that the best writing is done in situations where people feel comfortable expressing their deepest values and commitments. Although religion is one domain of life that may cause discomfort for some instructors, Doña Josefina's spiritual writing illustrates the value of openness toward student life experiences, whatever they may be.

Guerra's presentation of Malú's work is more problematic. It's easy to see why he is interested in her essays, because (unlike Doña Josefina) she is typical of many minority students who struggle in college composition classes: in her own words, "caught between two cultures." Furthermore, as Guerra states, she carries "the burden of setting an example." Although he is referring to the example she sets for younger relatives, he also makes her writing serve as an example for extended, out-of-school, written discourse capable of showing the literacy "competence" of her entire community. He wants composition instructors to see Malú's texts as representative of "the discursive and rhetorical practices that students bring with them." However, Guerra's description of the process he went through to obtain Malú's writing makes it clear that she would not have produced the pieces without his strong encouragement: Writing autobiographical essays is not a traditional literacy practice of the Chicago *mexicano* community.

Moreover, Malú seems to have been enrolled in college composition classes during the time she wrote the pieces for Guerra, and her work displays the influence of "essayist" organizational features such as the thesis statement in her third text. As Guerra himself says, the autobiographical pieces she did for him look like "first drafts" when compared to finished essays that she wrote for college classes. I would argue that the "digressive thinking" she displays in the work for Guerra has nothing to do with the fact that she comes from a *mexicano* community but rather is typical of first-draft writing regardless of culture. On the other hand, the most striking commonality Guerra notes about her early autobiographical pieces is that they all end on a note of "transformation." Pointing out that her essays written for college classes express a contrasting sense of "stalemate," he implies that it may have been the freedom to make mistakes and switch languages that allowed her to describe such transformative experiences. Perhaps Malú's example should encourage instructors to read first drafts carefully in order to help student writers find ways to incorporate compelling "digressions" that are at risk of getting lost once the organization is tightened.

In the end, all the intriguing and instructive ethnographic evidence presented by the authors cannot quite carry the burden of "proving" an entire community's "competence." Perhaps it doesn't need to. While students such as Malú may well experience a greater discontinuity than do "mainstream" students between the rhetorical practices of their families and those typical of academic discourse, it is also important to remember that "essayist literacy" is, for *all* learners, a set of conventions primarily learned in schools rather than homes. In mainstream as well as minority communities, few people write "extended discourse" except to meet academic and professional requirements. Even the personal letter is a dying artform. Therefore, while it remains important for college composition instructors to "understand and respect the communicative competence of their students' communities," it should be recognized that the production of extended written discourse in out-of-school settings is not and should not be a prerequisite for college success.

CRIS GUTIERREZ RESPONDS

Poems! Songs! Letters! Raps! Journals! Stories! Young people write in the privacy of their notebooks, on sheets of paper tucked inside books, sometimes in the margins or on the back of class handouts, stating their mind in the huddled minutes or hours away from school demands. These creations often reveal stimulating thoughts and obvious, if not stunning, talent. As a high school teacher of social studies and English, I am always amazed at what kind of writing adolescents do as they pour their feelings into their questions and ideas on a page when not writing for an analytical assignment. Born of imagination and experience and distilled in funny, excited, confident, vulnerable, or adamant voice, their language is honest and clear. Their words, phrases, and sentences stand as intelligent compositions, demanding to be heard and understood. As youth express themselves freely, their literacy resounds.

Unfortunately, it is also, too often, belied by the analytical prose required by academic standards. Throughout the 16 years I have taught in public or private high schools, I have found this contradiction to be true for most young writers, but it is particularly the case for my inner-city students—Latino, African American, and Cambodian American. Ironically, those who come from poor and minority backgrounds, many of whom are recent immigrants, can show literate capacities when and where we least look for them, when and where some of us may least expect to find them, but in exactly the time and place anyone who espouses support for lifelong learning would hope to see literate behaviors thrive—in the everyday goings-on of home, neighborhood, job, and community. How do we open our eyes and ears to recognize the power and potential of literacy in the lives of our students beyond the classroom? How do we incorporate that talent into their scholarship? How do we help youth admit this talent into their academic reasoning and writing?

Having been fascinated with this challenge for a long time, I am delighted to find it to be the concentration of Juan Guerra and Marcia Farr in this chapter. Setting out to present "documentation and description of communicative competence," these two researchers find strong features of literacy and critical thought in the "communicative competence" expressed in nonacademic writings of two *mexicanas*, Doña Josefina and Malú, at home in the United States and connected to families in Mexico. Guerra and Farr's discussion of these literate capacities is significant for two reasons. First, these investigators establish healthy evidence of assets for scholastic undertakings, especially the kind of writing known to researchers as "essayist literacy," essential for college retention and graduation. (I suspect the same is more and more true in high school.) Second, the capabilities evince bilingual and biliterate strengths while still conveying important cultural assumptions, attitudes, or beliefs particular to Doña Josefina's and Malú's native and familial backgrounds, which can pose healthy challenges to teaching and learning, K–12 or college, because, as Guerra and Farr admirably point out, "whenever classrooms include individuals (students and/or teachers) from different cultural backgrounds, the potential for miscommunication increases."

I am impressed with how clearly and consistently Guerra and Farr keep in mind what I see as honoring the person, indeed the voice, who matters in writing and other literate practices. Such honoring begins with respecting and remembering that context, meaning, and purpose—personal, cultural, and communal—impel communication, hence literacy. Understanding how to embrace natural, even necessary, contexts, meanings, and purposes important to individuals and groups of students underlies successful schooling in "essayist literacy" and classroom discourse. This essential dimension of quality teaching and learning empowers both students and teachers. At the heart of Guerra and Farr's research and chapter lies a high regard for authenticity in how one learns and knows and what one learns and knows.

Typically, K–12 teachers have been pressured much more than college faculty to change and improve practices affecting writing instruction and a myriad of other curricular dimensions. For K–12 there is the National Board for Professional Teaching Standards, which addresses the kinds of pedagogy that draws on the learners' reservoir of understandings and capacities, especially in heterogeneous groups of students. We need to leverage that work and other ways to document quality teaching and learning as forms of scholarship for college and K–12 teachers to advance and to collaborate on in their professional practice. We have far to go to strengthen essay writing by incorporating and valuing other forms of students' writings, yes, even as accountability measures. Most important, we need to help foster the inner voice of the writer. That depends on a writer's believing that he or she has something important to say and good reason to say it. Grades and graduation will not be enough to bring out the best in a student; the quality of our relationships as teachers with students and theirs with each other will be the difference that makes the difference.

Building community is imperative not only for quality writing but for quality teaching and learning in K–12 or college. Guerra and Farr show how such community-building also enriches research. Their chapter reveals many insights and much hope. For as it asks us to honor the person in writing, Guerra and Farr's chapter enlightens us about the human talent and intelligence active in life, the truest test of quality education.

Part III

LITERACY IN AFTER-SCHOOL PROGRAMS

5

STRUGGLE

A Literate Practice
Supporting Life-Project Planning

ELENORE LONG, WAYNE C. PECK,
and JOYCE A. BASKINS

What is the role of an urban community center at the turn of the 21st century? We at the Community House, a settlement house with a 90-year history on Pittsburgh's North Side, believe that one such role is to set forth practices of renewal—community-based educational practices that build human capacity while simultaneously working to lift the performance of community groups.

In the Introduction to this volume, Hull and Schultz ask how educators and researchers can build coalitions that help to bridge the digital divide. Likewise, we recognize that the issue of how communities best foster renewal is heightened by the advent of technologies that claim to widen the franchise for learning. Computer technology centers provide one model for community work in this technological age: Be a catalyst for connectivity by providing access to the Internet (Miller, 1998). Proponents of this model tend to focus on building a technological infrastructure within community-based organizations, leaving community residents to identify the uses to which they will put the computer technology. However, access to computer technology does not immediately translate into use, let alone empowerment. Community residents often remain dubious of the value of computer technology. Characterizing one aspect of the digital divide, Krieg (1995) has documented that children in wealthy neighborhoods tend to use computer technology for complex problem-solving activities, while children in poorer communities are more often expected to use computers for drill and practice. In *Losing Ground Bit by Bit: Low-Income Communities in the Information Age*, the Benton Foundation issues the following challenge: "Creative ways will have to be found to make . . . new technologies . . . a part of the social lives of people in low-income neighborhoods" (Goslee, 1998, p. 12). Our purpose in this chapter is to offer a model for computer-supported community-based education, one that uses computer technology to strengthen relationships and to support project-based learning. We call the model STRUGGLE.

STRUGGLE and Mainstream Culture

Our society invests deeply in youth as consumers, as Eidman-Aadahl observes in Chapter 8 of this volume. Our popular culture sells urban teens manufactured images of "success" (the athlete, the celebrity, the CEO) on the one hand and demonizes them on the other (West, 1993). In constructing personal identities, urban teens must daily negotiate competing versions of themselves as problems, troublemakers, and even criminals.

Interactions with adults constitute another forum in which teenagers' identities are enacted. The urban teenagers we know tell us, and educational literature bears out, that the most pervasive cultural forms tend to restrict and often silence teens; individual encounters with adults are often limited to a few seconds each day (Nettles, 1991). Encounters tend to be authoritarian in nature, with the adult issuing a command or set of instructions and the teen choosing to be either obedient or recalcitrant. Our observations extend to conversations between teenagers and well-meaning adults who fall back on well-practiced testimonials, scare tactics, pep talks, and minisermons. Lacking the shared respect and dynamism of mutual exchange, these forms secure the adult's authority and silence the teen, cueing him or her to serve as listener, a grateful (or at least quiet) recipient of the adult's codified wisdom. STRUGGLE is designed to support teens in challenging adults' naive or reductive impressions of who they are and what they are up to in life.

STRUGGLE: A Response to our Local Cultural

STRUGGLE emerged in response to what John Dewey called a "felt difficulty": Our local culture was doing too little to cultivate identity-creating dialogues with people, particularly with the young people and the people who support them in our community.

Home to a worship community and several public service agencies, the Community House is located at the crossroads of a large urban hospital, a shopping district, several housing complexes, and several public schools. So people come to the Community House through any number of portals, community-based educational projects ranging from dance to multimedia design and work readiness. (For an extended discussion of the Community House and community literacy, see Peck, Flower, & Higgins, 1995.) In the afternoons and evenings, teens shoot hoops in the gymnasium where the elderly play Bingo every Wednesday at noon. Professional and aspiring artists make pottery in a basement studio; a dance troupe practices in a far wing.

Over the past several years, people at the Community House have repeatedly mourned the dearth of meaning—and of meaningful conversations—in their lives. Parents complained of too little time with their children, particularly once children became teenagers and were involved in sports or after-school jobs. At a baby shower held for a community resident, Debbie, a working mother of two teens, observed: "Few of us [as parents] observe the nightly 'family dinner hour' that we knew as kids: Though change may be well and good, in the case of nightly dinners, I hate to see them go." The parents sitting next to Debbie agreed. None had found adequate contemporary alternatives for staying in touch with their children. Another group of community residents met weekly for several months to discuss Michael Lerner and Cornel West's (1996) *Jews and Blacks: A Dialogue on Race, Religion, and Culture in America*. Summing up the book's significance to himself, Lewis, a single father and engineer from the Caribbean, theorized that if one is seeking a commonality that cuts across race, gender, and socioeconomic standing in our community, we need look no further than our frenetic consumer culture. He commented: "It corrodes efforts to find the promise in our own lives. Instead, our culture tells us the promise rests in wearing the Armani suit, the Nike tennis shoe—in running around in the name of Making Ends Meet, finding something to sell, to buy."

Many teenagers told us they were tired with the "same old, same old" at school. In a series of literacy projects examining ways to restructure Pittsburgh's public schools, teens wrote analyses with such titles as "Why I Sleep in Class" and "Whassup with Suspension?" They explained that they were looking for—and not finding—footholds that would let them chart meaningful paths in school, to see school as a place of promise (Flower, 1996; Long, 2000). Along with the other contributors to this volume, we want to avoid demonizing formal schooling through overly simplistic characterizations. At the same time, we do hear in these teens' observations sets of concerns similar to those McNamee and Sivright document (see

Chapter 6, this volume)—students' frustration with tedious assignments and unfair practices of social control.

Community residents, including some educators, voiced a frustration with the punitive nature of public discourse in our city regarding teenagers. As Eidman-Aadahl reviews in Chapter 8 of this volume, the past decades have been characterized, in part, by policy makers' attention to "the 'problem' of young people during non-school hours." Our city's administration, for instance, recently invested hundreds of thousands of dollars in a detention center for minors caught on the street after curfew. The discussion was void of creative alternatives.

Goals and Theoretical Commitments

We have designed STRUGGLE to create possibilities in direct tension with current public discourses and practices that cast urban teens as problems and American families as dysfunctional. Guided by the Freirian principle of action and reflection (Freire, 1986/1970), we aim to use the best thinking of the day to inform our action and to use tools for observation to inform our subsequent reflections on that action. Our inquiry focuses on the following questions:

- Is our educational intervention up to the task of influencing the meaning-making process of identity construction?
- If so, where can we, as reflective practitioners, locate evidence that other educators might find credible?
- What do the texts and voices of participants tell us about the process of identity construction?

To frame our inquiry, this chapter draws on cultural production theory and rhetorical theory to analyze the outcomes that STRUGGLE supports. In particular, it examines the cultural forms, habits of mind, and literate practices that STRUGGLE cultivates.

STRUGGLE draws from cultural production theory to account for the process by which "identities are given meaning in context" (Eisenhart, 1996, p. 169). Interested in the "resources for, and constraints upon social action," Levinson and Holland (1996) write: "Cultural production . . . provides a direction for understanding how human agency operates under powerful structural constraints. Through the production of cultural forms . . . , subjectivities form and agency develops" (p. 14). The uncharted crevices between scripted schemas and institutional structure can be characterized by their "openness" (Holland & Cole, 1995, p. 480). Despite the virtually indomitable effects of hegemonic structures, openness allows for (in some contexts invites) interpretation, choice, response, even inventiveness. In the language of cultural production theory, STRUGGLE is an educational intervention directed toward the openness that makes possible the creative production of local identities.

As a literacy project within the Community House, STRUGGLE configures the link between writing and agency from a rhetorical perspective as well. Flower (1996) defines literate action from a cognitive rhetorical perspective:

- First, it [literate action] is a socially embedded, socially shaped practice.
- Second, at the same time, literate action is an individual constructive act that embeds practices and conventions within its own personally meaningful, goal-directed use of literacy.
- And third . . . literate action . . . is often a site of conflict among multiple goals, alternative goods, and opposing shoulds; it calls for negotiation among unavoidable constraints, options, and alternatives. (p. 249)

From this rhetorical perspective, a writer taking literate action cannot rely on well-practiced patterns of discourse. The problem he or she wants to address through writing does not fit typical characterizations, for instance, and his or her readership is likely more varied and complex than codified practices assume. Thus, the writer must work inventively to negotiate competing concerns. Flower, Long, and Higgins (2000) argue that strong rhetorical action constitutes acts of agency because readily available patterns of discourse (and, by extension, the social institutions that support them) come up short. Only by inventing dynamic, hybrid solutions can the writer effectively negotiate the demands of the rhetorical situation.

An Overview of the STRUGGLE Project

STRUGGLE is a member of a family of literacy projects at the Community House that have focused on building human capacity through collaborative social action. Over the last 8 years, we at Pittsburgh's Community House, in partnership with Carnegie Mellon University, have been crafting a process of community literacy. We have discovered that community literacy is effective when it develops and sustains the capacity to solve problems, to cope with obstacles, to commit with others, to imagine new possibilities, to achieve what seemed impossible—to act, to trust and to hope. The

STRUGGLE project has emerged as our best effort to integrate strategy-based, project-oriented, technologically attuned literacy instruction within the Community House, as a loving and hospitable context for community-based education.

The STRUGGLE project typically takes 6 weeks to complete and has four phases, as detailed in Table 5.1. The textual dimension of STRUGGLE is vital to the design of the project, for in STRUGGLE, people talk in order to write. The project stresses that the documents participants write are provisional, never finished, yet the project also evokes the classical defense of writing: Write down your thoughts so they can be revisited, revised, updated, clarified, shared, and responded to.

In their description of the Fifth Dimension, McNamee and Sivright (Chapter 6, this volume) identify Michael Cole and his colleagues' interest in fostering opportunities for problem-solving. So, too, at the Community House problem-solving strategies are taught as resources for systematically thinking through complex problems. Within the framework of community literacy, then, writing is a tool for building human capacity. Writing joint documents distributes expertise in many directions, gives voice to those whose perspectives often go unheard in public discussions, and stresses action.

There is, however, one vitally important caveat. Just as students in McNamee and Sivright's study resisted taking the Test of Written Language because of its association with formal schooling, so, too, in a community center, as elsewhere, people often bring with them anxiety-ridden school-based notions of writing as a venerated art. As we stipulated above, in STRUGGLE, people do talk in order to write. But that is not the end of the equation. Participants talk and write together in order to build new kinds of relationships, relationships in which they invite one another to compose compelling life narratives.

Teens and adults in the program are trained in collaborative planning (Flower, Wallace, Norris, & Burnett, 1994). In phase 2—the collaborative writing phase—everyone works with someone other than the person with whom they came. You will see in the following vignettes, for instance, that Janine's aunt Marlene (all names are pseudonyms) writes with a young man named Terrell. Jamaal works with Debbie, Jason's mother. As collaborative planning partners, pairs of teens and adults take turns as Writers and Supporters. The Supporter is trained to help the Writer develop his or her own rhetorical purposes. The Supporter grants the Writer "the floor" and helps the Writer build a more elaborated plan of the rhetorical problem. In STRUGGLE, both parties, the teen and the adult, write their own life plans. Within any given project session, the teen supports the adult Writer, and they switch roles. In the context of STRUGGLE, collaborative planning signals a new set of priorities, priorities that privilege mutuality rather than the

TABLE 5.1: The Four Phases of STRUGGLE

PHASE	DESCRIPTION
1. Gathering	Participants meet as a large group for dinner, for an overview of the project and its goals, and for training in collaborative planning.
2. Collaborative Writing	The core practice of STRUGGLE, this phase combines conversation and writing. Teen–adult pairs map their thinking to date on five questions:
	1) *Who are the people "at my table"?*
	2) *What am I going through?*
	3) *What am I up against?*
	4) *What am I up to in my life?*
	5) *What are the ways to be together in this?*
	Pairs work from laptop computers that house STRUGGLE's multimedia writing environment.
3. Presenting	Teenagers and their sponsoring adults come back together to present their documents to one another. The focus is on presenting discoveries and making new covenants with one another.
4. Renewing	Participants come back together to revisit the experience of writing about one's life as struggle. The goal is to maintain conversation between teenagers and adults grounded in solidarity and filled with possibility.

hierarchical relationships characteristic of well-sedimented, institutionalized discourse (Hopper, 1988).

Culture, Form, and the Construction of Personal Identity

In "The Cultural Production of the Educated Person," Levinson and Holland (1996) describe the role of cultural forms in the process of identity formation. They include forms "rang[ing] from actions, practices, and ritualized behaviors to expressive artifacts and concrete objects" (p. 12). Such forms work to link people to their social and material circumstances. Through cultural forms, people interpret and enact who they are and where they fit in the world around them.

STRUGGLE's Computer-Supported Writing Environment: A Cultural Form

As a tangible artifact, STRUGGLE's writing environment has the status of a cultural form. This multimedia environment has been designed to structure and support participants' writing. See Figures 5.1 and 5.2 later in the chapter for sample pages. The colorful template is divided among (1) written and spoken prompts, (2) supporting images to frame each section, and (3) expandable spaces for writing. Participants print their documents as they would any other Word document. In the printed versions, the icons that structure the writing environment (e.g., the logo and icons for Quicktime video inserts) now serve as illustrations. (See Figure 5.1.)

We chose to include Figure 5.1 in order to direct the reader's attention to the computer-supported writing environment that characterizes STRUG-GLE. The reader probably noticed that the environment is in no way "slick." The drawing of the table is obviously amateurish and the layout rather blockish, lacking an elegant use of white space. Not only does this design (or, arguably, the lack thereof) fit our do-it-yourself budget, it also is an implicit argument for the provisional nature of identity building: STRUGGLE argues that we all are works-in-progress; even the writing environment stakes that claim.

Central to STRUGGLE are its core five questions (see phase 2 of Table 5.1). They don't change. They are the gifts of theologians, primarily the 16th-century activist reformer St. Teresa of Avila and contemporary libera-tion theologian Dorothee Solle. However, the writing environment's design is provisional, so simple that we are always tinkering with and revising it. The fluidity of this cultural form also invites each document to be personal-ized and updated with digital photographs of participants and other images they supply.

So far, we have been trying to detail what STRUGGLE brings to the process of cultural production. We are emphasizing that the writing envi-ronment itself constitutes a cultural form indigenous to our local culture. We are also arguing that the cultural form is embedded, to the best of our ability, within a context that tries to signal a new day for community-based learning. As mentioned above, each STRUGGLE project kicks off with a dinner. Participants sit together, elbow to elbow, around a large oval table

FIGURE 5.1: Front Page from the STRUGGLE Writing Environment

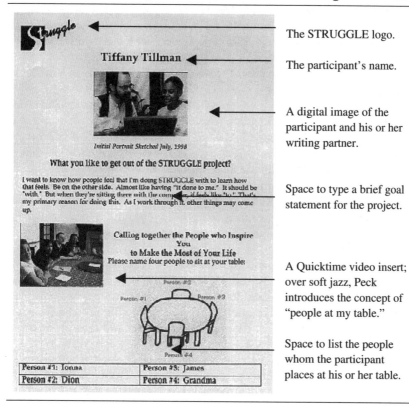

The STRUGGLE logo.

The participant's name.

A digital image of the participant and his or her writing partner.

Space to type a brief goal statement for the project.

A Quicktime video insert; over soft jazz, Peck introduces the concept of "people at my table."

Space to list the people whom the participant places at his or her table.

covered with an African-print tablecloth. The music, the food, the gentle teasing, the storytelling that we deliberately weave into each iteration are our efforts to signal a hospitality so robust as to reframe writing outside the (often punitive) context of schooling and within the existential context of life-planning and relationship-building.

Teens Composing Compelling Life Narratives: Acts of Cultural Production

We are suggesting that the writing teens generate within STRUGGLE constitutes a cultural form distinct from (not merely an extension of) the writing environment itself. Previously, we tried to establish with our readers a shared assumption: In public and private spheres alike, the dominant culture shortchanges urban teens by offering too few opportunities to consider seriously who they are and what they are up to in life. If readers grant us this assumption, they would likely agree that participants' extended responses to STRUGGLE's core questions may very well constitute inventive, constructive acts of resistance and promise, existing—from the moment they are uttered—in tension with the market-driven interests of our dominant culture.

Below are excerpts from two teens' STRUGGLE documents. Like other teens in STRUGGLE, Janine characterizes herself as a decision maker. That is, when she writes about what she is up against and what she is up to in life, she identifies her own acts of agency in places where choices make a difference. Consider, for instance, her response to the STRUGGLE prompt, "What are you struggling through?" Janine introduces a dilemma she faces. She professes a deep love for her mother. Yet Janine knows that her mom's drinking too often requires her to mother her own mother. She writes:

> I am struggling between my grandmother and my Mom. I love them both, but my mother wants me to move back with her. I know if I go back, I will go back to the way I was cutting school and doing nothing all day and making no real use of my life, whereas with my grandmother, I go to school everyday and my whole life has completely turned around. . . . I know my Mom does bad things—I still love her. But I don't want to have to choose between living here or there. The greater struggle is being torn between my grandmother and my mother. In a nutshell, they just don't get along with each other and that is my problem. Sometimes I kind of think it is my fault. . . . If I am with one, I am not with the other, and they get mad and hurt.

While Janine's grandmother has arranged for Janine to live with her, Janine writes that this solution is hardly satisfactory, for she feels that the arrangement betrays her mother and intensifies the stress between her grandmother and mother, leaving Janine feeling responsible and guilty. In the opening pages of her document, Janine charts the complex space in which she is working to center her life.

Now consider Terrell, a laid-back, soft-spoken teen, paired in a collaborative writing team with Janine's rather boisterous aunt, Marlene. Without encouragement, Terrell seems content to type in one-sentence, even one-word, responses to some of the STRUGGLE prompts. Initially, he insists on stock phrases: that he is "up to" becoming a professional basketball player and he is "up against" the fact that he's neither particularly tall nor athletically talented. But with Marlene's gentle insistence that he elaborate, Terrell gets specific, even operational, in his written description of what he is struggling through: his relationship with his father and his own efforts to improve communication between himself and his father. He writes:

> I'm trying to make him [my dad] a part of my life by talking to him on the phone. Quit being shy in front of him. He started getting me a little bit. After a while, when we haven't talked for a while, I start missing him. I try to call him. We have a good conversation, and after a while he calls me to come over. He hopes for me to stay in school and that—to be in college. Don't be in the streets. Come see him more often.

Terrell's mother was in the STRUGGLE project with him. Fluent in 12-step recovery discourse, she gave rehearsed responses to each of the STRUGGLE prompts (see Cain, 1991). She had a habit (as perhaps many of us, as parents, do) of speaking for her son in group settings: primarily insisting that he was not to become a basketball player but rather a white-collar professional. However, we noted that her recovery discourse was not her son's. Yet in order to hear him elaborate on his life for himself, his collaborative writing partner needed to be patient, quiet, and persistent.

Several years ago at a town meeting held at the Community House, Pittsburgh's mayor addressed the theme of renewal—specifically, renewing the city's commitment to its teenagers. He admitted that in the 1980s "we stopped investing in teenagers, and we started building buildings instead—high-rises, stadiums, office complexes." To renew a commitment to young people, teens' STRUGGLE documents suggest, adults must find ways to attend to the stories teens tell of their lives. The documents suggest that in the face of a popular culture that relentlessly broadcasts reductive images of success, renewal includes valorizing stronger and more sustaining identities, ones that connect young people with the supportive people in their lives and to the best selves they want to become.

Habits of Mind: Conceptual Aspects of Cultural Production

Cultural production theory emerged, in part, in response to the limits of structural arguments that people within institutional frameworks typically had just two options: to reproduce the status quo or to resist it. Cultural production theory raises the possibility of a whole range of alternatives. Thus it shifts the focus of analysis from social structures and discrete discourses toward people operating within complex webs of institutional and discursive practices. As such, cultural production theory seeks a fine-grained analysis of people's lived experiences. This theoretical orientation does not assume, as strict advocates of cultural reproduction have, that the mind is a "black box," beyond the reach of systematic inquiry. Instead a cultural artifact (one outcome of cultural production) has both an ideal— that is, conceptual—and a material dimension (Holland & Cole, 1995). It is toward the conceptual dimension of STRUGGLE, as a culture-creating enterprise, that we now turn our attention.

As writing researchers, we draw from a social-cognitive tradition that we think has something to contribute to a theory of cultural production. In particular, we refer to Flower's (1994) theoretical account of the construction of negotiated meaning. Negotiation theory accounts for the ways in which writers build dynamic representations of complex rhetorical problems and negotiate the competing—often conflicting—"voices" that operate within those representations in order to construct plans and prose that reach some provisional resolution. Negotiation theory is significant to cultural production theory because it speculates that if we are interested in how people attempt to do something besides either reproduce or resist the status quo, we need to investigate real people, within their own settings, wrestling within sites of contested meaning. Our extended inquiry assumes that given the existing cultural milieu, urban teens' claims of personal identity constitute such a site.

From this theoretical orientation, STRUGGLE, as a pedagogical intervention, deliberately commends two habits of mind: the dialogic imagination and strategic thinking. Though we have strong theoretical reasons for incorporating these features into the project, below we characterize how participants might internalize these constructs, bringing them to life for themselves.

The Dialogic Imagination

In his landmark work by the same name, Mikhail Bakhtin (1981) characterizes the dialogic imagination as the chorus of voices that breathe meaning into people's lives and that call them to participate in the world. Bakhtin uses the phrase to capture the ways in which voices of the public sphere mediate individual subjectivities. While Bakhtin's work characterizes the project of the novelist, in STRUGGLE we evoke the dialogic imagination as an image of everyday solidarity. In response to the postmodern cry of fragmentation (see Faigley, 1993)—and in tension with the adolescent feelings of alienation—STRUGGLE suggests that one is never really alone in the world. Moreover, STRUGGLE encourages participants to think deliberately about the dialogues they entertain in their imaginations: One can choose to be in conversation with those people who inspire and transform; likewise, at least in one's imagination, one can deliberately distance oneself from voices that degrade or depress.

To make more operational the notion of the dialogic imagination, STRUGGLE is grounded in the image of the dining room table. As described earlier, participants meet for the first time for a meal around a dining room table at the settlement house. And one of the first prompts in the STRUGGLE writing environment asks each participant to set an imaginary table at which to call together several important people in his or her life. STRUGGLE partners then take turns as Writer and Supporter, developing portraits of each of these fellow pilgrims in life (see Figure 5.2).

Below are excerpts from participants' portraits of people at their table.

FIGURE 5.2: A Portrait of "Someone at My Table"

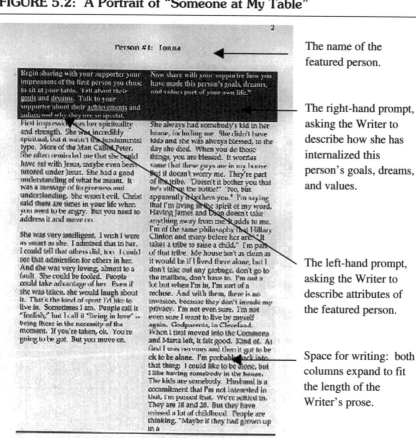

The name of the featured person.

The right-hand prompt, asking the Writer to describe how she has internalized this person's goals, dreams, and values.

The left-hand prompt, asking the Writer to describe attributes of the featured person.

Space for writing: both columns expand to fit the length of the Writer's prose.

As the reader might predict, the people who participants include are often family members and friends, people who participants know intimately, people who often protect or call forth treasured traits or talents that others may overlook: "Grandma believes in me." "Uncle Eddie loved that I would sing, no matter what the occasion." Participants also include (though less frequently) figures from more public spheres—popular culture or literature, for instance. Participants often describe these figures who inspire them in more general terms: "Congresswoman Barbara Jordan sits at my table to remind me to fight racism everyday, even when I'm so, so tired."

An Everyday Hero. Embedded in the portraits are tributes to moral values and shared aspirations. Articulated both to oneself and to others—written down often for the first time and now available for subsequent reflection—these stories serve as a basis for renewing participants' senses of identity, as well as for building the conditions for hope, mutual respect, and achievement.

Marcia places at her table her preschool teacher, Miss Beasley. In the portrait, Marcia commemorates a teacher who saw promise in her as a 4-year-old and who nurtured that promise in the years that followed. Below is an excerpt:

> She [Miss Beasley] is caring, devoted to children and respected by them. She makes a difference in children's lives. By that I mean that children who weren't even in my preschool class know her and know the good work she has done on behalf of children of all ages. I was genuinely covered with smiles growing up, especially when my mom was sick. . . . All of my life she has inquired about the things I have done, from age 4 until now. Somebody who was just a teacher for me a couple of years actually took the time to think of me as one of her own children and to look out for me.

The portrait Marcia sketches depicts hope. It characterizes the willingness of an adult to show a young person the strength of his or her own potential. Taken together with other similar portraits of other everyday figures, the profile also suggests that despite criticisms launched against schools and families in general, individual caretakers, teachers, and parents are finding ways to inspire and nurture young people. Such portraits underscore the communicative power of mutual respect as it gets translated into everyday actions.

An Enigmatic Father. The next vignette highlights another version of how the familial dinner table gets translated within the imagination of urban youth. Because the teen's dialogue with his Supporter is integrally connected to the text he composes, that dialogue is included below as well.

Placing people at his table, Jamaal quickly lists his mother and two grandmothers then pauses before naming his father. He announces, "I would love to have him at my table. I'm going to make him the first person." Rearranging the symbolic name cards at the table, he writes as he talks: "The first person I would choose is my father, he died in jail." The next computer prompt asks Jamaal to describe the person's goals and how he has made those goals his own. But Jamaal counters: "I really didn't know his goals or nothing 'cause he was always in jail and stuff. I just used to see him on and off, every now and then."

Apparently a bit confused, his adult partner asks: "Why, then, would it be important for you to have him at your table?"

Jamaal gets right to the point: " 'Cause I know he would tell me not to go through what he went through in his life." He then writes:

The last time I saw my dad before he died, he was trying to tell me some stuff. That it's tempting to make easy money. Then he died. In jail. I know he would tell me not to go through what he went through in his life.

Later in the conversation, Jamaal broaches the topic again with his Supporter, saying, "It's easy to make easy money."

Jamaal's partner, Debbie, is a mother of a younger teenage son, Jason, also in the project. As Jamaal writes the portrait of his father, Debbie takes more interest in and shows increasing respect for the young man's insights into negotiating the street—knowing how to "speak, think, and act" in various situations that arise in urban neighborhoods (Gee, 1989). Later she cited Jamaal's insights as one of the project's benefits to her as a parent. She drew a parallel between the experiences of Jamaal and those Jason needed to prepare for, since both are young African American males growing up in a socially challenging and economically challenged urban neighborhood. Debbie's participation in Jamaal's composing process underscores another characteristic of the dialogic imagination as it is translated within STRUGGLE: Texts capture one set of dynamics within the dialogic imagination; the collaborative planning process introduces other sets of voices and commitments.

A Public Figure. While Marcia and Jamaal choose family and friends to sit at their tables, STRUGGLE participants often also invite public figures to their tables. Whether referring to Barbara Jordan's public addresses, Frederick Douglass's autobiography, Margaret Mead's reflections, or James Weldon Johnson's anthem, in commending these figures participants also frequently describe how they have integrated into their own lives the contributions associated with the public figures. For instance, a teenager named Questa places Maya Angelou at her table. As she does so, she dramatizes the role that her own poetic imagination has played at a critical juncture in her life: the summer after high school graduation. Questa credits Angelou's poetry for helping her build a bridge from high school to college. In placing Angelou at her table, Questa recites Angelou's poetry from memory as she types it into her STRUGGLE document: "I look through the posture and past your disguise /And see your love for family in your big brown eyes." She then writes this explanation:

> I hear Angelou talking to me—directly. It's [the poem] was really
> written for the Million Man March. But the poem speaks to what's
> on my mind as I go away to college. It's easy to feel like you've
> gotta be all hard on the outside. But, inside, I don't want to leave my
> mother all alone. She never married, and I have been her companion
> for eighteen years of her life. Now, I must live my own life. I'm sure
> she wants me to. Angelou urges me to take this next step. At the
> same time, she tells me that I am right to keep making my fam-
> ily—my Mom and her Mom—a big part of my life. When I recite An-
> gelou's poetry in my head, what she writes about my big brown eyes
> showing my love of my family, I know she is talking to me, too.

Participants' portraits are typically tributes to the contributions others have made to their lives—a teacher's vision, a father's tenacity, a prophetess's inspiring poetry.

As community educators, we have been interested in the dialogic nature of participants' stories. Much has been made of personal narratives, or self-stories. Bruner (1990) explains that such stories are the basis for "action based on belief, desire, and moral commitment" (p. 9). Such folk narratives enable people to structure their experiences and to reflect on and to communicate that knowledge. Similarly, Eisenhart (1995) argues that "[P]ersonal . . . stories serve as guides to individual actions, goals, and interpretations. . . . These stories create continuity over time, affirm social relationships, and illuminate the 'good' self, that is, the moral value of self" (p. 18). Bruner's and Eisenhart's theories are corroborated by the portraits participants write. Yet something else strikes us about these portraits as well. These "self-stories" are also "other stories," stories of others at the table.

Our reflections lead us to see that there is all the difference in the world between holding in one's imagination the story that "my Dad died in jail" and "My dad died in jail wanting something better for me." In the mix of participants' talk and texts is the potential to tell stories—to craft experience—in any number of ways. A primary goal of STRUGGLE is to call forth compelling stories—not overly simplified, not naive, but rather constructive, promise-filled life narratives. Herein, we believe, lies the redemptive value of the dialogic imagination.

Strategic Thinking

We turn now to the second intellectual orientation: strategic thinking. It is important to note that neither a dialogic imagination nor strategic thinking dictates to someone how to figure out a tough problem, but both encourage people take the time "to go figure." Thus STRUGGLE is a tool to help each participant develop a sense of him- or herself as someone equipped with tools for thinking through tough problems. The question such an aim raises, of course, is whether such instruction transfers to situations in which teens themselves actively seek expanded sets of options.

Conversations with teenagers bring to the fore an important shortcoming in contemporary philosophy on human agency. Such philosophy is typically grounded in the comfortable assumption that our choices exist as fully articulated distinctions (choices are between éclairs or mille-feuilles on a dessert plate or, as in Jean Paul Sartre's favorite dilemma—tending to a sick mother versus joining the Resistance). But teens at the Community House tell us that the world they experience is far less articulated. Try to start a conversation with the question, "Who do you have to talk to about the stress you're under?" and you are likely to hear, "Nobody." Ask, "What else could you have done in that dangerous situation?" and you are likely to get the response, "Nothing." Such responses from teenagers are not uncommon and—like the research on adolescent decision-making—they suggest how important it is for educators, parents, and other adults to help teenagers learn to consider alternative courses of action (Fischhoff, Furby, Quadrel, & Richardson, 1991). Although in general the decision-making processes of adults are not much different or better than those of teenagers, Fischhoff and Quadrel (1990) document that adolescents in particular often consider only one course of action. For instance, when 150 teenagers were asked to describe difficult decisions in their lives, these teens typically described their decisions in terms of single alternatives, say, whether or not to attend a party at which alcohol would be served; whether or not to take a ride with a friend who had been drinking.

Our conversations with teenagers at the Community House suggest that decision-making is often not as simple as choosing "whether or not." In their lived experiences, decision-making seems often to be a matter of constructing alternatives when none seems to exist and of making choices in the face of competing sets of negative consequences.

To support STRUGGLE participants, both the STRUGGLE training materials and the project's writing environment make use of the problem-solving strategies that have become the hallmark of community literacy (Peck et al., 1995); see Table 5.2. These strategies have emerged from our own field experience, as well as the research and theory of writing researchers and social and decision scientists (Fischhoff et al., 1991; Fischhoff & Quadrel, 1990; Flower et al., 2000; Flower et al., 1994).

Participants are introduced to and practice these strategies during the initial training session. The strategies are woven within the project in other ways as well.

Collaborative Planning. As discussed above, throughout the second phase of STRUGGLE teens and adults work together as collaborative writing partners, deliberately taking turns as Writer and Supporter. At the end of each session, participants come together to reflect on discoveries they made while assuming these roles.

TABLE 5.2: Community Literacy's Problem-Solving Strategies

Strategy	Brief Description
Collaborative Planning	Deliberately taking turns, within a dyad, as Writer and Supporter to develop the Writer's ideas for carrying out his or her rhetorical purpose
Seeing the story behind the story	Dramatizing for readers the hidden logic of an unfamiliar perspective
Using rival-hypothesis Thinking (or "rivaling") to generate alternatives	Considering rival viewpoints and how those viewpoints would interpret the evidence at hand
Examining options and outcomes in decision-making	Evaluating alternative courses of action and the consequence—both positive and negative—associated with each decision path

Rivaling. Problem-solving strategies also structure several prompts built into STRUGGLE's writing environment. Consider, for instance, references to rivaling. Take the section "Expanding Your Options: Bringing Other People's Wisdom into Your Own Life." Click on a Help button, and you will hear Peck urging STRUGGLE participants to rival their own thinking regarding the options available to them:

> Rivaling is a kind of thinking in which you talk it out before someone at your table and predict what that person would say and the advice that person would offer. These imaginary conversations let us bring other's wisdom into our own lives. This section asks you to create a dialogue with someone at your table by predicting what he or she would say in response to what you've written—and what advice he or she could offer you.

The subsequent section of the writing environment is crafted to help elicit imagined responses of someone sitting at the participant's table. It asks the participant to choose one person from those he or she imagines to be sitting at the table and to predict how that person would respond to what the participant has previously written. To encourage well-specified predictions (as opposed to overly general accolades or criticism), the writing environment copies into the left-hand column what the participant wrote in response to the three previous questions. This feature permits the participant to easily revisit and refer to specific passages in his or her evolving document. The right-hand column is reserved, then, for the Writer's imagined response.

Options and Outcomes. Supporters are trained to use the options and outcomes strategy when they think their partners may benefit from considering a wider range of alternatives. The following is a brief example of the strategy at work.

You will recall Janine, the young woman struggling with whether to live with her mother. While writing her document, Janine decides to devise a plan to get her mother and grandmother to talk to each other. With support from her Supporter, the plan becomes rather detailed, laying out option A and option B and finally pulling in Uncle Paul for a third option. However, the Supporter also skillfully employs "options and outcomes" to help Janine not only to think of her responsibility to the adults in her life but also to seize the opportunity to think about and plan her own life.

Janine diagnoses the situation: "Well, my Mom is very stubborn. And she is frustrated easily. That will be a barrier. I have to create the conditions where she will not give up, and I have to let both of them get to know themselves in new ways and respect themselves." She writes:

> *Plan A:* It's going to be rough. My mom is the type who will listen to you, and then her temper will flare up. I will say: "You and grandma aren't on good terms. If you want your children to look up to you, then you are going to have to try to be a better role model."
> *Plan B:* Not be so direct, much kinder. Put my mom in a room with my grandmother and make her talk to her. And count on her. Tell her ahead of time: "It's not what you say, but how you say it."

Then she considers a third alternative: "Maybe I could get Uncle Paul. They both trust him."

The Supporter and Janine continue their exchange:

> *Supporter:* What would you like Uncle Paul to do? Explain it to him?
> *Janine:* I'd say something like, "Uncle Paul, I want to try to get them together to talk again because the falling out that they had is one that can destroy their whole relationship. . . . The *sorry*'s don't work anymore. We have to find some way for them to come together and talk it through. They are allowed to shout and scream, but they have to work it out."
> *Supporter:* How are you going to coach Uncle Paul to take his best shot at this?
> *Janine:* His best shot will be his ability to get them to talk eye to eye. Start with easy things, like coffee. If it gets hot, let them go at it, and don't let others get involved, because my grandmother needs her daughter to talk to her. Have them talk without interruptions. Not about how she screwed up, but about the future.

So at least in Janine's mind, a conversation is renewed between her mother and grandmother.

However, there is another breakthrough in all of this: Janine begins writing a plan for her own life after high school. The imaginary conversation between her mom and grandmother—this magnificent feat—lets her set aside, at least temporarily, the very real tension between these two figures in her life. The Supporter is then able to prompt Janine again, still using options and outcomes, to do some serious life planning:

> *Supporter:* What's the outcome you have in mind here?
> *Janine:* I see a family reunion. . . .
> *Supporter:* What would follow from that for you?

Janine: The two people I love the most would be closer, and I
   wouldn't have to worry about being torn between them.
Supporter: And what would you be free to do with your life?
Janine: That would free me to worry about the little things in life,
   like school and what my friends said and . . .
Supporter: And how would it free you to do the *big things*?
Janine: It would free me for new things. It frees me to find out
   where I am going after school. Am I going to college? Or into
   the army and then college? How well will I do on my SATs? It
   would free me to find out if I want to be a nurse first . . .

In the context of STRUGGLE, problem-solving strategies are designed to
support teenagers like Janine learn to give priority to the plans they have
for their own lives.

   Some Evidence. To get a sense of what community literacy strategies
might mean to teens outside the life of a literacy project, Baskins interviewed a cohort of 14 Community House alumni who had, 3 years earlier,
completed a project together. She structured the interviews with the following prompt:

   Remember your experience at the Community House—what you
   learned there about problem-solving strategies, about collaboration,
   or about community issues. Now think about what is going on in
   your life—at school, at home, on the streets or at work. Problems,
   struggles, accomplishments. Or think about goals and life plans for
   where you want be going. *Can you describe any specific instances—actual events—in which you used what you learned here
   about collaborative planning, seeing the story behind the story, using rivaling, or considering options and outcomes?*[1]

In their responses, alumni included specific instances and examples in
which they explicitly referred to using what they had learned at the Community House. Of course, we were not there to see what really happened
or what they thought during the situations they describe. At best, these
examples reveal a combination of changed behavior and changed perceptions about their behavior. These changes suggest that these teenagers see
themselves transferring learning from the Community House to situations
in their own lives that demand decision-making.
   In Table 5.3, alumni's descriptions of situations are on the left. On the
right are their descriptions of how they used specific strategies to think

TABLE 5.3: Examples of Teens' Strategic Thinking

Illustrative Examples: The Kinds of Problems Teens Are Solving	Strategic Action: Literate Practices Teens Use to Solve These Problems

Chrystal:

Charting a life path:
"There is too much pressure out there for you not to use drugs, like family, friends and boyfriends. Life itself is pressure. It is hard for us teenagers now. I can't see me having a baby and just letting my baby grow up into this society, 'cause it is wild. It is wild out there. It is very hard."

Having used options and outcomes:
"It helped me to sit there in the room by myself and just think. Just to think. The outcomes of what I'm gonna do. How I'm going to do it. Who is going to help me."

Peggy:

Avoiding sexual harassment at home:
"My step-dad is getting on my nerves. 'Cause my mom, she kicked him out 'cause he was trying to feel over me and stuff, and he was trying to say it didn't happen, and it did."

Having used rivaling:
"I used rivaling at home with my step-dad and with my mom 'cause for a minute there, I thought my mom didn't believe me. I told her the reason why I didn't want to come home, and he was out of town that day, so she changed all the locks, so when he came back, he couldn't get into the house."

Tony:

Resisting easy money:
"People ask me, do I want to sell drugs, use them."

Having used options and outcomes:
"It hasn't been a big decision about using them [drugs], but selling them. At the time, they would ask me like when I really needed money. But I just looked for a job. That is my way of work."

Considering unprotected sex:
"My girlfriend asked me to have sex without a condom."

Having used options and outcomes:
"I'm afraid of getting her pregnant. And she might have something . . . a disease. The options were to wait for a better time. Wait 'til we have protection."

through the problem. The stories the alumni told in response highlight how they saw themselves using literate strategies to navigate daily life.

Baskins's interviews with Community House alumni suggest that community-based education, at its best, fosters renewal by supporting learners in constructing viable options for living experimental modes of life; "creative responses," that is, "to novel circumstances and conditions" (West, 1993, p. 23). Levinson and Holland (1996) see a similar promise in authentic formal education. They "use the . . . concept of 'cultural production' . . . to show how people creatively occupy the space of education and schooling. This creative practice [cultural production] generates understandings and strategies which may in fact move well beyond the school, transforming aspirations, household relations, local knowledges, and structures of power" (p. 14). In these aspirations, we hear echoes revealing a shared heritage in American pragmatism. This intellectual tradition holds that words, ideas, and languages are not mirrors of reality, "but rather tools with which we cope with 'our' world" (West, 1989, p. 201).

Literate Practices and Identity Construction

Levinson and Holland (1996) credit "the focus on practice" with informing the action-oriented aspects of cultural production theory. Pushing against "reproduction theory" in which "subjects were imagined as being 'interpellated by ideology' and without agency," Levinson and Holland contend that cultural production frames "the larger question [to ask] . . . how historical persons are formed in practice, within and against larger societal forces and structures" (p. 14). From our view as writing researchers, we are particularly interested in literate practices and their consequences. This final section considers how STRUGGLE attempts to support identity construction in practice—in the day-to-day actions through which people enact who they are in the world.

Cultural Border-Crossing

Community literacy draws on what West (1993) commends as an experimental mode of being that permits people to cross cultural boundaries. Among its primary goals, community literacy seeks to extend multicultural awareness to include intercultural inquiry and problem-solving (Peck et al., 1995). Community literacy frames cultural differences as resources for collaborative, purposeful social action. That is, intercultural inquiry serves as a "strategy for making something—a new understanding, a document, public literate act" (p. 210). As a community literacy initiative, STRUGGLE asks

participants "[to] engage in . . . boundary-crossing encounters that go beyond mere conversation to the delicate exploration of difference and conflict and toward the construction of a negotiated meaning" (p. 209).

Although the media tend to focus on the territorial practices of urban
teenagers, the young people who come to the Community House are very
often among the most adept at crossing cultural borders. They are used to
navigate among cultural and class codes that characterize the school hall,
classroom, athletic field, and bus stop. Structured reflections have helped
us better understand the thought processes of teenagers as they work to
connect with people different from themselves.

Below, Tyrone—a Muslim teenager—views video footage of himself
and his collaborative writing partner. Tyrone's interpretation of the footage
was recorded as part of a larger effort to understand what border-crossing
looks like from the perspective of the youth who come to the Community
House. As such it complements the reflections of university participants
who enter the Community House via a service-learning project (Long,
2000)—reflections similar to those of Sally and her classmates in Chapter
6 of this volume.

To interpret for Peck the dynamics captured on the tape, Tyrone walks
Peck through the process he used to dispel a cultural stereotype that was
inhibiting him from working with his Asian American Supporter. Moving
from self-awareness to action, the teenager first recognizes a stereotype and
then begins a conversation that moves him beyond the limits of his own
experience.

> *Tyrone*: When you see [your writing partner] for the first time,
>   some curious feelings and ideas float through your mind. . . . Seri-
>   ously now, I'm an African American male, and I am wondering:
>   What if I am assigned that Chinese American female? Will we be
>   able to communicate? I am wondering about myself and her and
>   how she might feel about me. I come from a male-dominated
>   home. Can I work as well with a woman as I would with a
>   male? Put on top of that an ethnic difference. I dunno. . . .
>
> *Peck*: [Do you have anything to say about] how to approach a cul-
>   tural stereotype and go beyond it without just accepting it?
>
> *Tyrone*: . . . My [partner] was the first Asian American. Through TV,
>   I had always associated being Asian American with karate and
>   Bruce Lee. . . . I wanted to figure out if my stereotype was true.
>   I wondered first whether I should approach it. And then how to
>   do it without offending her. I wanted to know: Do all Chinese
>   people know karate? . . . I didn't know if it was a racist remark,
>   but whatever. I was always under the impression that everyone

who was Oriental knew karate because I don't know any Orientals personally, and every movie I ever saw—I mean with Orientals. I know there are all kinds of Chinese, Japanese. They are intelligent, and they like electronics. But I never met anyone close up. Now I had this first-time experience.

Tyrone forges a new literate practice of border-crossing, a practice he initiates in order to expand his own cultural horizons:

Peck: Tell us about the conversation. How did it emerge?

Tyrone: I really didn't come out and say, "Do you know karate?" because someone might not know, like me. Someone might ask me, being a black male—"so what's going on?" or "which gang do you belong in?" when I don't belong to gangs. So I was thinking of a way to approach it. . . . So I asked her if she watched movies. She said, "Yeah." Did you see the Bruce Lee movie, *The Dragon*? She said, "Yes." It's nice how she did that. Later, I told her that one of my friends was teaching me Akido and did she know any karate or anything. She says, "No, no, no." I told her, then, how I was all tied up by that, and how my parents didn't teach me that [stereotype]. I just kind of picked it up off the street.

Peck: We are always being surprised by each other. What did you take all of that to mean?

Tyrone: It means I can maneuver around a situation without making it tense or racial. I didn't want it to be that way. It showed me that I could break the ice, and I could work with someone who was not a male. I didn't need a male to be my companion.

Tyrone suggests that intercultural inquiry involves turning the obligation to work with someone unlike ourselves into an opportunity for mutual learning.

Intercultural inquiry implies a cultural value: mutual learning, a vision for an educational community in which everyone has something both to learn and to teach. The phrase isn't meant to suggest that everyone at the Community House should be working on precisely the same set of objectives or that for everything you learn, another person has a parallel educational experience. However, the phrase does mean that all of us, as learners, are developing our own literate repertoires for confronting and disarming the hatreds and fears that fuel racism and homophobia.

Practices for Bringing Teens and Adults Together

We began our inquiry by wondering whether STRUGGLE could effectively bring teenagers and adults back to the table to reimagine the world together as a place of possibilities. Upon reflection, we speculate that cultural forms and habits of mind are necessary but insufficient to transform teen–adult relationships. Cultural forms and habits of mind may serve as catalysts for change; literate practices enact the change. In the context of STRUGGLE, we consider sharing documents, making covenants, and grounding communication patterns in mutual respect are literate practices that create new possibilities. Below are three vignettes that dramatize some of the consequences of these practices.

Sharing Documents. STRUGGLE encourages parents and teens to share their written statements of their life plans. Consider, for instance, the significance of this sharing in the following relationship between father and son. Travis Jr., a teenage son, was living with his father in Pittsburgh for the summer. Travis Sr. enrolled his son and himself in STRUGGLE as a way of structuring some of their time together. He explained to Baskins that he and his son weren't close; he wanted them to be closer.

While writing their documents, each made reference to the other. Travis Jr. told his Supporter that his father was an alcoholic. He wrote: "I'm really proud of my father because he hasn't had a drink in 8 years." Likewise, the father made clear in his document: "I want to reassure Travis Jr. how much I love him."

At the closing meal when teens and parents share their documents, the father–son pair was especially engaged in each other's documents. They both seemed amazed by how much each thought about the other. Travis Sr. read of the pride his son took in his efforts to stop drinking and asked: "Are you really?"

Travis Jr. returned home at the end of the summer, with hopes of returning soon for an extended period. But a few months later, we were told by his shocked employer that Travis Sr. had "drunk himself to death."

After the news of Travis Sr.'s death, we were all the more glad that the father and son had been in the project the previous summer. For one thing, Travis Jr. had had the opportunity to know his father a little better, to know that his father loved him very much. Very likely that would not have happened had they not shared their STRUGGLE documents with one another.

Making Covenants. Mrs. Martin was, as she put it, "road weary." For her, STRUGGLE invited a covenant between herself and her daughter, a covenant that renewed the energy she needed to revise her life plans. Early in the project, Mrs. Martin wrote that she "despised" her civil service job and "hated" her kids. The two were part of the same equation she had been maintaining for almost 20 years. She was tired. A recent marriage and baby hadn't reinvigorated her as she had hoped they would.

Upon reading her mother's story, Mrs. Martin's teenage daughter, Peggy, began seeing glimpses of her mother's life from her mother's perspective. Over time, the two worked out an arrangement that renewed their family life: Peggy agreed to baby-sit explicitly for the purpose of freeing her mother to go back to school. With evenings away from the baby, Mrs. Martin attended a nearby community college. When she called the Community House to share her grades from her first term, she commented that school brought her so much joy because it let her consider a new career path. She added that she and Peggy were getting along better, too. Mrs. Martin had found new appreciation for her daughter.

Constructing Innovative Communication Patterns. While the above vignettes are quite dramatic, other parent–teen dyads remind us that practices of mutuality are often constructed in more subtle yet equally important ways. Consider, for instance, Debbie, who forges new communication patterns with her son as a result of working with her teenage partner, Jamaal.

As Debbie tells it, she manages a very busy, civic office where she "direct[s] other adults and make[s] critical decisions that impact the whole operation." But her involvement in STRUGGLE demanded a different literate practice, one that overtly challenged her. In STRUGGLE, Debbie strengthened her own parenting practices while working to build a more mutual relationship with her teen partner.

As mentioned earlier, when it was Jamaal's turn to seat the people around his table, he included his father, grandmothers, and mom. But once he placed his mother at the table, he came up short. He had much to say about his Grandma Lois, for instance; however, when it came to elaborating a profile of his mom, he became silent. He was hesitant. Perhaps he didn't want to be too critical of his mother (also in the project) in front of Debbie.

Consider that at this point in time, Debbie is a virtual stranger to Jamaal. Jamaal's silence posed a problem for Debbie because, as she later reflected, she saw the silence as a problem for Jamaal. Debbie describes the dilemma she faced:

> Is it more respectful to take the lead from the silence and let Jamaal skip over talking about his mom? Or is it my role as a Supporter to respect the fact that *he* brought her up, that *he* seated her at his table? After all, he was the one who had broached the topic of his

mom. So maybe it's my role to help him get the fullest out of the conversation, not to drop it. But if so, how do I do that Supporter role without playing the heavy?

For Debbie, figuring out how to follow up posed a real challenge.

Her role in STRUGGLE as a collaborative planning partner required that she listen to what Jamaal had to say. As Debbie describes it, she was learning to listen—to really listen—to a teenage boy. Early on, she was direct and asked leading questions, such as "Don't you think that your mother loves you?" Yet rather than hold to this pattern, she kept experimenting with ways of opening up the conversation so Jamaal would say what was on his mind. For instance, she learned to ask more open questions: "What do you mean by saying, 'We don't get along'? Can you tell a story about that?" She later commented that, yes, she wanted Jamaal to hear what he had said, but she also wanted to let what he had said "sink into [her] mind."

Debbie's story suggests that she constructed an identity for herself with Jamaal that transferred to her relationship with Jason. In the presenting phase of the project, while all the participants were gathered for dinner, Debbie was excited to share with the other adults at the table something that had happened between herself and Jason. She said that it was "so much easier to get along with Jason these days; there isn't as much friction between the two of us." As she described the change, Jason was more willing to cooperate with her in their home, rather than positioning her as an authority figure to resist. She attributed that change to the fact that her son had worked through the STRUGGLE process. In a follow-up interview several weeks after the project, Debbie elaborated. She, too, had changed: "I'm getting to know my son, Jason, in a whole new way now. Our relationship is based more on shared respect than on my authority over him."

Debbie's story is one of conflict and negotiation. Jamaal is a source of productive upset for her. He pushes her not only to rethink her relationship with her son, but also to experiment with new ways of relating to him. The story dramatizes that learning new literate practices may constitute subtle yet significant acts of personal agency.

Conclusion: A Lover's Quarrel with the World

In its efforts to address the digital divide at a local level, STRUGGLE stands as an argument against alternative models that enshrine connectivity, computer applications, and work readiness as ends in themselves. Rather, the project responds to a specific felt difficulty: the need for a set of compelling literate practices to support teens' personal narratives and life plans. STRUGGLE uses digital technology to support the configuration of those practices.

Our experiences with STRUGGLE have underscored, on the one hand, the fluid nature of identity and the provisional nature of life plans. On the other hand, STRUGGLE has also underscored the existential power a person finds in articulating long-term goals, in following one's North Star.

Since conducting the research behind this chapter, we have continued experimenting with ways of integrating digital technology into STRUGGLE; for instance, by supporting teens as they translate their documents into digital montages or brief digitized movies. Yet we continue to have the same end in sight: to capture the communicative force and vision of the compelling narratives teens tell about their lives. Our experiences and experiments have brought home several lessons that we will attempt to articulate succinctly here.

As an identity-creating enterprise, STRUGGLE works on several levels at once: For teens, STRUGGLE offers a literate practice that gives them repeated opportunities to rehearse and revise how they articulate their life plans to others. We have seen that a teen's chance of moving a relationship with an adult in a constructive direction is often contingent on the teen's ability to tell his or her story, to declare his or her life plans, to that adult. That adult may be a new teacher, a community mentor, an employer, or a college admissions counselor. In each respective discourse situation, the adult is likely to rely on a poorly fleshed out representation of "the urban teen" unless the teen can provide a more robust alternative.

For adults, we speculate that STRUGGLE supports intergenerational, intercultural working relationships that are so rare that they may let participants construct new dimensions of their identities. This is particularly true when adults are schooled in rhetorical strategies, such as collaborative planning, and are willing to reflect on and challenge habits and impulses that otherwise serve as defaults.

Finally, just as STRUGGLE is transformative for individuals, so, too, it holds this potential for organizations. A critical problem for contemporary community organizations is to find ways to sustain their vitality and vision. When STRUGGLE's core questions are posed to leaders of such an organization, STRUGGLE becomes a collaborative writing process that aids in envisioning strong purposes and in building consensus. In its home community, STRUGGLE remains the driving force behind our efforts to reimagine the identity and purpose of the urban settlement house itself. As a literate practice, STRUGGLE continually challenges us to consider what it might take to sustain an "inspired context" for literate action and reflection (Willinsky,

1990). It asks us to continuously reconsider how to reform our organization so those who seek sanctuary here can continue to reimagine the world together as a place of possibilities.

Note

1. Linda Flower was instrumental in developing the interview questions. We thank her for her contributions.

References

Bakhtin, M. M. (1981). *The dialogic imagination* (C. Emerson & M. Holquist, Trans.). Austin: University of Texas Press.

Bruner, J. (1990). *Acts of meaning*. Cambridge, MA: Harvard University Press.

Cain, C. (1991). Personal stories: Identity acquisition and self-understanding in Alcoholics Anonymous. *Ethos, 19*(2), 210–253.

Eisenhart, M. (1995). The fax, the jazz player, and the self-story teller: How do people organize culture? *Anthropology & Education Quarterly, 26*(1), 3–26.

Eisenhart, M. (1996). The production of biologists at school and work: Making scientists, conservationists, or flowery bone-heads? In B. A. Levinson, D. E. Foley, & D. C. Holland (Eds.), *The cultural production of the educated person: Critical ethnographies of schooling and local practice* (pp. 169–185). Albany: State University of New York Press.

Faigley, L. (1993). *Fragments of rationality: Postmodernity and the subject of composition*. Pittsburgh, PA: University of Pittsburgh Press.

Fischhoff, B., Furby, L., Quadrel, M. J., & Richardson, E. (1991). *Adolescents' construal of choices: Are their decisions our "decisions"?* (Report). Pittsburgh, PA: Carnegie Mellon University & Eugene Research Institute.

Fischhoff, B., & Quadrel, M. J. (1990). Adolescent alcohol decisions. *Alcohol Health and Research World, 15*(2), 43–51.

Flower, L. (1994). *The construction of negotiated meaning: A social cognitive theory of writing*. Carbondale: Southern Illinois University Press.

Flower, L. (1996). Literate action. In L. Z. Bloom, D. A. Daiker, & E. M. White (Eds.), *Composition in the twenty-first century: Crisis and change* (pp. 249–260). Carbondale: Southern Illinois University Press.

Flower, L., Long, E., & Higgins, L. (2000). *Learning to rival: A literate practice for intercultural inquiry*. Hillsdale, NJ: Erlbaum.

Flower, L., Wallace, D. L., Norris, L., & Burnett, R. E. (1994). *Making thinking visible: A collaborative look at collaborative planning*. Urbana, IL: National Council of Teachers of English.

Freire, P. (1986). *Pedagogy of the oppressed* (M. Bergman Ramos, Trans.). New York: Continuum. (Original work published 1970)

Gee, J. P. (1989). Literacy, discourse, and linguistics: Introduction. *Journal of Education, 171,* 5–18.

Goslee, S. (1998). *Losing ground bit by bit: Low-income communities in the information age.* Washington, DC: Benton Foundation.

Holland, D., & Cole, M. (1995). Between discourse and schema: Reformulating a cultural-historical approach to culture and mind. *Anthropology & Education Quarterly, 26*(4), 475–489.

Hopper, P. (1988). Discourse analysis: Grammar and critical theory in the 1980s. *Profession, 88,* 19–26.

Krieg, R. (1995). Information technology and low-income inner city communities. *The Journal of Urban Technology, 3*(1), 44–55.

Lerner, M., & West, C. (1996). *Jews and blacks: A dialogue on race, religion and culture in America.* New York: Plume.

Levinson, B. A., & Holland, D. (1996). The cultural production of the educated person: An introduction. In B. A. Levinson, D. E. Foley, & D. C. Holland (Eds.), *The cultural production of the educated person: Critical ethnographies of schooling and local practice* (pp. 1–54). Albany: State University of New York Press.

Long, E. (2000). The rhetoric of literate social action. In M. D. Goggin (Ed.), *Inventing a discipline, rhetoric and composition in action: Essays in honor of Richard E. Young* (pp. 289–313). Urbana, IL: National Council of Teachers of English.

Miller, P. (1998). CTCNet & AFCN: The shared future of community technology centers and community networking. *Community Technology Center Review.* Retrieved March 31, 2000. (http://www.ctcnet.org/r981afcn.htm).

Nettles, S. M. (1991). Community involvement and disadvantaged students: A review. *Review of Educational Research, 61*(3), 379–406.

Peck, W. C., Flower, L., & Higgins, L. (1995). Community literacy. *College Composition and Communication, 46*(2), 199–222.

West, C. (1989). *The American evasion of philosophy: A genealogy of pragmatism.* Madison: University of Wisconsin Press.

West, C. (1993). *Race matters.* Boston: Beacon.

Willinsky, J. (1990). *The new literacy: Redefining reading and writing in the schools.* New York: Routledge.

Marsha Pincus Responds

Too often high school students complain that school is not the "real world." They often explain their lack of interest or engagement in school by saying that what is happening in their classrooms has little relevance to their lives. While some of this may be attributed to adolescents' natural propensity to resist or rebel, as a high school teacher in an urban setting for the past 26 years, I have found that their complaints are often justifiable. While urban high schools are often called "neighborhood" high schools because of their location and the fact that the student body is usually drawn from the surrounding local population, there is often little meaningful interaction between the school and the community it serves.

Yes, sometimes, the gyms are open after school for neighborhood basketball leagues, or the computer labs are open to local residents after school hours. But it is rare to find community input into issues of curriculum, pedagogy, and evaluation. These decisions are made by bureaucrats in the central office or the local administrator. Parents in these neighborhoods are often made to feel unwelcome in schools. I have seen parents forced to stand in line for hours in hot crowded hallways trying to register their children at the beginning of each schoolyear without being offered a chair or a drink of water.

I was struck by the description of the new digital divide: that even when poorer urban schools obtain computers, the way in which these computers are utilized in classrooms is likely to replicate a pedagogy of remediation. Urban students are less likely than their suburban counterparts to learn to use computers to pose and solve their own questions and problems; they are often placed in front of screens displaying simulated worksheets supplied by expensive teacher-proof software packages.

The findings of this study offer hope for those urban school teachers who would like to make more meaningful connections between our students' lives and the work of school. The idea of *struggle* as a literacy practice can be very generative for those teachers who are trying to foster human agency in our students. The activities of the multimedia environment could easily be adapted by English teachers in our language arts programs, with or without the computers. The dining table activity, for instance, is a very powerful one that engages the students' dialogic imaginations and helps them breathe meaning into their lives. The collaborative planning aspect of the program builds in true purpose to the process. Learning to listen becomes as important as being heard. Hence response is seen as part of responsibility—to oneself and the one listened to. And the pairing of a teenager with an adult member of the community builds on the importance of family and community relationships.

This study is particularly illuminating in revealing to middle-class teachers of poor and working-class adolescents the complex webs of responsibilities and relationships that comprise our students' lives. Teachers' middle-class values, which emphasize individuals acting in their own self-interest independent of a cultural context, often leave us blind to the realities of our students' lives. Charles Taylor's (1985) powerful idea of looking at human agency in terms of "available choices" can be a very helpful one for teachers as we try to make the connections between school and life. Our students are individuals who are engaging in ongoing dialogues with their communities and their families as they are trying to make some sense of what is happening in their lives and plan for their futures. Teachers often don't understand the pressures these young people face, looking at their actions and decisions through a faulty lens and evaluating their performance through inappropriate measures.

Too often urban teachers approach the monumental challenge of our task the same way medics approach wounded soldiers on a battlefield. We perform a kind of educational triage, separating the critically wounded from those who can be saved. And more often than not, "saving" means working with those select students to "get them out." Such a winnowing process does even greater damage to communities already struggling to maintain a decent quality of life for *all* who reside there. It also can be harmful to the students, who know that their own lives depend on the complex web of relationships and responsibilities present in their communities. The nihilism that Cornel West (1993) describes *is* present in urban classrooms; however, urban teachers must not give in to that nihilism and the despair from which it springs. The findings of this program offer a paradigm of possibility. Teachers can help all students write for their own sakes. And all students' imaginations can be engaged as political acts of individual and collective transformation.

References

Taylor, C. (1985). *Philosophy and the human sciences,* Vol. 1. Cambridge, UK: Cambridge University Press.
West, C. (1993). *Race matters*. Boston, MA: Beacon.

Marty Williams Responds

The new man and the new woman will not be constructed in the heads of educators but in a new social practice, which will take the place of the old that has proven itself incapable of creating new persons. (Freire, 1978)

Literacy as Social Action

I am drawn to the way in which STRUGGLE of Pittsburgh uses the spiritual concept of renewal as a social practice that builds human capacity and lifts up the community. Many educational programs offered to low-income or marginalized individuals identify the community and its pushes and pulls as the problem and are geared toward lifting the individual up, but away from the neighborhood, the community, the dining room table. Call it brain drain, theft, escape, alienation, or exile, opportunities are presented as an invitation "to climb out" of the limitations of working-class poverty and marginality rather than to transform them (Shor, 1980, p. xiv).

Ah, but the dining room table around which participants seat their ancestors, their inspirers, those who have cradled and guided them, their own movers and shakers! Here the invitation is to lift up those who have helped shape and inspire the literacies participants bring to the table and to celebrate those literacies. The authors of this chapter also name and invite their co-inspirators, a rich congregation of theologians, educators, sociologists and philosophers. Together they set the table with questions of human capacity and agency, with leadership and making-meaning, with challenges to social injustice and inequity, and with practices to help make maps to live by, urgings to learn how to live "with creative anxiety."

STRUGGLE begins with the wisdom of a community, the lived experience of its people, and the literacy practices that are grown and nurtured there. These they apply to a project of great urgency, that is, equipping teenagers with hope and skills for their active struggle against hopelessness and despair. Mixing caring adults and accessible technology, they have created a curriculum that challenges participants to create a life path for themselves using a "vocabulary of worth."

Technology and the Listening Witness

The poet and English teacher in me loves the use of prepositions in the multimedia environment prompts. Prepositions physically locate the subject and show relationship. The questions, designed to help participants understand their relations to others and to locate themselves on the life path they are articulating, make the narrative self portraits STRUGGLE participants create situated narratives, showing connection, always negotiating relationship. Each question is a rich prepositional metaphor that opens out in several directions. They work, then, not as static definitions of identity, but as openings to possible ways of being.

> What am I going *through*? What am I in the midst of? What is the nature of the water in which I swim?

> What am I *up against*? What blocks my path, what is in my way? What wall defines my path? What is the rock and the hard place I am between?

> What am I *up to* in my life? What am I doing, what am I capable of? What am I willing to take on? Am I up to it, ready for the task, prepared?

> What are ways to be together *with others* in this? Who is my "we"? Who can help me? Who has passed on what to me? What/whom can I hold on to, turn to? Who will I watch and who will witness my work?

These are absolutely appropriate questions for young people in schools to be addressing and grappling with in their reading, writing, and discussions with teachers and one another. What must be reimagined is the role of teachers and other adults in the school community, perhaps along the lines of Nel Noddings's (1991) definition of the "caring relation," which is based on trust between the teacher and learner, and which "requires that we look at education from a different perspective," asking teachers to "learn how to engage in genuine dialogue . . . and develop teaching strategies that provide students with opportunities to care for each other" (pp. 167–168).

Along with furthering technological literacy embedded in an empowering literacy practice, the computers seem to act as a mediating object for the dialogue among the participants. There is nothing necessary about the computer for the dialogue to occur; the prompts could be written on actual rather than virtual cards. I suspect, however, that something about the presence of the laptop computer creates a mediating object through which the intimate naming and knowing of experience can deepen. The Writer and the Supporter look not only at one another, but at the story as it emerges on the laptop and becomes a part of the texture of the relationship between the storyteller and her or his listening witness.

Apprenticeship Model of Learning and Strategic Instruction: Making the Invisible Visible

The apprenticeship model of learning identified in STRUGGLE, where "a more proficient other is present to support the beginner" (Schoenbach, Greenleaf, Cziko & Hurwitz, 1999, p. 21), is used quite extensively in productive classrooms. Here teachers unveil their own skilled practices as readers, writers, creators of art, and participants in the world and invite students to do the same.

The specific literate practice outlined in this chapter is a practice of action and reflection. Learners identify their situation, articulate a problem, invent an action, reflect on possible outcomes, and so on. This shifts the paradigm for literacy from the consumption/production of text to understanding/imagination/action in the context of real issues and concerns in the learners' lives. It equips them with a set of strategies that can be broadly applied to their unique situations as well as the opportunity to practice these applications with a learning adult. Again, this is the challenge to a school community: to begin to redefine literate acts as a practice of social action.

Urban Sanctuaries

As I read the chapter, of course the kind of questions that any practitioner would want to know came to mind. Over what period of time do folks gather and how often? When is the first conversation in front of the computer? What is the training prior to this conversation? But these are the questions of detail. The important questions, the ones I would bring to the dining room table to hash over with folks, have to do with larger issues. How might the beliefs about literacy and human agency underlying this exemplary practice begin to find their way into the discourse around school reform? What conditions need to exist in a school or community for something like this to be proposed? By conditions I mean both the understanding and beliefs of the educators as well as the physical conditions and structure of a class or the day, number of students, availability of other caring adults, computers, and so forth. In short, what does it take for a school to reimagine its classrooms and reshape itself into an urban sanctuary?

Renewal versus Reform

The story of STRUGGLE, rather than proposing a blueprint for change, offers a window on one project within the frame of a larger gathering for social action and empowerment. With this context in mind, I can imagine a series of challenges to a school community that might wish to reconstruct or renew itself. To borrow from the wisdom of STRUGGLE, a teacher in a school or the whole of a school community would have to develop a similarly deep level of theoretical understanding and carefully structured practice toward a literacy for social action. Such an effort would require a group of facilitators, collaborators, or teachers as knowledgeable and committed as those who have crafted the work of STRUGGLE.

Are there schools that have dedicated themselves to a concerted curriculum of hope and change? Are there individuals, as well, working their small projects, alone or with a handful of other teachers, in the classrooms of our schools waiting for a larger call to action? I know there are, having met many in my practice as a teacher, but they are quite fragile in the face of current trends in education: increasing gatekeeping, high-stakes testing, and corporatization of the public arenas of learning. Most reform efforts are called on to prove themselves by ever more narrow standardized tests. The tougher, more resilient programs or schools are often dependent on one or two visionaries to hold them to a path.

There is no question in my mind that people will form communities to create caring classrooms and use them to engage in hopeful dialogue about real content, real issues, and important situations. And each of these efforts, however small, is worthy of great support and celebration. I would suggest, however, that short of a sea change in how education and oppression are tackled in this country, these hopeful projects are likely for quite some time to be swimming against the tide and therefore might remain small and somewhat marginal—a much needed, if not widely heeded, visionary voice in the structure of schooling.

References

Freire, P. (1978). *Pedagogy in process: The letters to Guinea-Bissau* (C. St. John Hunter, Trans.). New York: Continuum.

Noddings, N. (1991). Stories in dialogue: Caring and interpersonal reasoning. In C. Witherell & N. Noddings (Eds.), *Stories lives tell: Narrative and dialogue in education* (pp. 319–348). New York: Teachers College Press.

Schoenbach, R., Greenleaf, C., Cziko, C., & Hurwitz, L. (1999). *Reading for understanding: A guide to improving reading in middle and high school classrooms.* San Francisco: Jossey-Bass.

Shor, I. (1980). *Critical teaching and everyday life.* Boston: South End Press.

6

Community Supports for Writing Development Among Urban African American Children

GILLIAN DOWLEY McNAMEE
and SARAH SIVRIGHT

Dear Wizard,

My mother and my father are in my family, but my dad do not live with me. My grandfather do not live with me too. But I still love them. I'm sorry that I did not write back to you either. Alex do not like the Wizard but I do. I love you very much. It is rainy outside today. The date is April 19, 1993. My teacher is named Miss Hart. Today we got our measles shots. It didn't hurt at all. Some of my classmates were crying. They thought it hurt. The boys said it didn't hurt. The boys said all the girls was crying and they were crybabies. I didn't cry. I had to sit on somebody's lap but I didn't cry at all. Some of the boys were crying. I saw them. They said they weren't crying. They told a tale.

Love,

Darlene

This letter to the Wizard was dictated by a 7-year-old African American girl to a Wizard assistant in an after-school computer club program called the Fifth Dimension. The Fifth Dimension is an international computer telecommunications network for school-aged children situated in community-based after-school programs that vary widely in cultural and economic settings. Developed by Michael Cole and Peg Griffin at the University of California, San Diego (see Cole, 1996; Griffin & Cole, 1987; Nicolopoulou & Cole, 1993), the Fifth Dimension is a context of play and communication coordinated by the Wizard[1], a fantasy figure who the children believe exists in the telecommunications system. The Wizard is portrayed as both woman and man, timeless in age and growing younger all the time. The Wizard establishes the activity structure for computer clubs through Wizard assistants: program staff at the various Fifth Dimension sites. The Wizard sends messages to the children frequently, receives complaints as well as requests, encourages and coordinates intersite activity, and is interested in what is going on in the children's lives both in the computer club and outside of it. Since communication with the Wizard and others at distant Fifth Dimension sites takes place in writing, it provides an ideal setting for studying children's development as writers.

When children join the Fifth Dimension in after-school programs, they are introduced to a network of children and adults in the United States and Russia brought together by the Wizard or Wizardess. He/She introduces a constitution in which the parameters and ground rules of activities are described. Participation in the Fifth Dimension involves using computers to play a variety of games that are displayed on a game board allowing children to proceed from one to another by a set of rules. The computer games involve math concepts, geography, science, word games, and solving mysteries. Games are explained to children through Adventure Cards that guide children's activity at a level of difficulty they choose: beginner, good, or expert level. The higher the skill level a child chooses and succeeds at, the more options the child gains for future activities. The computer games are represented on a mazelike game board structure; children move toy creatures through the physical structure representing their progress in mastering Fifth Dimension activities.

The adults assisting the children in Fifth Dimension activities are called Wizard Assistants. Their job is to oversee the carrying out of the constitution on a daily basis, facilitate activities, and invoke the Wizard's help in mediating difficulties of any sort alongside the children. The Fifth Dimension provides children and adults with a common authority figure to whom all are accountable. Participants in the Fifth Dimension represent a wide range of social, economic, and cultural backgrounds. At the U.S. after-school sites (which have included programs in North Carolina, Louisiana, Michigan, Illinois, and California) as well as in Moscow, the structure of the Fifth Dimension and the Wizard's role are adapted to fit local circumstances. The Wizard's voice at each site is enriched by the individual and cultural nuances specific to each locale, and yet it reflects an evolving set of beliefs about the Wizard's role in adult–child interactions held by project organizers.

This chapter describes writing development among African American children living in a community known as Garden Homes who participated in the Fifth Dimension over the course of 5 years. Garden Homes became a participant in the Fifth Dimension when McNamee introduced the opportunity to community center staff. They eagerly accepted because the project fit with goals community members had set for themselves and their children. Garden Homes and Erikson Institute (an independent institution of higher education focusing on child development) had been involved in a community–university collaboration since 1981. During the 1980s, community leaders sought partnerships with businesses and educators that would bring skills and knowledge to community residents (McNamee, 1990). They also sought opportunities through which the knowledge and expertise for running innovative programs such as the Fifth Dimension would become a permanent part of the community.

The questions guiding Chicago's research agenda were: What are the effects of Fifth Dimension communication opportunities on the children's writing development? Could the children in this community, who were considered "at risk" for succeeding in school and particularly in the areas of reading and writing, benefit from participating in written dialogues that included peers from a variety of backgrounds in the United States and Russia under the guidance of a playful, caring adult figure known as the Wizard?

The Fifth Dimension as a Context for Research

The first goal that prompted the development of the Wizard and Fifth Dimension was to create a setting for children that would simulate a cognitive psychology laboratory—a place where researchers and educators could explore the constraints and possibilities of children's thinking and problem-solving through repeated performance on tasks. Cole, Griffin, and colleagues at the Laboratory of Comparative Human Cognition (LCHC) at the University of California, San Diego had attempted to set up such a partnership in research on children's development and learning with schools because they, too, define tasks and attempt to measure performance and developmental outcomes in a consistent and rigorous way. However, school personnel were not in a position to invest in such a research partnership, because demands on teachers' time and expectations for children's performance on standardized tests did not afford them the option to experiment with curriculum and instruction. Therefore, Cole and colleagues turned to after-school settings as a context for exploring curriculum innovations and a place for creating controlled variation in tasks with participants over time (Cole, 1996).

Cole and colleagues quickly realized that after-school programs do not carry the legal responsibilities and obligations that schools do (Cole, 1996) but rather are set up to complement schools, emphasizing time for play and socializing as well as providing time for children's interests and hobbies. Therefore, putting the Fifth Dimension into after-school program settings meant merging children's interests in play and informal interaction patterns with activities that had educational goals and objectives.

The growing national awareness and debate regarding women's and minorities' access to and involvement in computer technology and related career opportunities also influenced the design of the Fifth Dimension. The underrepresentation of women and minorities in fields requiring computer expertise was well documented by the early 1980s (Cole, Griffin, & LCHC, 1987; Griffin & Cole, 1987). Therefore, a second goal for the Fifth Dimension was to establish opportunities for girls to become involved with computers alongside boys and for children from a variety of cultural and economic groups to interact with one another.

The Fifth Dimension project was designed with a third overriding goal—to study the process of implementing educational innovation, the process of institutional uptake and sustainability of the innovation over time. This was a central goal for implementing the Fifth Dimension activity system in after-school settings across the United States and in Moscow; it made for an ideal fit between the goals set by Garden Homes community leaders and the goals of Fifth Dimension project developers and funders.

A fourth goal Cole (1996) and colleagues had in mind was "to create an activity thick in opportunities for written and oral communication about the goals and strategies used in problem solving" (p. 290). The opportunity to have children communicate understandings to others (adults and peers), to do so more than once, and to do so orally and in writing could provide important sources of data on the children's reasoning and thinking, and the roots of their development. Collaboration among Fifth Dimension participants around program development, implementation, and evaluation of various sites is carried out in open dialogue through e-mail. Correspondence is invited, encouraged, and solicited from children, after-school program staff, and university partners within and across sites. The system maintains the equivalent of old-fashioned telephone "party lines"; anyone can "listen in" on correspondence within and across sites, and jump into a conversation at any time.

There are a number of theoretical underpinnings to the Fifth Dimension activity system, but particularly salient are roots in Vygotskian theory of development. One of Vygotsky's unique contributions to psychology is the idea that development begins in interactions among people (1981); it does not begin within individuals themselves. Vygotsky proposes, "It is through others that we develop into ourselves. Development does not proceed toward socialization but toward the conversion of social relations into mental functions" (1981, pp. 161, 165). To follow the development of mental processes, educators need to track how thinking carried out among a group of people is transformed as more competent and experienced members in a group make expertise available to junior members, and how junior members appropriate (with or without permission) the means by which others have directed their thinking.

When implementing and documenting children's experiences at the Chicago site, our first and primary focus was relationships mediating the children's experiences in the Fifth Dimension—relationships between and among children, the Garden Homes staff, the Erikson research staff, as well as participants from other Fifth Dimension sites. To evaluate children's writing development in the context of the Fifth Dimension, Vygotskian theory led us to study how the adults' interpretations of the possibilities for Fifth Dimension communications guide the arrangements made for children's entry into written correspondences with the Wizard, peers, and staff at other Fifth Dimension sites. We also watched children closely to see what possibilities they saw in the setup, what they gravitated toward and worked to master.

A second area of Vygotskian theory that influenced the development of the Fifth Dimension is the importance of play in making development possible. For Vygotsky, play is fundamentally social and symbolic (Nicolopoulou, 1993), and it is the arena in which the give-and-take in relationships can nurture change for all involved (Vygotsky, 1978). Such thinking is certainly the essence of writing and reading, where a text is the springboard for author and audience to consider ideas beyond the here-and-now.

From a Vygotskian perspective, experiences in play do not contribute to an increase in specific skills or abilities, but rather are instrumental in instigating "reorganizations of psychological functions that may take years to come to fruition" (Nicolopoulou, 1993, p. 11). This aspect of play is related to the third aspect of Vygotsky's theory of particular interest at the Chicago site: the process of "transformation" or "revolution," which Vygotsky (1978) describes as characteristic of the developmental process. He hypothesizes that development does not follow a linear progression of incremental steps as a child masters skills or aspects of a task. On the contrary, development is more likely to follow a path of leaps forward and then what appears to be regression: steps that seem to indicate the child is losing ground in the process of development.

This conception of development as transformation is particularly relevant to the study of writing and its development through computers. Vygotsky and those that have interpreted his work in studies of literacy development recognize that learning to write (and read) is not a matter of acquiring, accumulating, and mastering motor skills that make possible communication through print. Learning to write involves a transformation of one's understanding of human symbol-making potential: that humans can create symbols (print) for symbols (spoken words). Thus writing becomes a second-order symbol system (Vygotsky, 1978).

Writing development from a Vygotskian perspective looks at relationships mediating children's interactions in a goal-directed activity. The mediation guides children to new insights about writing as a tool to shape relationships and a tool that can provide new opportunities for interacting with others. Writing is defined as a social-cultural enterprise of making, interpreting, and communicating meaning, using written language as the currency for exchange of ideas and messages among people across time and space (McLane & McNamee, 1990). In this view, writing represents entrance into new forms of mediation.

The Fifth Dimension program brings computer technology into after-school settings within a closely orchestrated plan hypothesizing that computers in and of themselves will not produce literate, problem-solving, imaginative youngsters. Rather, as with paper, pencils, and other writing tools, the ways adults organize the setting and activities in which computers are used, and the purposes created for using them, determine the literacy and computer skills that children develop.

The Chicago Fifth Dimension Site: Garden Homes

The Chicago site, Garden Homes, is located in a community center surrounded by about 650 families living in low-rise public housing. The Garden Homes Community Center offers a wide variety of activities to neighborhood families, including Head Start, after-school day care, programs for teenage parents and senior citizens, GED programs, and special food programs. The Fifth Dimension became part of the after-school day-care program that serves approximately 20 kindergarten children and 45 school-aged children. Erikson staff supported the community's carrying out of Fifth Dimension activities at the highest level of participation and practice that they could manage. Community center staff gave continuous feedback as to when things were going well, when there were problems or conflicts in the work, and when help was needed.

The after-school program has six staff who participated at various times in facilitating children's Fifth Dimension activities. They are African American women in their late 20s and early 30s who live in or near the community. All six are parents or grandparents of children in the community center programs. One has finished a 2-year college degree, three have high school diplomas, and the other two are working to finish high school. The community center staff came to this project with no prior experience with computers and with little experience using extended writing in the context of their jobs. During the first 9 months, the staff participated in labor-intensive work sessions with us planning the program; acquiring, assembling, and learning to work with computers; and evolving a routine for computer club sessions with their children. This was followed by 2 months of on-the-job tutorials to learn the logistics of telecommunications.

During years 2 and 3 of the project, the staff participated in paid tutorials (during their nonwork hours in the community center) to practice writing as the Wizard and writing to people at other Fifth Dimension sites. In years 4 and 5, two of the staff were part-time paid research assistants facilitating their children's Wizard correspondence, documenting children's writing and reading activities during computer club sessions, and assisting with beginning- and end-of-the-year testing of the children.

At the Chicago Fifth Dimension site, the first letter that children received from the Wizard upon entering the program asked them to tell the Wizard something about themselves and their neighborhood. The responses of children in second through sixth grade had common themes: They were aware of danger and violence in their neighborhood and Chicago, but they also loved their home.

> I go to a school called Hastings School and my neighborhood is bad. It's a gang across the street from us but my grandma's house is great. (Joyce, age 8)

> I live in a big house with three floors. It's very big. I go to a school named Hastings. I live in the city of Chicago. There's a lot of violence in Chicago, and gangs, and children being abused. But in some places, there's a pretty scenery. In other places, there's a bad scenery. I wish I could move out of Chicago cause there's a lot of violence. I really don't like it. Sometimes I do and a lot of people here are friendly. (Andrea, age 11)

The descriptions of their school and classrooms were mixed; some found school a nice place to be while many did not.

> In my house, I have a gray couch. I have a thin green table. I have a gray door. Sometimes it be terrible. I have real nice trees. We have a nice white ground. At our school under are windows we have red

mix with oranges. In side our school we have real nice seats. We
have real nice light brown mixed with dark brown. (Patrick, age 7)

I live in row house made for blacks. My neighborhood is very violent
place to be for kids. My school is a nice school but the teachers are
so ugly. The Fifth Dimension is a very nice place to go after school
and the teachers are so nice in some ways. (Arlene, age 11)

The children in this African American community tended to come from
families who had lived for two and even three generations in the neighborhood. One child's mother described having goats in her yard 20 years ago
when she was growing up in the neighborhood. A staff member told stories
of neighborhood children having sleepovers as a group on the rooftops of
the two-story row houses when she was a child.

Several features of Chicago's Fifth Dimension context were unique in
comparison to other sites. Most of the after-school activities that Chicago
children participated in were ones that the staff choose for them. When
children arrived at the center, they were told what they would do and when
it would happen. The children participated in activities as a group: They
arrived, ate a snack, had outdoor time, homework time, time for art projects, and so forth. Children were assigned a computer club day, when they
wrote their responses to the new Wizard letter that had been prepared for
them and to other Fifth Dimension people who had written to them. This
was followed by group discussions, after which children could work on
computers in pairs on games of their own choosing. Children chose whatever program they wanted to work on, and staff would troubleshoot problems getting programs to work and helping children work more effectively
together. One community center staff person and one Erikson research person led each computer club session with seven to eight children. For the
last 2 years of the project, we experimented with hiring high school Fifth
Dimension alumni from the community as an additional source of help for
children while they worked on computers. This proved very effective for
the children and the high schoolers alike.

The structure of life in the community center parallels what we observed in the community where the children and most of the staff lived.
Adults are directive as caretakers of their children, and they cherish and
respect their children and want to provide for them. Within Garden Homes
and the community center, even though children would move through activities and routines as a disciplined group, the children's individuality was
valued and nurtured, as will be evident in case study data below (see also
McNamee, 1995). Though the group structure was emphasized, children
found their own reasons and motivations to participate in activities. The

goodwill and kindness of staff left children feeling that the activity that everyone would do next was likely to be one that they would enjoy and one that would fit their needs.

This chapter presents profiles of children's writing at the Chicago Fifth Dimension site in order to understand the children as writers in this setting and to look for changes over time in their writing—and, if possible, in their sense of self as writers. It addresses the following questions: What evidence do we have that the Garden Homes children do in fact progress in their development as writers? What were the configurations of support facilitating their daily activities? How did peers, the Wizard, and people at other Fifth Dimension sites provide reasons for children to write? What did the ups and downs of relationships in the Fifth Dimension look like over time? What kind of social supports can be constructed outside of school to facilitate children's development as writers? Finally, how do our findings in this out-of-school setting contribute to discussions of these African American children's learning to write in school?

This chapter draws on a database that includes both descriptive data (what children wrote, the frequency of their writing, characteristics of their writing) and qualitative data (daily fieldnotes from community center and Erikson research staff on the context for writing and the children's actual texts). In addition, children's performance on the Test of Written Language (TOWL) (Hammill & Larsen, 1988), a standardized test of writing development administered at the beginning and end of the computer club (and academic year), are reported here. As part of our larger research effort, we along with other Fifth Dimension sites took on the challenge of looking for external validation of children's development as well as validation from children's performance on activities within the Fifth Dimension. We chose the TOWL because it examines children's awareness of and development in regard to mechanical aspects of written discourse (such as word usage, spelling, punctuation, capitalization, and grammar) and also the degree to which children can compose and convey ideas to others in writing in clear, concise, and even creative ways. Because the test is designed to assess children's writing development from ages 7 to 18 at 6-month intervals, it was applicable to the age range of children in the Fifth Dimension (7 to 13 years).

Data on Children's Writing in the Chicago Fifth Dimension

During the 1992–1993 schoolyear, when the Garden Homes site was fully up and running, 27 children in second through sixth grade participated in the Fifth Dimension; 10 boys and 17 girls. Eleven were in second grade, 7

TABLE 6.1: Amount of Writing Sent to Chicago Children during 1992–1993 Year

Letters sent to Chicago children by the Wizard	149
Letters sent to Chicago children as a group from the Wizard	8
Letters received by individual children from Fifth Dimension people outside Chicago	58
Letters sent from other Fifth Dimension sites to Chicago children as a group	3

in third, 2 in fourth, 1 in fifth, and 6 in sixth grade. The children were divided into four groups, with each group assigned to one afternoon per week. There were 91 computer club sessions held that year: 43 sessions held in the fall and 48 held in the spring. Tables 6.1 and 6.2 summarize the flow of writing between Garden Homes' children and other participants in the Fifth Dimension during that year.

TABLE 6.2: Amount of Writing Done by Chicago Children during 1992–1993 Year

Individual letters written to the Wizard	220
Letters written to other Fifth Dimension people	80
Group letters written to other Fifth Dimension sites	2
Other kinds of writing (on word-processing programs)	71
Print Shop projects such as banners, signs, and greeting cards	85

As was true in all other years of computer club at the Garden Homes site, correspondence with the Wizard provided the most compelling reason for children to write and read while in computer club. There were ongoing attempts by the Wizard to cultivate intersite communication among children, but this was hard to sustain. After the initial exchange of personal greetings and inquiries about each other, correspondence usually died out. Often children did not receive a response to a message for several weeks, and this rapidly diminished their motivation to write peers in other cities. Pen pals could never compete with the reliability and personal investment the children felt in correspondence with the Wizard.

The next most compelling computer club writing activity after Wizard correspondence was the word-processing and graphics program Print Shop, used to make greeting cards, posters, and specially decorated messages. This program combined children's interests in drawing and play with the graphic features of written language (for example, using different fonts and layouts) and their love for making and sending notes and messages to people they care about. Finally, there was writing that occurred among children as they worked on programs, for example, writing down clues when solving mysteries in games such as 221 Baker Street or writing hints for others on how to play games successfully at higher levels of expertise.

Did these opportunities for writing in the Fifth Dimension systematically contribute to Garden Homes children's development as writers? To answer this question, we looked at data from children while working on Fifth Dimension writing tasks as well as on the standardized test.

Test of Written Language

The Test of Written Language was administered to children in October and again in May to see if we could measure changes in children's written language development during the time they were participating in the Fifth Dimension. The test scores, unfortunately, do not reflect positive change in children's development; on the contrary, they portray negative growth, as shown in Table 6.3.

Of the 27 children who participated in the Fifth Dimension during the year and were tested on the TOWL in the fall, only 20 were available for testing on the TOWL at the end of the schoolyear. Of those 20, 7 children's test scores went up (3 boys and 4 girls), while 8 children's scores went down (3 boys and 5 girls). Five children's scores stayed the same (2 boys and 3 girls). Among the children whose scores went down were several whom we knew to be strong students in school; we would not have predicted that they would do as poorly as they did on this end-of-the-year testing. In both October and May, Garden Homes children scored poorly: in

TABLE 6.3: TOWL—Two Standard Scores for Chicago Children (Group Averages)

	October 1992	May 1993
Contrived Writing Tasks (mechanical aspects of written language)	36	40
Spontaneous Writing Tasks (written composition)	37	30
Overall score	73	70

the 6.87 percentile nationally. When we had piloted the use of the TOWL in the preceding year, test results showed that Chicago children improved, particularly on the spontaneous writing task in which children compose a story in response to a stimulus picture. This finding interested us since that task most closely resembles the open-ended writing opportunities offered in the Fifth Dimension.

The results of the TOWL were discouraging. We knew from daily experience with the children and our pilot testing that the children would not easily accept the request to take standardized tests administered by staff of Garden Homes or Erikson Institute. The TOWL resembled testing associated with school and interests of adults that are far removed from those of children. It was particularly hard on the children when they were letting go of the structure and routine of their schoolday to be asked to work on a task that epitomized school. On testing days, we went out of our way to help children have a good afternoon. We had ample snacks and numerous opportunities for choices before and after testing. We had the children complete test tasks over a 2- or 3-day period, depending on their stamina for working on them on any one day. The children worked on test tasks in small groups of five to eight; they had a lot of food as well as adults to encourage them. Even with this effort, the children could not be cajoled, coaxed, or even bribed into doing better on the testing tasks!

Knowing that the test score data by no means told the whole story of children's writing development in the Fifth Dimension, we turned to examining children's experiences through case studies. The following case studies present a cross-section of boys and girls at different ages describing how they used their time in the Fifth Dimension, how they benefited from participating in the program, and how writing and reading played a part, if any, in their experiences. Each case study helps illuminate how play and relationships contribute to change in children specific to their development as writers.

Case Studies

Scott. Scott was 7 years old and in second grade. He was a child for whom computer club was a place of respite as well as stimulation. He was a bright boy and, from what we knew, a good student in school. Scott came into computer club wanting to play Mario Brothers and only that. He was not particularly invested in writing, but he dutifully answered letters when he had to. Other than seven exchanges with the Wizard, he did no writing for the entire year. At the beginning of his weekly computer club session, he headed for his favorite computer; and if it was not available, he was sad but patient. When he finally got on the computer, he spent the rest of the afternoon playing his favorite game. He was in heaven; he played alone but kept up an audible commentary on his progress: groaning or cheering.

In March, he began asking an adult worker to sit by him and watch his efforts. In time, he asked the adult to record his scores at each level. In Scott's Fifth Dimension file, we have several pages filled with scores representing his efforts to track his progress in mastering the game over several weeks. One week, he requested the adult's presence at the beginning of class. The adult could not oblige immediately, but Scott was politely persistent until he had his wish. In subsequent weeks, he extended his conversation to peers around him while still choosing to work on Mario Brothers by himself. He showed signs of wanting more connection with others, and yet he protected computer time for himself; he knew just how he wanted to spend it—alone and in charge. As Scott began to reach out to others tentatively, the Wizard wrote to him and asked what game he would play if he could not play Mario Brothers. The Wizard did not want to deprive Scott of his beloved game but to lead him to other possibilities. Scott answered:

Dear Wizard
How do you know about a game about Mario? I'm good at
Mario Brothers. Why don't you know how to play Mario Brothers?
How do your world look? Is it nice outside in your world?
The End.
From Scott
P.S. And I would play Outnumbered if I couldn't play Mario.

The next week, he wrote to the Wizard:

> Dear Wizard,
> I love Mario Brothers, and I start playing Ancient Empires because I
> want to see how it goes. Ancient Empires was a fun game when I
> play it. On board 2, it was hard. The End.
> Love, Scott

None of the children or adults was experienced with Ancient Empires, but
Scott became determined to figure it out. His method was trial and error,
a strategy that had served him well with Mario Brothers. He replayed one
level 10 times before he mastered it. He was frustrated but not discouraged;
he only quit when it was time to go home.

Near the end of the spring term, Scott chose a new game: Outnumbered, a game familiar to many of the children. He again chose to play alone
but soon realized he would need help. He was quick to pick up a strategy,
but the math involved in this game was often too difficult for him. One
child, Brian, came to his aid. Brian was adept with math problems but also
a thorn in Scott's side. They quarreled often and generally seemed unable
to work together. However, when it came to this new game, Scott was able
to accept this boy's help, and Brian in turn eagerly gave it. This interaction
was an achievement for Scott.

Scott grew in several important ways during the year. He began the
year playing only Mario Brothers (a game requiring no writing or reading)
and quickly discovered that his wish to play only that game would be honored until he decided to try something new. He played uninterrupted for
an hour and a half at a time on his game of choice for months. He completed his responsibilities to Fifth Dimension correspondence with minimal
bother and concentrated on what was important to him. As the year pro-
gressed, he moved beyond this one favorite game to try new ones, and as
he did, his connection with people slowly widened to include adults and
finally his peers, who posed more of a risk to him.

Computer club was a setting where the adults were willing to accept
Scott's choices of what he thought was good activity for him. Within this
atmosphere of confidence in his choices, Scott explored tasks and created
challenges for himself as he felt ready and moved into collaborative relationships with adults and then peers in these new activities. These relationships
supported his rising to new challenges. His end-of-the-year TOWL score
went up 8 points, from 81 to 89. This put him 19 points above the Garden
Homes group average score and on the brink of the 50th percentile ("average") for his age group in the national norms. To attribute this change in
score to writing experiences in the Fifth Dimension would be overstating

the case, since he did so little writing in that setting. Where he did grow in the Fifth Dimension was in his willingness to open up to help and enter relationships in which he could trust and depend on others.

Darlene. Darlene was 7 years old and in second grade when her family moved to the community. She entered the community center program halfway through the year. From the first day that Darlene came to computer club, she had the group's attention. During snacktime, she began talking about Harriet Tubman and held the group spellbound with her story. Her use of language was powerful and vivid. She took great pains to communicate expansive ideas in conversations and, eventually, on paper. She was kind to other children and eager to know about them and computer club. The Wizard was a wonder to her, and she immediately wanted to know the personal details of his life. Did he have a wife and children, what did he look like, was he coming to visit? Her letters to the Wizard were full of personal information about herself; she wanted him to know her (see the letter at the beginning of this chapter).

Darlene was hungry for the new experiences computer club offered, but her reach often exceeded her grasp. The adult workers were crucial to her initial successes. Because she was new to the community center, and because she was so open, sweet, and eager to communicate, the other children initially made fun of her, but the group also quickly developed respect and affection for her spontaneous and expressive nature. This reaction could be seen in two comments made during snacktime by the same boy. After Darlene had spent several minutes telling us about famous inventors, he said, a bit disgruntled, "She sure does talk a lot." A few minutes later, after listening closely to her comments, he said, "She sure does know a lot of information." The tension between these two responses to Darlene sometimes made it necessary for the adults to protect her and the other children. She and they needed reminders that computer club was to be a safe place where they could express themselves, ask questions, and be taken seriously. The Wizard, who met children wherever they happened to be and guided them in the directions they seemed to want to go, reinforced this accepting approach.

If Darlene's spirit was sometimes dampened by the other children's reaction to her, she was never inhibited in her correspondence with the Wizard. Her birthday message to the Wizard, written 2 weeks after joining the Fifth Dimension, reads:

> How do you look? Is you nice ot you dad [to your dad]. Can you make this a better plase Darlene

The Wizard responded:

Dear Darlene,
I try to be a good Wizard and I love to make things better for every
child in the Fifth D. I'm looking good with a big smile these days
with all my birthday messages around me!
Love, The Wizard

Darlene had very high standards for her writing, and dictating her letter
was often the best way for her to achieve them. There was no stigma
attached to the dictation process in this setting for her (or the other children), and for Darlene it meant that the very words she wanted would get
down on paper. She wanted to be able to spell each word correctly (no
process writing for her!); once she burst into tears after being repeatedly
encouraged to "sound it out the best you can." Dictating to an adult was
the satisfying solution for her.

Darlene was curious about the workings of the computers and the
games. She was particularly taken with Print Shop, where she could make
cards and pictures as well as write stories. Her occasional frustration came
when she had a definite idea of what she wanted to create and could not
figure out how to use the computer to realize it. Her determination and
willingness to seek help from the adults and other children usually carried
the project to satisfactory completion.

Darlene's end-of-the-year TOWL score was 76: 6 points above the Garden Homes group average score. She was in the 7th percentile nationally,
hardly indicative of the potential for writing she presented. Darlene benefited from computer club by having a place where her storytelling and ideas
were heard and valued by computer club staff, her peers, and the Wizard.
Her appetite for learning was met with the opportunity to learn about computers and software as well as to find new means for expressing her expansive ideas, which she now composed on word-processing programs. This
articulate, expressive, eager 7-year-old finished 4 months of computer club
with computer skills that had become second nature to her.

Alex. Alex was 9 years old and in third grade. Alex's letters to the
Wizard told his story; the first was written at the end of March and the
second in mid-April.

I hate you. I do not leibe Alex wizard because I am to big to beleibe
you and I do not care about the games or you. I am 10 years old and
that's why I hate you. I am made [mad] at every one. Good bye. I
got hit by playing ball and in here. You are not my friend.

> I don't know what to say. I don't believe anything but myself and
> my family. I don't believe in you or anybody. Can you send me a pic-
> ture?

Alex was mad at the world and had reason to be. He lived with his grandmother, who frequently told him (and his older brother, Lawrence) that
they would have to live somewhere else because she could not cope with
them. His mother was a drug addict who had many children by different
fathers. Alex loved her very much, and his constant hope was that he could
return to live with her. His relationship with this brother, who also attended
computer club, was, at its best, indifferent. More often, it was openly hostile, lacking the bond of typical brotherhood. While his brother was a dark-
skinned black, Alex was light-skinned with wavy, glossy hair.

Alex's response to chaos and abandonment was to fight. He fought
with girls and boys, young and old, big and small. When asked by a peer
why he was always fighting, he answered, "Because that's what Alex can
do." He sabotaged other children's games by hitting keys randomly on their
computers while running through the room. If he was actually playing a
game with another child, he delighted in the child's mistakes and was a
merciless tease during the play. If, for a brief moment, Alex and another
child seemed to be enjoying each other's company, he could not bear it—
maybe out of fear that it would end any moment. He would figure out a
way to ruin the play.

Alex did not understand cause-and-effect sequences. He did not seem
to understand that computer operations have logic, that games have instructions, that keys pressed randomly would produce nothing. The world he
knew did not operate logically or consistently. In February, Sivright's fieldnotes read, "Alex needs a consistent, patient adult presence to settle down
and focus; he does it beautifully if that element is there." "That element"
for Alex was his Garden Homes staff person, Angela. They had known each
other for years, and Alex had spent time at her home playing with her son.
Angela had, as she said, "a soft spot for Alex." She hugged him, kissed him,
comforted him when he cried, held him until his waves of anger passed,
teased him, and laughed with him. She was the reliable, loving adult in his
life who also had the strength to discipline and teach him.

Angela was consistent: She never disciplined him physically and she
did not allow him to abuse her physically. When he misbehaved, she
hugged and talked, hugged and talked. The other adult workers modeled
this same behavior, but Angela was Alex's anchor. His letters to the Wizard
paint a picture of a boy who has been prematurely pulled out of childhood.
"I am to big to beliebe you." But, " . . . can you send me a picture?" For the

Wizard's birthday card, Alex wrote the following message on a card that was e-mailed to the Wizard:

> this is Alex could you please come to see me I no that all of my friend come to see me now could you please come to see me now that is a good friend
> bye-bye good friend

The Wizard responded:

> Dear Alex, I do see you every day and I'm here for you any time you want to send a message. I'll be waiting, friend! And I love to watch you play 1 on 1[2]: you're good!
> Love The Wizard

Alex pushed people and the Wizard away but wanted them close. This pull-and-push kept him and the people around him constantly edgy and frustrated. A letter to Mike Cole, project director in California, revealed this self-protective distancing:

> I been to California once but I didn't stay all night.
> Sike[3] I never been to California.

Alex sometimes threw up a screen with Angela, too, but never for long. For better or worse, he was real with her and she with him. Communication with Fifth Dimension members was almost nonexistent for Alex, and correspondence with the Wizard revealed anger and lies. His relationships with his own computer club peers were mostly destructive. Angela was the bright spot in his experience, and that became ever more clear in late spring when Angela was promoted to an administrative position at the center in the front office. Alex fell apart; the fighting and physical violence increased, as did his crying. Angela did her best to intervene when she could; we called her away from her desk more than once. Angela understood where she needed to put her efforts with a child whose life was as desperate as Alex's was. Alex needed a real Wizard, a flesh-and-blood miracle worker instead of a more distant source of fantasy, friendship, and support. Alex recognized that Angela was offering exactly what he needed.

Alex's TOWL score went up 7 points, from 45 to 52; his final score was 18 points below the group average score of 70. He scored in the seventh percentile nationally. Alex demonstrated that he could use writing as a medium of expression as long as there was a seamless experience of support, encouragement, and guidance from a caretaking adult that could anchor him in the immediate here-and-now. The potential was there; his life circumstances, however, made it hard for him to cultivate that potential.

Andrea. Andrea was 12 years old and in sixth grade. She was a tall, willowy teenager with a shy, sweet smile. She had two sisters who were also involved in computer club: a 7-year-old sister and an older sister who began the year as a youth worker. Her parents were loving, attentive, committed, and hardworking. They took immediate action to protect their older daughter when they discovered her premature sexual activities. Andrea's equilibrium seemed to reflect that care from her parents. She spent much of her time at the side of her best friend, Tatanya. They had known each other since they had entered Head Start in this community center when they were 3 years old.

Andrea usually came into the community center with a story about school events that day. The character of life during and immediately after school took on the feel of daily battle. She told stories of sexual harassment by teachers, nonresponsive administrators, and constantly being physically intimidated, if not beaten up by, classmates. She related these details matter-of-factly, and the other children chimed in with similar stories of their own, nodding knowingly at the names of offending adults and children. However, Andrea was not passive. She fought back physically and verbally. She would tell her parents and go to the principal to report incidents. She wrote to the Wizard one day:

> Dear Wizard,
> It teaches you a lot of fun and it teaches you skills that you never had. It is very fun. I love to come to after school and I like to go to school for studying and learning. I live in a big house on Maplewood. It is very big. I have 3 floors and its real wide. Neighborhood is very bad. It is where all the gangs are. School is very bad. I don't like it. The teachers be hitting us and hitting us in some places we don't want to be hit in. I am tall, love shopping, [have] long dark brown hair, love to wear jewelry, brown eyes and skinny.
> From Andrea

Andrea enjoyed making cards for her family and friends with Print Shop. She stayed oriented to the peers and staff immediately around her and loved to show them anything she happened to be doing. One day she began typing her name on the computer and continued until dozens of *Andrea*'s filled the screen. She called staff over to see her work in progress and again when she was finished. Her delight in seeing her name repeatedly was something a child much younger might have enjoyed, but it also seemed to reflect the sense of pride and pleasure she took in being Andrea. In her birthday message to the Wizard, she wrote out the words to "Happy Birthday" (two verses) and then signed her name. In each of these cases, she seemed to enjoy filling a computer screen with print, the kind of play with the generative principle of written language younger children explore when using new writing tools and discovering what they can do on paper with them (Clay, 1975).

Andrea's TOWL score stayed roughly the same from October to May: her pretest score was 73, and in May it was 70, right at the group average score, which put her in the seventh percentile nationally. The fact that her score stayed the same could be said to reflect her time in the Fifth Dimension, since the club provided her and her peers with a setting for the healthy development of early adolescent friendships and activities. Andrea did not seek challenges and did not push to achieve in this setting. Rather, computer games and word-processing programs provided her with satisfying ways to spend time with peers; they engaged her interests along with other activities, such as dancing and singing, that were fluidly weaving together in the children's after-school experience. She and her friends were in a safe place where adults valued them.

Lawrence. Lawrence was 12 years old and in sixth grade. Lawrence spent the fall being the coolest, baddest dude in the neighborhood. He portrayed a strongly negative, sarcastic, rebellious nature in the after-school program and computer club. He and his half-brother, Alex, lived with their grandmother, who threatened to put the boys in foster care because she was overwhelmed trying to care for them. Lawrence's mother was in and out of his life. Like his brother, Alex, he remained loyal to his mother and desperately longed for her.

Lawrence began the year working to poison any good feeling in relationships around him, including that with his brother Alex. He also quickly became interested in computers, telecommunications, and particularly in typing itself. He became involved in productive activities when paired with the male high school youth worker, and then with the Garden Homes staff person Angela, just as his brother did (although he and Alex had computer club on separate days). These relationships seemed to allow him to start a dialogue with the Wizard and "play along" with the group fantasy while devouring the opportunity to learn the ropes of computers and telecommunications.

Dear Wizard,
The reason I have not wrote you yet is because I was in a hurry.
And when you write me don't call me homey. Because that isn't my

name. In if that was my name I would tell you to call me that but I din't tell you to call me that so I suggest you don't call me that. so sense were still friends I'm not going to be so hard on you. In you have not done any thing it's just that I don't be wonting to do it. From Lawrence and learn how to spell homey.

One week later, Lawrence dictated a letter to Sivright for the Wizard, responding to a message he had just received. He then went to the computer and, with help, got online to type an e-mail while Sivright read his text back to him. Sivright read the first couple of lines and Lawrence typed in a few words just as he had written them. To the adult, the sentences were unclear, but after a few unsuccessful attempts to help him improve them, she stopped trying to edit. At that point, Lawrence began to elaborate and create something new with his letter. Not only did he add to the original text, but he also expressed his ideas more clearly in the second version. In his dictated draft, he asked the Wizard a rather pointed question: "Is you Angela?" In the final copy, he softened the question while also making it grammatically correct: "Are you really someone who works at this center?" The final text read:

Dear Wizard,
How are you? I hope you are fine. I just wrote to you to see how are you. I said happy birthday and thank you for our treat you said you was going to give us. I hope we have treats. And also I just wanted to ask you are you A person in the center. And I also hope that we have A cake or something. That is A treat.
From Lawrence

In early April, Lawrence got online again, this time to answer a letter from two girls in New Orleans. His ability to understand the directions for signing on to telecommunications had grown such that he did so almost completely independently. He sometimes needed a hint in the process but usually not. He was very proud of mastering this. The children who had written to him had sent some "Hinky Pinkys."[4] Lawrence had never heard of these, so Sivright explained the idea and made up some to illustrate. He was mildly interested at first and began his response with the intention of thanking the letter writers and being done with it. As he wrote, he became curious about the New Orleans children and asked them questions about themselves. Then he decided it was only polite to send them a Hinky Pinky. Once he got the idea, there was no stopping him. When he finally had to finish the letter (because another child needed the computer), he thought that this game should have a name. He came up with his own Hinky Pinky: "Mind Combined."

The story does not end there. As he was sending the letter, he pushed a wrong key and half the letter disappeared. Nothing he or Sivright did could retrieve it, so they were forced to piece it back together with the half that remained as clues. Lawrence stayed calm and focused. He dictated back to Sivright what he remembered while she typed. However, he typed in the commands to send and log, and ended the activity with deep satisfaction.

> Dear Lisa and Charmaine,
> I just wrote to say thanks for the game Hinky Pinky. And I also wrote to ask you who is, or what are you? Are you a child or adults? But anyway! We have a few of our own.
>
> What do you call a pencil that's passed away?
> Dead lead.
>
> What do you call dust that falls to the ground?
> Hurt dirt.
>
> What do you call a parent that gets angry?
> Mad Dad.
>
> What do you call a man with a mattress on top of him?
> Bed head.
>
> From Lawrence and Sarah.
> The name of our game is Mind Combined.

A few weeks later, conversation at the snack table turned to Lawrence's rap group, Out of Control. He said the group chose that name because they rapped fast and did not care if they made mistakes. "We just go, we mess up sometimes, but we don't care." On that particular day, Lawrence felt comfortable enough to perform a few of his original raps. Some of the older girls danced to his oral beat. Lawrence's raps were eloquent, clever, angry, and evocative. One line that stuck out vividly described a man who hit his girlfriend and how he explained his violent behavior as being the result of being beaten by his own father—being "a critter from a litter."

The last Wizard letter was written in May; the Wizard asked the children to send information about themselves that he/she could take along while traveling in the Fifth Dimension over the summer. Lawrence chose to dictate to Sivright and started out by giving nonsense, smart-alecky answers. When he saw her writing these down, he stopped and told her not to write down that "silly stuff." He sobered up and answered the questions seriously and thoughtfully. Corresponding with the Wizard was not his favorite activity, but expressing himself in writing was serious business, no matter what form it took.

> May 26
> Dear Wizard,
> I would just like to say that I have joined a basketball team. And I am getting better at school. And today we played a game and it was me and Neil against 2 boys. And we was doing lots of passes and we also won.
> LAWRENCE
> D
> A
> M
> S

Lawrence finally got an answer to his Hinky Pinky letter. His pen pals had been so impressed, they wanted his home address and photograph. He was initially worried that his girlfriend, Arlene, would object, but when she did not, he agreed. A later letter revealed that his photo now sits framed atop the dresser of one of the pen pals.

Lawrence benefited from many parts of computer club. His relationship with the Wizard was peripheral (as was true for most of the children over 9 or 10 years of age), but the writing, even to the Wizard, was not. He took it all seriously. He formed close attachments with adults and with his peers; both were a lifesaver to him at a time when his home situation was painful and precarious. He had the bravado—the "attitude" and poses—of boys his age that made them easy prey for life in the streets or in a gang. However, he also had the chance to develop a poetic, expressive voice in writing through computer club. His computer club experience demonstrated the potential of educational experiences within his community to offer him an alternative direction for developing his bright mind and linguistic talents. With all of this achievement, his TOWL score went down 13 points, from 64 to 51; his final score was 19 points below the group average score of 70. He was in the seventh percentile nationally.

Discussion of Data: The Context of Children's Writing

The Fifth Dimension is, for all who hear about it and who have visited or participated in it (adults, youth, and children), a remarkable invention: a creative, appealing, and fun activity setting. The Garden Homes Fifth Dimension provides insights about what it takes to find the voice of these children and this community in writing. The project also shows how far we have to go to create a setting that can elicit the potential of the children. The case studies show that the Fifth Dimension activities, embedded in the larger context of the Garden Homes Community Center, can offer opportunities for play with peers, adults, and the Wizard (some of which included writing) while also learning about computers.

The Garden Homes staff believe the benefits of the Fifth Dimension for their children were many. The children learned basic computer operating procedures, including word-processing programs and telecommunications. They developed favorite games and expertise at playing them. Children participated in positive interactions with peers and adults that helped them manage particular life experiences. The Fifth Dimension provided opportunities for extended conversation that also included reading and writing about ideas. For these children, each of these benefits was significant; they had a place and time each day when they could count on adults and peers being together in an unpressured way to listen and be heard.

Vygotsky's hypothesis about transformation in the course of growth in a zone of proximal development as a function of relationships in an activity setting is relevant to the data we collected on children's writing development in the Fifth Dimension. Children appeared to make progress, but it often followed a circuitous and unpredictable path. As educators working with groups of children each day, it was often hard to know whether or not to worry about a child's course of activity for periods of time. How might we have known whether a child's lack of progress or repeated choice of one activity alone was a prelude to a transformation—a reorganization of previous knowledge, skill, and understanding—or whether it was a signal that development was stuck and needed new forms of mediation to get things going again?

The Fifth Dimension offered the possibility of looking at children writing for different purposes, for a range of people, and with a variety of supports. The environment—which included computers, all types of paper, pens, markers, pencils, scissors, dictionaries, calculators, and rulers—helped children explore and solve problems in their mostly self-appointed tasks with support and encouragement from adults and youth workers. Helping others with the computers and writing activities was encouraged and expected. Writing by dictation, receiving spelling help from adults and peers, copying, and borrowing were part of the ethic of the environment. In order to get the best out of the children, we had to know something about their concerns and interests and to make room for them within the context of the Fifth Dimension. In making a place for more play and more of children's personal selves than might normally be brought to the school context, writing became a creative and sometimes effective tool for managing the issues and concerns that preoccupied the children. Children who were not interested in writing, such as Scott and Andrea, seemed to maintain a benign disposition toward writing.

Two of the five case study children wrote at least once, if not more often, in every session of computer club. For Darlene and Lawrence, writing was satisfying and compelling, enabling their inherent strengths, skills, and preferences to emerge. The other three children wrote less frequently, seemingly reflecting their predilections. Scott tended to be a loner, avoiding relationships with others much of the time. Alex wrote in 17 out of the 22 computer club sessions he attended, and his writing was closely connected to Angela's efforts to channel his energies productively. Andrea wrote in 14 out of 17 computer club sessions she attended while she tried to balance her attention to peers, adults, and Fifth Dimension friends.

For all the children discussed, the bulk of their writing was invested in Wizard correspondence; this group of five produced 82 pieces of writing, 50 (61%) of which were letters to the Wizard. This follows the pattern of data presented in Tables 6.1 and 6.2, which show that the primary use for writing among Chicago children was communicating with the Wizard. The Wizard has two important qualities: The Wizard offers each child friendship that reflects care and a willingness to listen and respond to the child. The Wizard also represents an opportunity for play and fantasy.

We recognized that the Wizard was not as appealing to the older children as to the younger ones because of the increasing importance of peer relationships and their lack of belief in such fantasy figures. However, even for boys like Lawrence who had so much pain to deal with, playing along with the Wizard fantasy was more appealing than not having this opportunity for play and dialogue. Particularly on occasions such as the Wizard's birthday (Valentine's Day), no one worried about the truth-value of the Wizard when presented with cakes, small treats, and e-mail messages. Writing in the context of such satisfying play was an incentive to write.

The reasons and incentives for writing were different for each child. What comes through in the children's letters is evidence that the arrangements of activities and the creativity of the adults involved did facilitate the children's finding some connections with writing. Writing in this setting does not look foreign or uncomfortable (although the pre- and post-testing on the TOWL certainly did!); the children could find continuity between themselves in their daily lives and an expression of themselves in writing.

What were the significant transformations in writing development? Our present work suggests that there is far too close a symbiosis in the areas of a child's functioning and self-expression to try to separate them and account for specific developments. The children's rejection of our attempts to use evaluation measures that belong to school contexts is a reminder of how inappropriate it is to try to assess these domains of development separately. When we see what was required to get boys in particular to write, and when we see what was troubling them so deeply, we question whether the children's issues and needs are not beyond the energy and skill of one teacher working with 25 to 28 children in a classroom. The Chicago Fifth Dimension experience suggests that to effectively deal with the subjective life of children in pain and need, more adults are needed—adults who have the emotional imagination, patience, and strength to help children contain, manage, and creatively live with various difficult life experiences. We also learned at the end of the year's work that the problem of helping these children find a voice was going to be far more complicated than any of us had anticipated.

Conclusion: Garden Homes' Future in Practice and Theory

Even with the benefits of the Fifth Dimension for Garden Homes children, there were also glaring shortcomings. The staff specified four areas they feel need to change before the Fifth Dimension can make a difference in the lives of Garden Homes children and their development. First, they need software full of African American people and cultural situations from the past and the present. The staff want to see countless faces of African American people making contributions to society—and, as one staff member, Tina, said, "not just the people who earn a million dollars a year. They do not have to make a million to be important. Everyone wants a million dollars but that's not all there is in life. God put us here for all kinds of reasons. We want our children to see their culture and their people to be able to identify with them." The staff agreed that they wanted the Garden Homes children to grow in opportunities to succeed in mainstream society, but not at the expense of disowning or disregarding their home culture.

Related to this concern is the second need staff identified: the need for Fifth Dimension activities to address the children's low sense of self-esteem. Staff were disappointed and upset at how the children represented themselves to others in the Fifth Dimension outside of Chicago. They see a need to develop the children's view of themselves explicitly and intensively throughout their time in the Fifth Dimension and other Garden Homes programs.

Third, community center staff want to involve parents in the activities and goals of the Fifth Dimension project because overall, they feel that parents in the community are too hard on their children. "They tell children, 'your grades are important to me, not you.' They buy their children expensive clothes but then do not want their children to play hard and get dirty like they should at this age." The staff long to help parents become more attuned to their children and learn to listen and talk with them as opposed to only disciplining them.

Finally, and most importantly, the aspect of the Fifth Dimension that they want to change most is the voice of the Wizard. They see clearly that the Wizard voice needs to talk in more culturally relevant ways and talk with the children about being African American. The staff said that the Erikson Wizard voice asks too many questions and certainly never talks in dialect. Staff want to create a Wizard figure that their children will look up to and that will know how to reach the children concerning family and neighborhood issues that could make a difference to them in the long run. It was not easy for the staff to find their way with the Wizard's voice. Yet staff saw the possibilities for the Wizard voice and yearned for ownership of it.

There were many obstacles that staff and children struggled with on a daily basis that were part of the fabric of their efforts to implement innovative educational programs such as the Fifth Dimension in their community. The main factor that influences community life is economics. Jobs are hard to come by. Drugs and crime are visible. Gunshots can be heard in the community. There are drug dealers daily outside the community center doors. During one 3-month period, a 6-year-old boy's 3-month-old baby sister was beaten to death by his mother's boyfriend. A mother living with her three children across the street from the center committed suicide. A teacher in her mid-40s, who had worked in the program for many years and was the mother of five children, died of cancer. Illnesses—physical and mental—left staff and children exhausted on many days.

Family problems, illnesses, and tragedies are not reserved for inner-city communities. However, what was evident in this community was the absence of tangible supports and resources to help families manage these problems. There were no back-up systems in terms of child-care providers, financial resources, or mental health professionals. When staff were absent (as they frequently were), the community center did not have substitutes to fill in. The persistence of day-to-day problems that staff, children, and families faced had a tendency to stay in the foreground as opposed to the background of our daily work. The Erikson staff had to respond to, acknowledge, and contribute whatever wisdom and help possible before we could get to the Fifth Dimension work of the day. Often, all we could do was keep the daily program activities going, and this was sometimes a great relief to everyone.

Computer club also had to adjust to issues that the children brought with them each day. Most prominent were problems from school. The children arrived at the center full of complaints about the tedium of writing and reading all day, fights that occurred, and punishments and other treatment they judged unfair. The children rejected anything that reminded them of school. Whenever the weather was reasonable, the children were forceful in their wish to have outdoor playtime.

Research on learning and development in after-school settings does not automatically translate into insights and recommendations for writing development in schools, since the goals of the settings are so different (Cole, 1996). Still, when we undertook this project, we all believed the uniqueness of the Fifth Dimension would help illuminate aspects of children's development that we might not otherwise uncover. We hoped that findings in this out-of-school setting could help generate hypotheses as to what it might take to get such activity happening in school (Cole & Scribner, 1974). The case studies from the Chicago site show that the Fifth Dimension did not produce miracles as far as the children becoming voracious writers. The context did not make the children's life problems disappear or become irrelevant in their literacy development. We did, however, make progress in identifying elements of the setting, relationships, and tasks that had the potential to reorganize children's relationships with one another, their families and home community, and, eventually, communities outside of Chicago.

The Garden Homes staff recognize that furthering educational goals for their community in and out of school will require aligning literacy practices with relationships of power and voice for the community as well as meaningful community discourse patterns. As they discovered, launching new forms of writing and reading with their children was not going to be lasting unless at least some of the adults in the community find purpose in such communication and become partners in written as well as oral dialogues with their children. Exploring the nature and effects of this support is the work yet to be done to understand more fully the development of Garden Homes children as writers outside of school, let alone in school. For their research partners, the challenge is to further develop a theory of equitable opportunities for education and literacy development in American communities.

Notes

1. Also known as Proteus, Volshebnik, Golem, Sun Wiz, and El Maga in his/her various homes.

2. A computer game called Jordan vs. Byrd.

3. "Sike" to our kids means "I psyched you out!" —meaning that they fooled the person.

4. Hinky pinkys are riddles to be solved by guessing a two-word rhyme from two clues. The first clue is in the question. For example, What is sky-colored paste? The second clue is in the number of syllables given in the beginning. If an answer is two one-syllable words, it is a "hink pink"; if it is made up of two-syllable words, it is a "hinky pinky"; three-syllable words are "hinkedy pinkedys." The answer to the above hink pink is "blue glue."

References

Clay, M. (1975). *What did I write?* Portsmouth, NH: Heinemann.

Cole, M. (1996). *Cultural psychology: A once and future discipline.* Cambridge, MA: Belknap Press of Harvard University Press.

Cole, M., Griffin, P., & The Laboratory of Comparative Human Cognition. (1987). *Contextual factors in education.* Madison: Wisconsin Center for Education Research.

Cole, M., & Scribner, S. (1974). *Culture and thought: A psychological introduction.* New York: Wiley.

Griffin, P., & Cole, M. (1987). New technologies, basic skills, and the underside of education: What's to be done? In J. Langer (Ed.), *Language, literacy, and culture: Issues of society and schooling* (pp. 199–231). Norwood, NJ: Ablex.

Hammill, D., & Larsen, S. (1988). *The Test of Written Language—2.* Austin, TX: PRO-ED.

McLane, J. B., & McNamee, G. D. (1990). *Early literacy.* Cambridge, MA: Harvard University Press.

McNamee, G.D. (1990). Learning to read and write in an inner-city setting: A longitudinal study of community change. In L. Moll (Ed.), *Vygotsky and education* (pp. 287–303). New York: Cambridge University Press.

McNamee, G. D. (1995). A Vygotskian perspective on literacy development. *School Psychology International, 16*(2), 185–198.

Nicolopoulou, A. (1993). Play, cognitive development, and the social world: Piaget, Vygotsky, and beyond. *Human Development, 36*(1), 1–23.

Nicolopoulou, A., & Cole, M. (1993). Generation and transmission of shared knowledge in the culture of collaborative learning: The Fifth Dimension, its play world, and its institutional contexts. In E. Forman, N. Minick, & C. A. Stone (Eds.), *Contexts for learning: Sociocultural dynamics in children's development* (pp. 283–314). New York: Oxford University Press.

Vygotsky, L. S. (1978). *Mind in society: The development of higher psychological processes* (M. Cole, V. John-Steiner, S. Scribner, & E. Souberman, Eds.). Cambridge, MA: Harvard University Press.

Vygotsky, L. S. (1981). The genesis of higher mental functions. In J. V. Wertsch (Ed.), *The concept of activity in Soviet psychology* (pp. 144–188). Armonk, NY: M.E. Sharpe.

DIANE WAFF RESPONDS

As an urban teacher who has grappled with ideas about how to spark student engagement while supporting and stretching children's capacities as readers and writers, I read this chapter with a great deal of interest. The ideas presented resonated powerfully with my ideas of constructivist teaching and learning and showed how these ideas could come alive in an after-school computer club program. In the Fifth Dimension, computers were envisioned clearly as tools for learning, and the vision was set in the context of Garden Homes, a low-rise public housing development. The question of whether poor students of color who are considered "at risk" for succeeding in school would benefit from such an opportunity is answered in the evocative stories of students who made advances socially and academically. The fact that this improved performance was not captured on the Test of Written Language (TOWL), a standardized test of writing development administered at the beginning and the end of the computer club, calls into question the primacy of standardized tests in measuring student achievement. Throughout the chapter, the writers exhort the reader to look beyond standardized tests and school-bound activities to see the world of play and computers as a springboard for the most personal and powerful ways of learning.

The computer club provided a relational and environmental context that fostered student achievement and provides an alternative vision of what is possible in other educational settings. The descriptions of home/community environments marred by violence, abuse, and neglect as well as systemic problems of poverty, racism, and sexism enables the reader to see the complexity of the diverse lives of the computer club children. I was especially struck by students' awareness of the systemic oppressions they confront in their daily lives. The line from an 11-year-old girl's letter, "I live in a row house made for blacks," is especially poignant. In understanding the struggles and strengths of the young people in the program and the contexts in which they live, the reader begins to see the computer club as an intervention that has the potential to help students "contain, manage, and creatively live with various difficult life experiences."

By looking critically at their site, the community-based staff began to develop a shared understanding of what computer club practices were undermining program effectiveness. They called upon the Erikson staff to launch an initiative to institute practices and materials that would make the program more responsive to the needs of the African American students. Community staff began to ferret out less visible barriers to student achievement in computer club life, as evidenced in software devoid of African Americans and a Wizard voice that did not communicate in culturally relevant ways. They began to define areas of knowledge, skills, and support that would transform the club positively for students—emphasizing the need for cultural relevance, parent involvement, and raising student self-esteem. The authors point out that these dimensions of learning have tremendous potential for enhancing children's development and have been only minimally realized in the project. It is not clear from the chapter what steps the university partners took to address the legitimate concerns raised by the community center staff. However, the writers do indicate that future project research will focus on the nature and effects of parent and community support on students' literacy development.

While the Fifth Dimension did not produce "voracious writers," it did provide impoverished urban youngsters with a safe place to learn and grow in the company of adults who believed in their capacity to achieve. The work of the after-school computer club represents for me what Karl Weick terms a small win in "Small Wins: Redefining the Scale of Social Problems" (*American Psychologist*, 1984). I have come to respect the efficacy of incremental change while participating in the school district of Philadelphia's school reform movement. It is often the small gains that begin to slowly chip away at the barriers that prevent impoverished youngsters from achieving. The continued documentation of this program will be an invaluable resource for teachers, administrators, and policy makers who seek to create schools and other institutions that work for all students.

LEIF GUSTAVSON RESPONDS

Programs like the Fifth Dimension should always be supported. Any space that encourages youth, particularly at-risk youth, to express themselves creatively in writing and otherwise should be embraced and replicated. I also recognize the incredibly difficult task the Fifth Dimension set out for itself—providing a safe, secure, and warm environment for at-risk youth while also teaching them computer and writing skills. Perhaps the most difficult component of that task is designing a writing program that does not smack of the tedium that the children face day in and day out at school.

It has been my experience writing with all kinds of children that the act of writing, communicating something to someone else, is a potentially transformative act. I use the term *transformative* fully recognizing how slippery and problematic it is in the field of education because one of the goals of the Fifth Dimension is to "reorganize children's relationships with one another, their families and home community, and, eventually, communities outside of Chicago." One of the things that I find interesting is that the "network," as it is called by McNamee and Sivright, attempts to achieve this connectivity through a variety of activities, including writing, while often keeping the content of the writing instruction separate from the other activities. I would like to spend some time here exploring how the infrastructure of the program might possibly help or hinder transformation, specifically focusing on the idea of the Wizard as disembodied audience and the role of the community in the process of writing. I choose this focus because McNamee and Sivright's work has left me wondering whether the Wizard gets in the way of the goal of reorganizing children's relationships to people and writing. How does writing to an imaginary figure promote a communal awareness? And how does writing to the Wizard show the effect that writing can have on people and life?

McNamee and Sivright illustrate the difficult life circumstances of many of the children involved in the program. Children in the Fifth Dimension face drug abuse, sexual harassment, and poverty every day. The Fifth Dimension was constructed cybernetically and physically to be a safe haven for the children while at the same time to be a place to introduce them to the technology of computers and improve their writing skills. This multipurpose creates tension and offers interesting possibilities in terms of how writing can fit into a place and purpose such as this. Interestingly, I feel that the Wizard contributes to the tension and limits the possibilities. The interaction with the Wizard, because of its one-sided nature, does not set up the framework necessary to create a space for change to occur. I became aware of this, I think, when reading Alex's invitation for the Wizard to come visit since they are "good friend[s]." I wondered what Alex feels is the purpose of writing after that kind of exchange, particularly in light of the response he receives. The Wizard's reply reinforces the idea that writing is a disembodied act, much like school writing, and does not necessarily bring people together. While there is a transaction between Alex and the Wizard, the promise that the Wizard makes—"I'm here for you any time you want to send a message"—rings hollow because of the infinite distance between them. I often wondered while reading what would happen if the physical community of the Fifth Dimension wrote to and for each other? I raise this question because I think it is central to connecting literacy with a critical consciousness, something that I think is an important part of the Fifth Dimension's agenda. I see glimpses of the possibilities in the way in which the advisers dictate letters to the Wizard and the side performances that seem to happen on a daily basis.

Toward the end of the article, McNamee and Sivright write that the Wizard needs to become more culturally relevant, talking "with children about being African American." What could be more culturally relevant than the adults and the children in the Fifth Dimension writing to and for each other? For one, the children would be able to see the direct impact that their writing has on the community, similar to the way the community reacts when the children tell stories or rap. In addition, the children could see the adults in the community engaged in the same activity as they are. Through adults modeling the writing behavior, they could show how writing reflects an individual and a community and how it can be used to stimulate change. Ironically, while the latest buzz in education is how essential computers and the Internet are for connecting people and writing, this technology may actually limit the understanding of what writing can be, particularly for young children.

One year, I organized an e-mail exchange between my students and a class in Virginia. Our students were to write to each other weekly, exchanging stories and critiquing them as well as just getting to know each other in the process. The students started eagerly and enjoyed the exchange for the first month or so, writing diligently and frequently. Then it slowly ground to a halt with me becoming more and more dictatorial about doing the writing and continuing the connection. McNamee and Sivright's chapter has helped me realize that one of the myriad reasons the exchange petered out was because of the lack of performance involved in writing online. Writing, whether it be stories or essays, is a performative act, done in part to elicit a response from the reader/audience. This characteristic is particularly true when it comes to teaching young children how to write. I think my students lost interest because they were not getting the immediate feedback that standing up and sharing writing can get. When they performed their writing for the class, which we did often, they could sense how the group felt. They heard the laughter or the groans. They received much-needed encouragement for writing more.

At the heart of the Fifth Dimension is a desire to affect the way these children perceive writing and how they envision themselves as writers. Indeed, the authors write that reframing what writing means to these children will not endure "unless at least some of the adults in the community find purpose in such communication and become partners in written as well as oral dialogues with their children." While getting them to write, through e-mails to fantastical figures or children in other countries, is most definitely a part of promoting lifetime writers, I wonder what that does to the children's ideas of writing and who they think they are as writers. What will truly break them out of the mold that institutional writing so desperately wants to cast them in? Writing is not simple correspondence. Writing embodies all of the amazing things that McNamee and Sivright recount in this chapter: the stories Darlene and Andrea tell; the incredible raps Lawrence performs; the grammar of the TOWL test; the loving attention that Angela shows Alex. That is the most hopeful message of the Fifth Dimension for me—the material for changing how writing is done with the children already exists. It just demands a shift in focus from communicating outward to writing from within, expanding the idea of writing beyond e-mail letters and Print Shop cards by acknowledging and publishing in many different forms the "stories" that emerge in the everyday exchanges between the children and adults in the Fifth Dimension. If out-of-school writing projects can begin reframing the purpose of writing with young children, we may have a better chance of seeing that new vision reflected in how writing is conceptualized in the schools.

7

Contact Zones Made Real

ELLEN CUSHMAN and CHALON EMMONS

Against a wall painted with bright flowers and the name "YMCA," in a community center in the San Francisco Bay Area, a college student and a young girl sat on a bench reading a book together. Nearby, children and students from the University of California at Berkeley (UCB) gathered around tables, some working on homework, some writing cards to friends, siblings, and social workers, and some playing educational board games. Other children circulated between tables looking in on activities, joining them for a time, then moving on. In a corner of the YMCA multipurpose room, in the midst of laughter and playful activity, an undergraduate and a child found space for themselves: the book open and shared between them, Bernadette and Sabrina leaned close together. All the literacy events (Heath, 1983) unfolding that afternoon at the Y exemplify the kinds of hybrid literacies and social interaction that can develop in outreach courses and after-school programs, such as the one that brought Bernadette and Sabrina together. These images of children and young adults reading, writing, drawing, and playing together depict a very real contact zone, where individuals representing a university and community meet to read and write about topics important to them. We use the terms *outreach* and *service learning* to describe projects such as this, although we realize that many service-learning courses have purposes other than reaching beyond the university to community-based sites of learning. When service-learning reaches beyond the university setting, contact zones emerge in which individuals with different, yet overlapping, agendas and identities come together to create reading and writing practices meaningful to all involved.

In this chapter, we explore the complex literacies and teaching strategies that unfolded during the spring 1998 semester of a service-learning course we team-taught. We develop and illustrate a theory of hybrid literacies produced when youths and university representatives collaborated with each other at the YMCA. While these literacies served the YMCA members in important ways, they also influenced the undergraduates' knowledge-making and research. Yet this result glosses the complex ways in which students, teachers, and YMCA members viewed the merit and utility of these literacies. We find that service learning can enact the multicultural goals of contact zone pedagogies and can expand our understanding of literacy; along the way, we explain the difficulty of achieving these ends.

Theoretical Framework

Pratt's (1991) idea of contact zone pedagogy offers one way to begin thinking about the pedagogical issues and literacy practices that emerge in outreach or service-learning courses. In "Arts of the Contact Zone," Pratt describes the course she developed at Stanford in which students read both European and indigenous representations of the Americas. She defines the "contact zone" as including those "social spaces where cultures meet, clash, and grapple with each other, often in contexts of highly asymmetrical relations of power" (p. 34). Although in this article Pratt is primarily concerned with colonized peoples and their literacy, she goes on to describe a course she taught, called "Cultures, Ideas, Values," that enacted her version of a contact zone pedagogy. In this class, students read literature to understand the emic systems presented therein: "every single text [they] read stood in specific historical relationships to the students in the class," so "everyone had a stake in nearly everything [they] read" (p. 39). Texts and class discussion about them became the operative means for providing "contact" with other value systems.

Understanding a culture through texts alone seems oddly reminiscent of the methodology that armchair anthropologists employed before they developed ethnographic methods. When learning about a culture solely though texts that represent that culture, students may have less compunction to develop a respect for the culture studied. They can (and did in Pratt's class) read other cultures in ways that "horrified" the students in that culture and that caused "all the students [to] experience face-to-face the ignorance and incomprehension, and occasionally the hostility of others" (p. 39). Reading a culture from texts alone lends itself to facile, often invalid, claims, claims based on second- and third-hand information. It also lends itself to a contact zone pedagogy where a kind of violence is done to other learners who have to defend themselves and their cultures against their peers' harmful representations.

Perhaps the greatest shortcoming of Pratt's hypothetical contact zone pedagogy rests in the kind of interaction it encourages. Harris (1995) makes this point well:

> Taken either way, as hinting at conflict or connection, what is missing from such descriptions of the contact zone is a sense of how competing perspectives can be made to intersect with and inform each other. The very metaphor of *contact* suggests a kind of superficiality: The image is one of cultures banging or sliding or bouncing off each other (p. 33, emphasis added).

The superficial social interaction manifested in contact zone teaching that Pratt describes makes for a classroom where students have little stake in expanding their conceptions of others or in negotiating interpretations with those who are represented. Thus the contact zone pedagogy misses its multicultural mark because university teachers and students need, in Harris's (1995) words, to "learn not only how to articulate our differences, but how to bring them into useful relation with each other" in everyday interactions (p. 35). We believe outreach courses create one means by which multicultural and literacy issues can be mutually negotiated through face-to-face interaction and experiential learning.

In the context of the kinds of meeting places that Harris describes, and from a combination of collaboration and invitation, two forms of mutually informative literacy emerged in the service-learning course we taught. The initial interactions between students and YMCA youth generated what we are calling "hybrid literacies"—reading and writing activities occupying multiple categories that have typically been used to describe language. Hybrid literacies combine elements of oral and written discourse; include facets of storytelling, dialogue, letter-writing, and personal journals; and unite print and illustration. Of course, Dyson's (1999) research on literacy development reveals how children employ multiple media and social representations of themselves to create literacy artifacts that appear to be hybrid literacies. In fact, most children when learning to create literate meaning rely on interaction with others and multiple media to forward their literate goals (Dyson, 1999; Goodman, 1988; Harste, Woodward, & Burke, 1988). But hybrid literacies are officially sanctioned by institutional representatives who, in the context of this study at least, value all meaning-making activities and media equally. This value system is quite different from the one that children encounter in school, where children become gradually "more deliberate about using writing as a cultural tool to negotiate boundaries. . . . For example, children were becoming more sensitive to the cultural material appropriate in particular contexts" (Dyson, 1999, p. 390). Children use literacy in school contexts to identify and then carefully navigate the boundaries between competing value systems about what counts as a legitimate medium and activity for meaning-making. The school context must necessarily, given state mandates for curriculum standards, create borders between official and unofficial texts. Unlike the school context, the service-learning context creates an environment where those involved value all texts equally and therefore promote children's blurring of boundaries between official and unofficial texts in order to create meaning.

Hybrid literacies in this service-learning program emerged from a mutually rewarding interaction between adults and children, where both adults and children learn from each other in dialogic relations. Hybrid literacies are, in short, reciprocally rewarding—the undergraduates learned about language and learning by observing and interacting with the children, and the children learned to make meaning that was significant to them, their parents, and the YMCA staff. Hybrid literacies allowed YMCA members to redefine and affirm their individual senses of self-worth, to represent aspects of their culture they found important, and to delight immediate audiences. Hybrid literacies helped the UCB students initiate, maintain, and extend their relations with YMCA youths, and also helped complicate their thinking and writing. We found that academic reading and writing, when done in light of hybrid literacies, can involve university students in active, critical, and purposeful knowledge-producing. These literacies bring to the foreground and address language and learning issues as they arise in meeting places of mutual respect. Importantly, the community-based hybrid literacies served as a challenge to undergraduates' notions of what counts as schooled literacy, asking students to question their preconceived notions of the goals and purposes of reading and writing. In effect, outreach courses enact a socially responsible form of learning, where knowledge is made with community members.

To illustrate these points, we offer first a background of the Richmond Community Literacy Project and the course we team-taught at UCB, called "Social Issues of Literacy." We present numerous examples of hybrid literacy in order to characterize features of this literacy, and then focus on the hybrid literacies produced between Sally Viera, a college student, and Tanisha, a fifth-grader who belonged to the YMCA. While these hybrid literacies have their selling points, they also raised important questions regarding which teaching methods best fulfilled the educational and social responsibilities we all had. The final section describes how Sally developed a pedagogy that encouraged revision and attention to grammatical skills. In it, we analyze the literacy events and stories that emerge from Sally's revised pedagogy.

Background

The Cortez Community Center of the YMCA stands across the street from the Cortez Elementary School in a residential neighborhood of Richmond. Richmond has been described by a representative of the University of California Office of the President as the "forgotten inner city," because most of the university's outreach efforts have been directed toward Oakland: "Oakland's high profile. Nationally recognized. They're closer to the university, too." The Cortez neighborhood, in contrast, is a 20-minute drive from the Berkeley campus, tucked away off a highway exit not often frequented by drivers traveling between the East Bay and affluent Marin County. Cortez is a quiet neighborhood of single-family homes. Occasionally a preschooler will pedal his big wheel down the sidewalk, or a group of young adults will gather in a driveway to talk while one of them washes his car. A majority of the children who attend Cortez Elementary are growing up poor: in 1998–1999, 89.8% of the student body was eligible for the school's free or reduced-price meal program (Ed-Data, 2000). Cortez Elementary students' test scores between 1989 and 1994 placed that school in the lowest percentile in the state.

Despite the fact that the Cortez neighborhood has not shared in the economic success enjoyed by other Bay Area communities, individuals and agencies in the area are committed to the neighborhood and its young people. One such agency, the YMCA, offers programs for children, teens, and adults in the community; residents of all ages come to the community center for a game of basketball, for cooking classes, for Friday night videos, for homework assistance. About 60 children between the ages of 6 and 12 visit the Y each weekday afternoon. There they are free to set up a board game in the multipurpose room, grab a ball to shoot baskets in the gym, or eat a snack in the courtyard. The Y staff provide help with homework when they can and work to establish a quiet and orderly space where children can study. In addition, teen and adult staff members lead creative, educational, and recreational activities, so that there is always something new going on each day at the Y for the children who want to participate. Nevertheless, YMCA staff often have their hands full, as two or three teens and one or two adults try to keep track of and engage 60-odd children. While staff members try to keep in touch with children's caregivers and monitor their homework, to help ensure children's school success, they often don't have time to sit young people down in a quiet room and give them the assistance they need. In addition, the children themselves come to the Y pursuing their own after-school agendas: They come with siblings, with best friends, and with children they don't like or don't know, so that while they are engaged in officially sponsored activities such as homework and games, they are often simultaneously working out their place in the social world.

On Wednesday afternoons in the spring semester of 1998, the small staff of YMCA members and groups of schoolchildren would greet nine adults from the University of California at Berkeley—seven undergraduates and two instructors. Each of these adults quickly found a child or group of children and settled down to work and play. These adults from the university assisted YMCA staff in supervising the multipurpose room and gym, freeing staff members to interact more closely with individual children. Furthermore, the visitors from the university—whose arrival children would announce with shouts of "The tutors are here! The tutors are here!"—invited their young friends to draw, write, and work out math problems, sharing their own knowledge and enthusiasm for learning. The image that opens this chapter, of Bernadette and Sabrina reading together on a bench in the multipurpose room, is representative of many similar relationships that were nurtured over the course of the semester; these relationships between young adults and young children were nourished and sustained by a rich array of literate activities and practices.

Together, YMCA staff and members, along with the university students and instructors, were participating in a new collaborative endeavor, the Richmond Community Literacy Project. This project was initiated at a time when the University of California at Berkeley strongly supported outreach efforts as part of the chancellor's "Berkeley Pledge," a commitment to initiating and maintaining access routes between Bay Area communities and the university. Funded in part by the UC Links program sponsored by the University of California Office of the President, the College Writing Programs, and the Graduate School of Education, the Richmond Community Literacy Project aims to engage academics, social workers, young children, college students, and community residents in literate activities important to all involved. As a collaborative effort, the project has multiple aims and multiple constituents; it can be understood as drawing from two recent, related movements in higher education—outreach and service learning.

A central facet of the Richmond Community Literacy Project is a university service-learning course, "Social Issues of Literacy," first offered at UC Berkeley in the spring of 1998. This course is one of a growing number of service-learning courses and represents only one of several models of "service learning." The theoretical framework underpinning many service-learning courses posits that guided service opportunities enhance learning. In addition, Lillian Bridwell-Bowles (1997) points out that service-learning courses have practical benefits as well: Such courses help anchor university studies to the "real world," providing students with marketable experience in addition to their degree while providing universities with evidence of commitment and engagement with communities, businesses, and agencies beyond the campus.

The course we team-taught in the spring of 1998, "Social Issues of Literacy," conforms in some ways to a model identified by Heilker (1997), in which courses "construe the experience of doing community work as *research*—research to be used as a work consulted or work cited for a term paper or as a basis for criticizing an author's treatment of a given topic" (p. 74, emphasis in original). The course readings surveyed literacy theory and research; in addition to keeping a reading log and discussing this work in class, students wrote fieldnotes on their participant observation at the Y, then drew on both published work and their own experiences to write a detailed research paper exploring some aspect of literacy or teaching. At the end of the semester, the undergraduates presented their findings to members of both the Berkeley and Richmond communities.

Geisler (1994), Prior (1998), and Brandt (1990) have each in their own way charted how students become enculturated into academic discourse through the literacy needed to develop expertise with a topic and social involvement with other scholars. These studies of academic literacy focus on how students produce and consume texts solely in the context of the university. Expanding on this, the assignments in "Social Issues of Literacy" asked students to refine their academic expertise and social involvement in light of their engagement with literacies and children in the community context. The writing, thinking, and discussion done in class was reinforced and challenged by the writing, thinking, and discussion done in the after-school participant observation at the YMCA, creating a dynamic, mutually rewarding relationship between the two contexts for learning. In the end, the literacies created between the UCB undergraduates and members of the YMCA challenged fundamental notions of the schooled literacies in which students were becoming versed. The assignments and final papers reveal one way for service-learning instructors to integrate community with school literacy.

Many service-learning instructors structure curricula that eschew essay writing in favor of writing brochures, newsletters, or reports for community organizations. They do so in an effort to furnish students with audiences, tasks, and genres typically encountered in out-of-school settings (Brack & Hall, 1997). They find academic literacies moot exercises meant only to mold students into the image of a professor. Odell (1995) compares academic literacy to community service literacy: "Many academic literacy practices often allow—even invite—students to read passively, trying to extract meaning from a text rather than construct it. The reading and writing students do outside of school [in writing internships] often requires them to read more assertively and uncritically" (p. 50). Odell categorizes academic and community literacies in ways that value one over the other: One, academic literacy, seems all bad, while the other, community literacy, seems all good. We haven't just caught Odell in an ungenerous moment here—his comparison echoes widely held beliefs among community service scholars and teachers.

In fact, the backlash against certain forms of academic literacies prompted Stanford University to develop one of the nation's leading service-learning programs. Bacon (1997) observes,

> Because the classroom is such a contrived and atypical rhetorical environment— . . . where the purpose of communication is easily subordinated to the purpose of demonstrating mastery of a skill or satisfying a requirement—we tend to see the classroom as artificial, while we perceive an off-campus readership as real. We design CSW [Community Service Writing] assignments in an effort to create authentic acts of communication (p. 42).

Critiques of essay writing as passive, uncritical, inauthentic, vapid performances certainly have some validity. But do we need to throw the academic essay out with the bath water? Practice in academic writing prepares students for their future work in graduate school. At its best, academic writing engages students in the inquiry, data collection, analysis, and authoring that earmark knowledge-making. Service learning can provide students an introduction to the intellectual work of building on previous scholarship, of questioning the claims of other writers, of writing for authentic audiences—and of doing so with the confidence gained from drawing on first-hand participant observation experience with a variety of literacy practices in local settings.

Furthermore, with end-of-the-semester presentations, students have very real audiences made manifest before them, authentic audiences of interested professors, administrators, and community members. In our class, visitors to the students' presentations asked for anthologies of their writing to bring to the attention of other colleagues, university administrators, and funding agencies. The social workers at the YMCA used the anthology to evaluate the YMCA youths' progress. They also saw ways they could better integrate reading and writing into other programs and fieldtrips the YMCA conducted. Two months after the semester ended, one social worker said: "We're trained to intervene in crisis situations. But more and more our funding sources are asking us to help prevent these situations through education. I read this collection [of student papers] like mad because [in it] I'm seeing all sorts of ways to build up the academic part of my program." These anthologies and presentations, then, brought the students' learning full circle: Questions that began with their initial readings and led to more focused participant observation were then explored in their papers and disseminated to an interested audience of colleagues.

Like our undergraduate students, we were actively engaged both as participants and observers in this project. Cushman, a Lecturer in the UCB College Writing Programs, and Emmons, a graduate student in the Graduate School of Education, team-taught the course and collaborated with YMCA supervisors in coordinating undergraduates' work in the after-school program. In addition, we recorded and transcribed weekly class discussions, and collected students' fieldnotes and drafts of essays. Our aim was to discover and to describe the ways in which students negotiated their interactions with the children at the YMCA, paying special attention both to the kinds of literate activities that took place in the after-school program and to the ways in which the undergraduates represented their interactions to us, to their classmates, and to audiences beyond the classroom.

In the sections below, we discuss several literacy events (Heath, 1983) that took place at the YMCA, events in which Y members and undergraduates together created hybrid texts, drawing on a range of representational practices and conventions. Next, we describe the experiences of one university student, Sally Viera, as she struggled to develop an approach to her work at the Y—and a perspective on literacy—that would be emotionally, intellectually, and ethically satisfying. We focus on Sally because she consistently voiced concerns that stimulated the class as a whole to reflect on and reevaluate what we valued as good reading and writing and the methods for teaching it. The relationship Sally established with Tanisha (a fifth-grader at the YMCA), the texts she helped Tanisha compose, and her analysis of both the relationship and the texts shed light on some of the complex terrain between "school" and "out-of-school," the terrain on which Sally and Tanisha met each week.

While Sally participated in the project via a university class she was taking for credit and a grade, Tanisha was a member of a community center who visited the Y facilities after her schoolday was over. When Sally worried about Tanisha's performance on reading and writing tasks they did together, she often worried from her position as a university student minoring in education who planned to pursue a career as a teacher or school psychologist. Sally was concerned about Tanisha's performance in school and about the efficacy of her own efforts to help Tanisha. Tanisha, on the other hand, was willing to collaborate with Sally but was not obligated to work with her for the full 2 hours every Wednesday; occasionally she didn't show up at the Y or she left early with a group of her friends. Sally's task was to engage Tanisha without alienating her, to invite her to read and write sophisticated texts without denigrating her current ways of using language, and to prepare Tanisha for future success without losing sight of the present circumstances in which the two of them worked together. Their initial interactions generated a hybrid literacy, one not easily categorized because it includes characteristics of multiple modes, functions, and genres for literacy. Created in an out-of-school context, this hybrid literacy prompted Sally to reflect on the utility of schooled literacy and to develop a pedagogy aimed at creating a mutually influential relation between community and school literacies.

Hybrid Literacies

One model of the service-learning course, such as the one described by Peck, Flower, and Higgins (1995), connects universities with community centers in underserved urban areas. Peck and colleagues' community literacy project had begun 8 years ago as a "collaborative between the Community House and the National Center for the Study of Writing and Literacy at Carnegie Mellon" (p. 200); they concentrated on developing alternative discourses in multicultural exchanges and strategic approaches to inquiry and problem-solving. These alternative discourses Flower (1997) calls "hybrids," a term she uses to emphasize the potentially collaborative nature of multicultural community-based dialogue.

> The discourse of community problem-solving dialogue is not going to be anybody's home discourse. Aside from the emphasis on sustained analysis and writing, it cannot rely on the practices that are the property of any one group. It needs to create a hybrid discourse in which there is a collaborative structure that gives everyone a space, and in which multiple ways of talking and writing and representing problems and actions are privileged (p. 107).

Flower's provocative definition raises many questions. What literacy practices and artifacts actually constitute hybrid discourse? How does the collaborative structure created during community dialogue actually create a space in which multiple modes and channels of discourse have privilege? How did these hybrid discourses actually come into being and affect the audiences that received them? In asking these questions, the word *actually* appears again and again precisely because hybrid discourses need to be located in the time, place, and interactions from which they emanate. If we want to understand how and why these discourses are hybrid, we need to trace their formation back to the specific values and literacy practices that contributed to their formation. To expand the metaphor of hybrid, we need to know what features of each type of discourse were grafted together to produce this new fruitful discourse, especially if we hope to sustain current and generate new outreach projects. Thus, when Flower includes in her description of hybrid discourses the compelling literacy artifacts from the community problem-solving dialogue, such as the "CLC Urban Youth Report 14," the artifact itself could be better contextualized to illustrate its hybrid nature. For example, we wonder: What were the interactive processes that led to this piece? Whose language was used in what ways? How exactly were teens' and the larger community's voices brought to the table? How were the contact zones made real?

In part, we ask these questions out of methodological concerns. Literacy artifacts, such as the one Flower includes, appear flat—a mere snapshot of the social-cultural context in which they were generated—when they are extricated from the context of their creation. But we ask these questions, too, out of larger theoretical concerns. If hybrid discourses indeed promise one means to realize democratic expressions of multiculturalism, then we need to illustrate in some detail ways in which they do so. A theory of hybrid literacies could provide a framework others can use in their community–university collaborations.

The central problem, we think, in describing hybrid literacies is that they are relatively new to literacy studies. They are practices and objects that manifest themselves in fairly recent outreach efforts around the country that have come into existence in the last decade. Flower is right: While the language generated during outreach collaborations "draws on the kinds of expertise and distinctive literate practices associated with both university and community, a [community problem-solving discourse] is a hybrid that asks everyone to engage in new strategies" (1997, p. 107). Precisely what these new strategies are, what relations influence them, and who benefits from them all remain undertheorized. In what follows, we present a number of examples of hybrid literacies in order to take needed strides toward a theory and definition of them. We then closely examine the hybrid literacies that Sally and Tanisha produced together in order to illustrate the social complexities involved in encountering and teaching these new literacies.

Hybrid Literacies as Invitations

"The Kiss", by Samuel

Newman, a UCB undergraduate, and Samuel, an 11-year-old YMCA member, were reading and writing stories and cartoons together at a table in the YMCA's multipurpose room. Newman gave Samuel a sheet of paper he had folded and divided into quarters and asked

Samuel to make a story about anything he wanted. In his fieldnotes, Newman relates, "I had Samuel do a little cartoon where he would draw a picture, write about what the picture was doing, and draw another picture that responded to the original picture. He was open to the idea and drew a little cartoon that went in this fashion:

> (1) I am on a skateboard and I see a girl. (a figure on a skateboard)
> (2) The girl is on high-heels. (girl on high-heels)
> (3) The girl wants to kiss me. (no picture)
> (4) The end. (A picture of lips)"

As Samuel drew his picture and wrote the caption in the first cell, Newman asked who the "you" is and was told it was a picture of him. Samuel asked Newman questions about how to draw a girl on high-heels and then a kiss. Newman gave suggestions for the last two cells, and when Samuel was done, they shared the piece with a dozen people at the YMCA, including the social workers, other youths, and UCB students.

"Double Dutch," by Trisha

Newman describes in his fieldnotes another visit to the YMCA in which he met Trisha (a 10-year-old sixth-grader), and they chatted about things they wanted to do that day. When Trisha said that she liked Maya Angelou's poems, Newman asked if she wanted to write a poem, maybe about one of her favorite things to do. She told him she only really liked jumping rope, and he suggested that was a good topic. When Trisha finished the draft, she told Newman that she thought it was a stupid poem, "but after reading it aloud with her and telling her that I thought it was a good first draft, she thought better of her poem."

> Double Dutch, Double Dutch. I like Double Dutch cause you get to touch when you pay Double Dutch. When you jump for a long time you start to feel fine. When you move your feet, you start to hear the beat in Double Dutch.

Trisha showed Ellen the poem and Ellen read it aloud to her, trying to hit the rhythm of the words. Trisha's poem mimicked the actual beat the "twirlers" make (in double Dutch two twirlers swing two ropes in opposite directions as a third person jumps in the middle). When Ellen read the poem in time, Trisha smiled and said that it worked pretty well. She then showed her poem to her peers and asked them to read it to her.

Both Samuel's cartoon and the double Dutch poem represent different aspects of the youths' culture to audiences of interested peers. Although Samuel and his peers often joked with each other about their budding interest in girls, Samuel makes Newman the subject of this romance cartoon. Samuel had many comic books and shared them with other children at the YMCA and the male UCB undergraduates. In both content and form, Samuel reveals aspects of his gendered experience. Trisha, too, reveals aspects of what she values: the game of double Dutch, the form and rhythm of it, the touch of the game. She shows interested readers something about herself, the values of her peer group and culture, and her gendered experience.

These activities allowed Samuel and Trisha to display their cleverness, to reveal their understandings of their surroundings, and to entertain audiences. Samuel and Trisha shared their work with numerous other adults and children over the course of the day and enjoyed eliciting reactions of laughter and praise from their peers. Both youths generated these texts at Newman's encouragement, working with Newman in a give-and-take process that facilitated the generation of these artifacts, making social interaction the reason for and means to their drafts. Mutuality in the interaction and in the sharing of the final product sustain the creation of these hybrid literacies.

Hybrid Literacies and Affirmation

"My Schooll," by Edward

Edward, an 8-year-old YMCA member, greeted Steven at the door when we arrived from UCB. Steven, Ishmael, and Edward sat at a table and began working on homework and talking about what they wanted to do that day. Steven asked Edward to write him a story, and laid out two large sheets of paper for him to do so. The paper was lined with large spaces for big letters and also had open space for pictures. In his fieldnotes, Steven wrote, "Edward titled his story at the top of the page and drew a picture of his school. One thing that struck me about Edward is that he never asked me to spell any words to him besides the more difficult one[s]. His title, 'My Schooll,' was misspelled, although his spelling never affected the flow of his ideas. . . . He just tried to sound out the words the best he could and then he proceeded. His sentences showed structure

and he enjoyed writing his story. When he was trying to spell his favorite TV show, 'Cartoon Network,' he never asked for help. He
sounded out the word and wrote 'cartoonnat wert in my favrt cow-
sow.' Obviously spelling the words correctly was not Edward's first
priority."

Thomas's Top 10 List of Movies

Thomas took to Ruth after the second week of the semester, always
seeking her out when we arrived at the YMCA on Wednesdays.
Thomas's speech impediment and hyperactivity had landed him in a
behavior modification program at school. Ruth's fieldnotes reveal her
initial reaction to and interaction with Thomas: "He is a boy who at
first glance looks disruptive and very uncooperative. . . . A speech impediment makes it extremely difficult to understand what he's saying. This lack of understanding makes him get frustrated because he
has to constantly repeat himself. Thomas is made fun of because of
the way he speaks, and this makes him angry. Once you interact
with him you realize he is anything but that—he is intelligent, patient, and really sweet. . . . I didn't think he would want to write anything at first because I didn't think he would be interested. I was beyond wrong. When Thomas realized I wanted to sit there and work
with him, he was willing to try it all. Actually he liked the idea of
making up stories. First we made a top 10 countdown. He wrote out
all the movies and numbered them. We then thought about how the
story was going to develop, and I drew as he narrated. Once the
drawing was finished, Thomas colored it. He took so much pride in
that story we made up that he wanted a copy for Vicki [a social
worker] and he wanted the original."

Both Edward's and Thomas's interactions with the UCB undergraduates
reveal how an invitation to write and draw allow them to represent themselves. Steven just had to invite Edward to sit next to him, and Edward was
off and writing. For Edward, his self-view seems positive—in his story, he
writes that he likes his teacher and that he likes to read. He presents himself
as smart, and in his writing he sets the goal of studying hard. He created a
piece that used drawing and autobiography to express himself and called
it a story. When he showed it to Steven, Steven asked for a copy and then
showed it to Ishmael. Edward, pleased with himself, took his story home
to tape to his wall. Edward affirmed his sense of self when invited to do so
by Steven. This mostly positive image of himself stands in stark contrast to

Thomas, who was placed in a special program and who at first glance seemed disruptive.

Thomas, stigmatized by the other children at the YMCA and tracked into special education at school, acts in ways that left Ruth wondering whether he would even want to engage in reading and writing. But Ruth's invitation to him made Thomas realize that something he had to say mattered. He wanted to read and write, and he worked steadily with Ruth for an hour and a half producing two stories. His pride in these stories, and his desire to share them with other people, show that he came to see himself differently because Ruth paid special attention to him. She encouraged him to redefine himself in a literacy artifact that was part story, part newspaper movie review, part art. Taken together, both these works reveal the ways in which hybrid literacies used social interaction to promote positive self-images in the youths at the YMCA. They also show how an immediate and ready audience encourages these children to see themselves and what they have to say as important.

We find that hybrid literacies are produced in meeting places where social interaction not only prompts and sustains the language activity, but also becomes the final reason for the activity—these literacies are created *by*, *from*, and *for* social interaction. Importantly, this social interaction takes place between institutions that had not previously worked together, and between participants who cross age, race, class, and gender differences in order to meet together. In their form and content, hybrid literacies should be viewed in terms of the categories they straddle as opposed to the single categories they occupy. They are inviting literacies, inviting in two senses of the word: First, this reading and writing invites the audience to appreciate various aspects of the authors' worlds; second, this reading and writing invite the authors to represent their lived experiences to others inside and outside their community. Finally, hybrid literacies often provide individuals ways to redefine and affirm their notions of themselves and their capabilities. In all, hybrid literacies are invitations to enjoy the creativity involved in reading and writing, invitations to represent one's self or culture to an appreciative audience, and invitations to interact with different people in an atmosphere of mutuality and respect. Even with so much going for them, undergraduates wondered how these literacies and they as tutors actually served the YMCA members, as we illustrate in two hybrid literacy artifacts and events generated by Sally and Tanisha.

"The Poison Bottle," by Tanisha

In their second meeting together, Sally and Tanisha sat at a long table in the YMCA's multipurpose room. During the previous visit together, Tanisha had told Sally a story and Sally had written it down. This time, Sally brought out magnetic words (the kind put on refrigerators to encourage creativity) and asked Tanisha if she wanted Sally to chose a few words that Tanisha could then put into a story. Sally picked *old, poison, broke, bed, down, haunt,* and *peace,* and Tanisha began a story for Sally to transcribe.

> Once upon a time there was a old poison bottle. And a little girl had gave a man the poison bottle. And he broke it. And he started crying. And he went to bed. He fell down. And perhaps a ghost haunt him. And then he lives in peace.

Once it was written, Tanisha illustrated the story with a bottle, two characters, and a ghost drawn at the top of the page.

"Sally's Book," by Sally

During the fourth and fifth weeks of the semester, the undergraduates and children created personal journals. Large sheets of paper were folded in half, stapled, and bound on the outside by construction paper. The covers were colored, glued and glittered, stenciled, and written on to identify the writers and titles. Sally and Tanisha made a journal together, called "Sally's book," and began writing to each other in it. Sally wrote to Tanisha first asking how she was, what she did in school that day, and whether she wanted "to read a story or write one?"

In reply, Tanisha wrote "I am doing good. I did spelling and reading and Math. I do not know. Sally, today is my sister birthday." When Sally read Tanisha's response, she realized that Tanisha had answered her in decontextualized and brief sentences. Tanisha assumed that Sally would remember which question elicited which response. Sally recalls in her fieldnotes, "the letter wouldn't make sense if my letter wasn't around. So I asked her if she could tell me the same things in a ways that I would know what question she was answering." Tanisha agreed and revised her letter back to Sally, offering a bit more context for her answers.

The poison bottle story and journal dialogue, like the examples presented earlier, resist easy categorization because they encompass aspects of several types of literacy and language use. The story uses a type of vocabulary list like the ones found in "skill-and-drill" workbooks to prompt a creative work. While Tanisha called her piece a story, the vocabulary list drives the content and placement of the sentences (note how the sentences use the magnetic words in the order of their listing). The drawings included with the story are modeled after a children's book. The opening "once upon a time," along with "and then he lives in peace" provide appropriate fairy tale conventions. The coordinating conjunctions show an attempt to connect sentences together to form a chronological sequence of events. The story was spoken to Sally as she transcribed, bridging both oral and written narratives in a single gesture.

The journal dialogue collapses the spoken and written together in a form that includes aspects of the personal journal, letter writing, and conversation. The turn-taking movement between addresser and addressee in these letters echoes conversation, especially since they handed the journal back and forth to each other; yet the conversation is written. The conversational aspect of this piece makes the journal as literacy artifact more than a diary, despite the title "Sally's Book."

The dialogic journal as hybrid literacy differs from the dialogic journals typically used in teacher-researcher studies (Chiang, 1998) and classrooms (Rose, 1995). In classroom activities, the journals typically relate to texts being read or research questions under consideration. While uses vary widely, journals commonly function as a gathering ground for ideas, questions, and suggestions needed for early drafts of compositions. Dialogic journals that are situated within the context of outreach courses function more as a meeting place for individuals to engage each other. As a hybrid text, their purpose rested in easing the awkwardness that initially shy children and college students felt at their first few meetings together.

Hybrid literacy artifacts such as these occupy multiple genres, forms, and modes of communication. They should be analyzed in terms of which categories they straddle, as opposed to which category they occupy. Perhaps hybrid literacies can be expected in initial interactions between community members and undergraduates during outreach courses. If we see contact zones as meeting places, as Harris (1995) does, then hybrid literacies become a complex forum for initiating communication between individuals from different ethnic, class, and educational backgrounds.

Yet the nature and purposes of these literacies prompted students to question which types of reading and writing they should be doing with community members. With the UCB undergraduates, readers may be tempted to question the rhetorical utility of hybrid literacies because, at first blush, these literacies beg the questions: Whose ends do hybrid literacies really serve? What's their purpose? Literacy practices such as the two mentioned above were critiqued in class for their shortcomings in coherence, audience awareness, ill-defined purpose, and improvised grammar. Such critiques use as baselines for judgment both schooled literacies and progressive discussions about the need for skills and process writing (Delpit, 1995).

When students viewed hybrid literacies in the broader scheme of inner-city residents' educational needs, these literacies seem to offer little in terms of educational advancement and schooled literacy achievement. Before we discuss how these problems were considered during the class, we need to investigate the implications hybrid literacies had for the course specifically and for contact zones generally.

These literacies were necessary to the initial fostering of relations between YMCA youths and the UCB representatives. The dialogic journal served as a safe avenue for Sally and Tanisha to become acquainted with one another. When Sally learns about Tanisha's sister's birthday, Sally writes a series of questions in the journal that both ask for information as well as elicit further self-disclosure from Tanisha.

> Dear Tanisha,
>   How old is she today? Are you going to have a birthday party for her? How does it feel to have five sisters? Are you the oldest? Do you like all of your sisters?
> Your friend, Sally

Tanisha answered all these questions in a note following Sally's entry. Even though Tanisha had not been signing her notes to Sally up until then, her last entry is signed with "Your friend."

The dialogic journal serves the purpose of establishing axes along which Sally and Tanisha can begin to relate to each other, despite their difference in age (12 years) and ethnicity (Sally is Salvadoran American, and Tanisha is African American). The journal allows these two to take initial steps toward a mutually rewarding relation that lasted throughout the semester. When we all arrived at the YMCA on every Wednesday, a YMCA youth acting as a lookout would alert the other children in the gym and multipurpose room that we had made it. Before Sally could even put her backpack down, Tanisha and other girls would meet her by the door, hug her, and ask her to work with them. Almost every visit saw Tanisha and Sally learning together. The journals established lines of communication where none existed before and thus facilitated the early stages of Sally and Tanisha's relationship, a relationship that grew in depth and breadth throughout the semester.

The poison bottle story furthers the scope and tenor of their interactions because they cooperated in its creation. Tanisha suggested they work on telling and transcribing a story; Sally selected the words; Tanisha creatively linked them together; Sally transcribed; and finally Tanisha finished the piece with her drawings. The turn-taking and collaborative process manifested here suggests a mutuality that in itself was the reason and purpose for the literacy event. The story as a type of school-based literacy was not as important as the social relation that initiated and sustained it. Hybrid literacies provide necessary forums for socializing between groups of individuals who typically do not associate together.

These hybrid literacies and those described earlier exist solely from, by, and for social relations. Indeed, these literacies could not exist in and of themselves, could not exist outside the social interactions that initiated, formed, and propelled them. Literacies for socializing do exist, but typically outside of and separate from any curriculum. An ethnography of adolescent girls, Margaret Finders's (1997) book *Just Girls*, shows the deep chasm between social literacies, such as note-passing and 'zine-reading, and schooled literacies: For the adolescent girls from working-class families "literate practices were perceived as avenues to academic success; yet, beyond the sanctions, home literacy practices were constructed very differently from the school practices, and unknowingly, at times, worked against sanctioned practices" (p. 91). These girls' private and social literacies were viewed by themselves and by teachers alike as separate from schooled literacies. And the social interactions that created these literacies took place in contexts where girls and adults were separate from each other. We see in Finders's book, then, evidence of what Hull and Schultz term the newest great divide between schooled literacies and all other literacies (see Introduction, this volume). Service learning seems to provide one way for out-of-school and school-based literacy events to emerge between adults and youths. When service-learning programs are sustained, we believe these hybrid literacy events will become literacy practices between adults and youths (for the distinction between literacy events and practices, see Gee, 1992; Heath, 1983). Service learning seems to provide one way for out-of-school and school-based literacy to intermingle in productive tension.

Hybrid literacies are sustainable only when all the participants value meaning-making with multiple media and genres, and resist the inclination to privilege one kind of literacy to the point of excluding others. These literacies also require a context where adults and youths can interact together in ways that attempt to level the asymmetries typically found in adult–youth interactions without denying the differences in social roles altogether. As you may imagine, hybrid literacies produced tensions for students, instructors, and the YMCA staff as we grappled with the larger social and political effects these literacies may or may not have. Because literacies for socializing were sanctioned in this service-learning curriculum, what counted as literacy soon came up for grabs. Despite their social merit, YMCA youths, students, administrators, and the teachers saw a need to move forward with these literacies. Sally voiced her concerns in class one day during the sixth week when we were discussing their current activities with the YMCA members.

> I'm really questioning like if I'm making a disservice because . . . I sat down with another tutoring program that I'm involved in . . . and wrote a story. She's a second-grader and she wrote the most awesome story . . . six pages. It had a beginning, middle, and end . . . everything made sense. . . . Like she's in the second grade and Tanisha's in the fifth grade. Like there's a big difference . . . in how they write and their abilities to write.

Sally become concerned that she was doing a disservice to the YMCA members in general, and Tanisha in particular, because she was only engaging them in literacies for socializing. She wanted to move away from emphasizing just the social process of hybrid literacies without an equal emphasis on the story as a product and revision for an audience. She acknowledged the social value of hybrid literacies, however, as we'll soon see, and did not want to demean their value in her push to up the intellectual ante.

With Sally, we as teachers wanted to add more structure to the activities without re-creating a school-like environment. Before we even began the semester's activities, Steva, the supervisor at the YMCA, warned us that if we created a school-like atmosphere at the YMCA, we would drive the members away. "They get too much structure and not enough fun and joy at school. I want them to feel like they can move around and learn what they want to," Steva said. Steva's point is interesting because it highlights the schism between school environments for learning, which are by necessity structured around prescribed curricula and in which students don't "move around," and the YMCA's environment for learning, which is more flexibly structured around learning activities that children and adults initiate together, with much more movement between and among participants and workshop areas. Steva quite consciously wanted to make this learning environment something different from the one she perceives school to be. But toward the middle of the semester, Steva also wanted us to reach beyond these goals. In a mid-term meeting at the YMCA, she said that since we had obviously established solid working relations with the children, we needed to begin correcting their grammar more systematically, to get them writing and reading even more. She also asked us to work on small projects that would lead us to some final products that we could show to parents and other YMCA administrators. The YMCA staff and UCB representatives decided, and the YMCA children agreed, that an end of the semester presentation of the children's stories at the YMCA would serve as sufficient motivation for increasing the range of literate activities. The remainder of the chapter explores how Sally created a pedagogy that remained true to her values for hybrid literacies, even as she developed a teaching method to advance the reading and writing activities she did with the YMCA members.

School as a Contact Zone

Hybrid literacies illustrate only one type of reading and writing in one type of contact zone. In the contact zone created at the YMCA, young adults engaged children in a number of reading, writing, and drawing activities. In the course of these activities, participants had to negotiate their various positions—positions conditioned in part by age, education, ethnicity, socio-economic status, language practices—while at the same time negotiating form and genre to produce hybrid texts. But service-learning courses such as this one are predicated on multiple, and mutually sustaining, literacies and contact zones. For instance, the UCB students' reflections on their own experiences in school and with literacy shaped their literacy activities with YMCA members, as we show in this section. In turn, the literacy events at the YMCA shaped the ways students came to see academic literacy and their own writing and reading practices within the university, as we show in the next section. We believe that fostering a dialogic relationship between community-based and academic literacies should be one of the primary functions of service-learning courses.

The undergraduates enrolled in our course found themselves engaging in a number of different types of learning activities over the semester, as they read research reports and theoretical discussions of literacy, observed children's behavior and collected their writing, worked as tutors and mentors, and wrote fieldnotes and essays. As college students, they had had extensive experience with some of these activities—they had been reading and writing, and had been receiving "lessons" in how to read and write, since they were very young—while other activities, such as conducting ethnographic fieldwork or tutoring children, were less familiar. Within the context of a small seminar that provided frequent opportunities to talk and write, students were able to allow the strange and the familiar to inform each other; as they tried out new ways of gathering and creating knowledge, and as they experimented with ways of helping YMCA members learn, they also reflected on what they had been taught in the past and on their present approaches to their studies.

In particular, students offered us and their classmates accounts of their development as language users and as literate people, often prompted by discussions of autobiographical essays in which professional writers described how they had come to write. In this section, we examine a section from Sally's first paper, written in response to our prompt to write a literacy self-portrait; next, we analyze transcriptions of class conversations, in which Sally reflected on her perceptions of herself as a reader and writer. These self-portraits add to our understanding of how Sally approached and framed her interactions with Tanisha. From these examples, we unfold the complex ways both community and academic contact zones mutually reinforce and widen each other.

Sally's Literacy Self-Portrait

> The road to Literacy has been a long and significant journey for me. I immigrated to the United States at 6 years old to this strange new land that everyone back home always talked about. It was surprising to see that not everyone was Salvadorian and that I was the stranger who spoke in an alien tongue. Sure there were others like us, but even they knew a word here or there to communicate with all these new people. Having only preschool under my belt, first grade was a pretty scary place to go to. Although I had a curly-haired little Mexican girl assigned to help me understand things, I felt sad that I couldn't truly share with any of the other children. . . .
>
> The inevitable did happen—I learned English. How could I not when half my days were spent in school and the other half was spent on watching television. My ESL days were over in fourth grade. It was a great milestone in my life not to be taken out of my class to get "Special Help" and to finally enter the Ooh Soo exclusive group of the high reading levels. I wasn't embarrassed to read out loud in class anymore, in fact you could almost bet on my hand being the first one frantically waving in the air whenever the teacher asked for someone to read out loud. Those were the days.
>
> My Spanish was never forgotten though. It was a rule to speak only Spanish at home. Sometimes, though, I feel inept in both languages. I hardly write to the rest of my family in El Salvador because I fear I've spanglicized a word and won't be understood. In English I don't quite have the handle on the fancy terminology and decorative vocabulary that college folk often construct their sentences with.

The opening paragraphs of this essay offer, at first glance, a straightforward and familiar account of being educated as an experience of the American melting pot. The school and the surrounding society blur in these paragraphs: the United States is a "strange new land" and first grade is "a pretty scary place to go to." But after her initial disorientation, and as the result of both her desire and her effort, Sally is assimilated into the linguistic and educational mainstream, an assimilation symbolized by the end of her "ESL days" and her placement in the high track in reading. This "milestone" transforms Sally's attitude toward reading out loud from one of embarrassment to one of eagerness.

But even in these first two paragraphs, Sally hints that her story is not as simple as it might appear on the surface. She capitalizes and puts in quotes the "Special Help" she received in ESL, and similarly calls into question the status of the "Ooh Soo exclusive" reading group she is "finally" allowed to join. The ambivalence that these rhetorical flourishes imply is explored more openly in the third paragraph of the essay, in which Sally claims that at times she feels "inept in both" her languages. Sally's experience was common among her classmates: Five of the seven students enrolled in our course grew up in homes where at least one language other than English was spoken. All the students in the course had "succeeded" during their educational careers, as witnessed by the fact that they were attending a prestigious and exclusive university.

Yet, as Sally's early essay indicates, some of the students also brought to the university and to our project first-hand experience of struggling with language, of feeling unsure about how to speak or read or write, of failing to communicate with important others, especially in an academic context. Sally identifies fancy vocabulary and rhetorical flourishes as earmarks of academic literacy: "I don't quite have the handle on the fancy terminology and decorative vocabulary that college folk often construct their sentences with." Her account of her personal "road to Literacy" suggests the intricacy of her perspective on her own early education and language development.

Her ongoing reflections about her present experiences as a writer in the academy suggest both an embracing of traditional notions of "success" and a desire to honor community-based language. At several points in the semester, we conducted classroom workshops in which we read and discussed students' writing-in-progress. On other occasions, discussion of course readings about literacy and pedagogy prompted students to talk about their experiences of the writing process, both within and outside of the classroom. During these conversations, Sally often judged the lessons that she had learned from other teachers about writing against her own perceptions of how writing worked for her and what made a piece of writing succeed. For example, at the beginning of the semester we photocopied sections of each student's first draft of the research paper and then talked about the strengths of each section. One of the students, Hannah, had written an engaging introduction in which she described her own observations of "everyday" literacy. Many in the class, including Sally, were impressed and surprised by Hannah's skillful use of the first person. Sally had learned to avoid the use of first person in her essays and illustrated this to us through an unflattering imitation of her teacher: "This is your paper, and we already know that these are your thoughts, so why are you gonna put 'I'?" In looking at Hannah's introduction, Sally began to find answers to that challenge, and in subsequent drafts of her own research paper she used the first person to help her establish a thoughtful and personal voice with which to develop her argument. Using the writing and talking that she did in class to reflect on the lessons she had learned about in school, Sally was able to transform the potentially harmful contact zone of the academy where "I" is erased into a space where she could negotiate new understandings of herself in relation to academic writing. Her process of peer review in this academic contact zone contributed to her developing a process of revision in her work with Tanisha.

Respecting Language, Revising Texts

As Sally wrote in the final draft of her paper, she set out at the beginning of the semester "to respect the language that each child used to express themselves, whether it was through verbal language or written language, and not make them think that the way they talked or wrote was incorrect and 'improper.'" We saw earlier that such unconditional respect initially allowed hybrid literacies to flourish in an atmosphere where children and students could begin interacting around and through literacy activities. Sally's assessment of her first few meetings confirms this: "I did not want to offend [Tanisha] by being highly critical of her writing right from the start. This approach allowed her to see that I valued her as a person and that I respected the way she chose to express herself. Emphasizing [this] also helped in the establishment of trust between us as we also got to know one another more." Although she didn't comment on them to the children at first, her careful observations of children as they worked together on reading and writing revealed patterns of oral and written language use that were nonstandard and that began to trouble Sally.

Sally's observations led her to question her decision simply to encourage children without guiding them in any way:

> The mistakes that students made in their writing were being overlooked by me as I positively reinforced their writing and failed to take the responsibility to teach them the literary skills that society expects from each person.

By initially concentrating solely on literacies for social involvement, without revising or correcting grammar, Sally believed that she failed in her duties as an educator and member of this class who had obligations to the service goal of the course. These obligations, as Sally's fieldnotes make clear, do not constitute a one-way street; Sally expected YMCA members to honor her friendship and commit to spending time working with her, in the same way that she came to expect herself to help YMCA members produce texts that would be successful with a range of audiences.

Sally devised what she called the "unification pedagogy" for helping YMCA members in general and Tanisha in particular. To create this pedagogy, Sally engaged in a central aspect of knowledge-making: to build on the work of previous scholars. She explored in some detail Delpit's (1995) typology of "fluency" as opposed to "skills" instruction; she culled models of teaching both skills and fluency from Rose's (1995) *Possible Lives*; and she defined what Stubbs (1986) meant by "Standard English" and concluded "standard English should be taught in a way not to disparage students' native dialect. Finding the way to do this of course is the hard part." Sally went on to consider arguments for emphasizing the writing process and for focusing on "skills" and the final written product when teaching children; she concluded that neither approach was in itself adequate but that the two could be effectively combined.

As she developed this unification pedagogy, she practiced it in the last weeks of the semester. Sally and Tanisha collaborated on a final writing project, a story Tanisha called "The Animal Story." In doing this project, the pair gained experience with prewriting, drafting, and revising; they talked about the needs and expectations of readers; and they produced two distinctly different drafts.

Sally guided Tanisha through brainstorming and writing a rough draft of a story about a sheep dog, reassuring her not to worry about scratching out mistakes and offering to spell words that gave Tanisha trouble. Just as it had been at the beginning of the semester, Sally's stance was supportive, but her willingness to spell words for Tanisha was a shift from her practice at the beginning of the semester, when she encouraged children to sound out words or to spell as best they could. Sally wrote in her final paper that she wanted Tanisha to see her "as a resource whenever she needed help." Her final paper describes how she and Tanisha moved this draft to a more final version. "I asked if she would mind me helping her on spelling, grammar, and her sentences for her second draft. She said no and we got started." Sally's technique was to ask Tanisha a series of questions, evoking the needs and expectations of readers, and then reading Tanisha's work out loud to help her identify areas for revision. Sally had told Tanisha that the

YMCA would soon hold a party at which members could read stories they had written. Thus the two worked with a specific audience in mind and with a compelling incentive to produce a polished final draft. The final draft of "The Animal Story" demonstrates a more polished, audience-aware, developed piece, especially when compared to the "Poison Bottle Story" discussed earlier.

> Once upon a time there was a sheepdog named Sally. Sally's mother was black and white. They lived on a farm with a cow and the cow liked to eat and talk a lot. On Sunday there was a new animal coming to the farm and it was a pig named Babe. Babe wanted to cry because the other animals was talking about babe. Sally had came and said can you please stop talking about babe. Babe is new around here. Would you like if babe talked about you? They said No we are sorry can you forgive us? Babe said yes we can be friends. Sally moved away to new Fish city. Babe started to cry when Sally left. Sally Birthday came and she returned to the farm. Babe and the animals said happy Birthday friend. So Sally moved back to the farm they were best friend and they stayed together forever.

Sally's process of asking Tanisha questions about the story, and prompting revision through calling the writer's attention to a reader's possible response, allowed her, as she wrote in her final paper, to focus "on skills or product without being critical." Just as the initial hybrid literacies Sally and Tanisha created together in their early interactions worked to establish a relationship of mutual trust, so this final writing project helped fulfill the promise of that mutual trust, as each partner honored her obligations to the other. Before they began to write, Tanisha told Sally "that this time she wasn't going to leave me to go to the park and that she wanted to work on a story with me." Likewise, Sally reassured Tanisha that she would help her through the writing and revision process, essentially promising that she, too, "wasn't going to leave."

Contact Zones Made Real

Through our look at the multiple contact zones of the academy and the community, we have seen some ways in which our ideas about "literacy" in and out of school may be extended. Hybrid literacies allowed YMCA members to express their ideas, questions, interests, and concerns to a respectfully engaged audience of peers and adults. These literacies stem from, center solely on, and promote social interaction between the individuals involved in their creation. They're invitations to YMCA members to voice their own perspectives and to engage others as they do so. These literacies offer individuals, in the words of Harste and colleagues (1988), "one of the most valuable gifts we can give language users": the social interaction and resources necessary to "litter their environment with enticing language opportunities and guarantee them the freedom to experiment with them" (p. 334).

As the Richmond Community Literacy Project develops a collaboration with the Cortez Elementary School, we hope to further articulate the precise ways the after-school program relates to and expands on the curriculum teachers already have in place. Specifically, we believe service-learning courses introduce a collaborative, enticing, and respectful audience to youths who want to be listened to, addressed, and talked with, using both oral and written language. Hybrid literacies grow out of invitations to express one's self, to explore self-affirming literacies, to describe and characterize one's cultural and social world to immediate audiences of peers and university representatives. Other investigations in this kind of collaboration have revealed initial success and potential.

In order to offer ninth-graders an immediate and attentive audience for their writing, Heath and Branscombe (1985) established a teacher-researcher relationship in which they set up letter writing teams between the ninth-graders, upperclassmen, and Shirley Heath and her daughter Shannon. They ask: "are there ways the school can improve communicator-audience relations of students and thus advance the 'intelligence'—i.e., the social-relation capacity—of those who have been judged by previous measures of school intelligence to be inferior or unacceptable communicators and audiences?" (p. 4). All but three of the students in Branscombe's class had been in special education classes and had tested "between 75 and 85" on the Stanford-Binet Intelligence Test (p. 4). Yet when given an engaged audience to correspond with, these students "acquired writing instead of learning simply to imitate styles of a limited number of types of decontextualized academic writing" (p. 31). Branscombe's students' low test scores and cultural backgrounds parallel those of the Cortez YMCA members; and like Branscombe's students, the YMCA members developed written language skills in "a rich responsive context" (p. 30), where social relations with the audience presented both the means to develop, and the reasons for developing, communicative skills. School, university, and community collaborations make possible an array of writing activities, resources, and audiences that ask all involved to bring to bear their concrete linguistic skills in immediate communicative contexts.

Hybrid literacies also engendered the careful reflection of undergraduates on their own literacy experiences, leading students such as Sally to question lessons about writing learned in school and to define for themselves who an audience was and the sort of feedback they expected from readers. Thus this service-learning course helped students challenge, and ultimately reconceive, the decontextualized academic essay with its rigid rules (don't use "I") and its audience of one, the teacher or professor. Instead, Sally and her classmates wrote for an audience that actually showed up in our classroom to view students' poster presentations at the end of the semester; this audience included familiar supervisors from the YMCA and unfamiliar scholars and community members interested in the project.

The same experiences and opportunities for reflection convinced Sally and other classmates that there was a place for teaching and learning, even outside of school—indeed, the relationships that developed between UCB students and YMCA members obligated each to teach and to learn from the other. Consistent throughout the semester was the participants' commitment to establishing relationships of trust and support; but as students read, discussed, wrote, and worked at the YMCA, they began to see that they could provide close attention to the details of children's writing—details such as spelling, grammar, and topical coherence that would make a difference for readers—within the trusting and supportive relationships they had created. Indeed, Sally was particularly struck by a metaphor used by Delpit (1995, p. 18), which she related in her own words during class discussion mid-semester:

> I love that quote that . . . she was talking about comparing white teachers and black teachers. "White teachers say 'Let me . . . let me hear your voices. And let me hear the song that you sing. And I will, I will make sure not to criticize it.'" And then she said, "Whereas a black teacher would say, 'Great. I hear your song, but let me teach you different notes . . . so you can harmonize with the rest.'" And I really like that because it summarizes everything.

Delpit's metaphor might also be an apt image to keep in mind as we envision the contact zones created when people of different ages, ethnicities, linguistic histories, and educational backgrounds come together—and particularly when they come together to read and write. As university outreach programs grow in popularity and become more established, and as after-school programs spring up to address the local needs of communities and their children, classroom teachers may be asked to work more closely with university students and their instructors, with representatives of service agencies, and with the parents of schoolchildren. Our own experience suggests that such collaborations may be unfamiliar and uncomfortable for many—at least at first—as people redefine their roles and relationships and as they reconsider their goals and values with new collaborating partners. But such collaborations, we believe, can offer language and literacy teachers and tutors, at all levels, fresh perspectives on what it means to teach, to read, and to write. When outreach projects and service-learning courses provide opportunities for students to consider published scholarship in light of their own experiences (and vice versa), and when university, school, and community participants are able to establish mutually support-ive relationships, then the reading and writing that emerge from their inter-actions may harmonize with what we know as "academic" and "out-of-school" literacies. And in that harmonizing, these literacies may also help us listen for something new.

References

Bacon, N. (1997). Community service writing: Problems, challenges, questions. In L. Adler-Kassner, R. Crooks, & A. Watters (Eds.), *Writing the community: Con-cepts and models for service-learning in composition* (pp. 39–55). Washing-ton, DC: American Association for Higher Education.

Brack, G. W., & Hall, L. R. (1997). Combining the classroom and the community: Service-learning in composition at Arizona State University. In L. Adler-Kassner, R. Crooks, & A. Watters (Eds.), *Writing the community: Concepts and models for service-learning in composition* (pp. 143–152). Washington, DC: Ameri-can Association for Higher Education.

Brandt, D. (1990). *Literacy as involvement: The acts of writers, readers, and texts.* Carbondale: Southern Illinois University Press.

Bridwell-Bowles, L. (1997). Service-learning: Help for higher education in a new millennium? In L. Adler-Kassner, R. Crooks, & A. Watters (Eds.), *Writing the community: Concepts and models for service-learning in composition* (pp. 19–28). Washington, DC: American Association for Higher Education.

Chiang, Y. S. (1998). Insider/outsider/other. In C. Anson & C. Farris (Eds.), *Under construction: Working at the intersections of theory, research and practice* (pp. 150–165). Logan: Utah State University Press.

Delpit, L. (1995). *Other people's children: Cultural conflict in the classroom.* New York: The New Press.

Dyson, A. H. (1999). Coach Bombay's kids learn to write: Children's appropriation of media material for school literacy. *Research in the Teaching of English, 33*(4), 367–403.

Ed-Data. (2000). *California public school profiles.* ⟨http://www.ed-data.k12.ca.us/dev/School.asp⟩.

Finders, M. (1997). *Just girls: Hidden literacies and life in junior high.* New York: Teachers College Press.

Flower, L. (1997). Partners in inquiry: A logic for community outreach. In L. Adler-Kassner, R. Crooks, & A. Watters (Eds.), *Writing the community: Concepts and models for service-learning in composition* (pp. 95-117). Washington, DC: American Association for Higher Education.

Gee, J. P. (1992). *The social mind: Language, ideology, and social practice.* New York: Bergin & Garvey.

Geisler, C. (1994). *Academic literacy and the nature of expertise.* Mahweh, NY: Erlbaum.

Goodman, Y. (1988). The development of initial literacy. In E. R. Kintgen, B. M. Kroll, & M. Rose (Eds.), *Perspectives on literacy* (pp. 312-320). Carbondale: Southern Illinois University Press.

Harris, J. (1995). Renegotiating the contact zone. *Journal of Basic Writing, 14,* 27-42.

Harste, J. C., Woodward, V. A., & Burke, C. L. (1988). Rethinking development *and* organization. In E. R. Kintgen, B. M. Kroll, & M. Rose (Eds.), *Perspectives on literacy* (pp. 321-347). Carbondale: Southern Illinois University Press.

Heath, S. B. (1983). *Ways with words: Language, life, and work in communities and classrooms.* Cambridge, UK: Cambridge University Press.

Heath, S. B., & Branscombe, A. (1985). "Intelligent writing" in an audience community: Teacher, students, and research. In S. W. Freedman (Ed.), *The acquisition of written language: Response and revision* (pp. 3-32). Norwood, NJ: Ablex.

Heilker, P. (1997). Rhetoric made real: Civic discourse and writing beyond the curriculum. In L. Adler-Kassner, R. Crooks, & A. Watters (Eds.), *Writing the community: Concepts and models for service-learning in composition* (pp. 71-77). Washington, DC: American Association for Higher Education.

Odell, L. (1995). Basic writing in context: Rethinking academic literacy. *Journal of Basic Writing, 14,* 43-57.

Peck, W. C., Flower, L., & Higgins, L. (1995). Community literacy. *College Composition and Communication, 46*(2), 199-222.

Pratt, M. L. (1991). Arts of the contact zone. *Profession, 91,* 33-40.

Prior, P. (1998). *Writing/disciplinarity.* Mahweh, NJ: Erlbaum.

Rose, M. (1995). *Possible lives: The promise of public education in America.* Boston: Houghton Mifflin.

Stubbs, M. (1986). *Educational linguistics.* Oxford: Blackwell.

Porfirio M. Loeza Responds

As a teacher, I find captivating notions of contact zones, social spaces, and hybrid literacies. These notions paradoxically lead to alternative ways of viewing literacy practices. The paradox lies in that we normally connect literacy practices to school settings and Cushman and Emmons bridge these contact zones to out-of-school settings. The conceptual juxtapositioning of hybrid literacies and contact zones forges an intense portrait of literacy practices. While hybridity evokes reading and writing activities that occupy multiple categories, as Cushman and Emmons state, contact zones are social spaces full of tension and often reflect contexts where asymmetrical power relations exist. Seemingly, these contact zones also exist in the classroom, yet there are qualitatively distinct contact zones created in schools and classrooms. Given state mandates for curriculum standards, must the school context necessarily create borders between official and unofficial texts, as Cushman and Emmons assert? From my perspective as a classroom teacher, this type of research resonates with in-school literacy practices in a number of interesting ways.

Schools also contain contact zones where social spaces are disputed. In these social spaces cultures also meet, clash, and grapple with each other. In keeping with the notion of hybridity, these disputed contact zones in our schools, particularly urban schools, seem to be a consequence of hybrid social spaces. The asymmetrical power relations are also quite cogent: Texts stand in specific ahistorical relationship to students in our classrooms, and few have a stake in what they read. The concept of "hybrid literacies," reading and writing activities that occupy multiple categories, broadens the social space where hybrid practices can flourish. These expanded social spaces can also be re- and co-constructed in our classrooms. But how do we foster the dialogic relationship between community-based and academic literacies that was part of Cushman and Emmons's service learning courses? Part of the answer appears to lie in engaging students in a number of different types of activities, similar to what took place in the university service-learning course.

In my teaching practice, a reverberating theme from this chapter was Sally Viera's important question regarding how to fulfill our educational duty as teachers while meeting our social responsibilities as educators. I would like to think that embedded in literacies for social involvement are the technical aspects of literacy and that we indeed meet our social obligations as educators. This seems to be Sally's intention behind her "unification pedagogy." Yet, contrary to Tanisha, as a UCB student Sally is capable of embracing traditional notions of "success" and of honoring community-based language. This capability is strengthened by her personal experience of struggling with language and of successfully dealing with various academic contexts. It is precisely Sally's personal and academic experiences that allow her to foster this dialogic relationship between community-based and academic literacies. Indeed, this may be the very reason she enrolled in this service-learning course. Using Cushman and Emmons's words, she has access to multiple and mutually sustaining literacies and contact zones. Although Tanisha through Sally and the Y may also have access to these contact zones, her schooling experience is another matter.

Service-learning education makes available a certain dialogic authenticity that is missing in our public school classrooms. There are a couple of major advantages that the "Social Issues of Literacy" students had. First, they were able to juxtapose and contrast their two learning contexts. There is a crude but real distinction between both of these social spaces. In fact, the second advantage is that they were able to both physically and emotionally distance themselves from each of these contexts. Thus they were able to develop a contrastive discourse in one social space regarding the other one. This is a major advantage that is very difficult to replicate in our schools. Tanisha, for example, was able to take advantage of Sally's hybridity of experiences but was likely left with few resources to access what should be a dialogic curriculum in her classroom.

Just as Cushman and Emmons experienced in their service-learning university course, maybe in the classroom mutuality in the interaction and in the sharing of the final product can also nourish the creation of these hybrid literacies. This seems to be the intent behind the "career academies" that my school district is setting up. When I began my teaching career some 10 years ago, authenticity was a big issue. We were to seek authenticity in our assessment and instruction. Hybrid spaces and literacies evoke something much more real than mere authenticity. Hybrid literacies seem more inclusive. Whereas authentic assessment was simply to include the instructional practices of a classroom, hybrid literacies go further by including the participants in a dialogic classroom curriculum. What a noble idea to include in a dialogic relationship the literacy practices of those who will actually be practicing those literacies.

Given what I consider the real but major distractions surrounding issues of race, ethnicity, linguistic differences, and educational background, we also need a "unification pedagogy" that will come to serious terms with how to improve our schools. As a bilingual teacher in California, focusing on whether to teach in English or use a native language is a case in point. Teachers and students must begin to redefine their roles and relationships, as Cushman and Emmons declare. Hybrid literacies reconsider the goals and values of each collaborator in a new partnership. Learners (and yes, the teacher is also a learner) should be able to develop communicative skills in which the means to develop and the reasons to develop them are responsive to an alternative multiplicity of literacy practices. This premises a trustful and supportive relationship in which each partner honors each other. The net consequence has to be that social spaces are created where official and unofficial texts (oral and written) meet, clash, grapple, and ultimately converge.

Sarah Jewett Responds

Having coordinated and evaluated youth literacy programs situated within university-based community service programs in the past, I read Cushman and Emmons's piece with particular interest. Their text gave me the opportunity to celebrate that which is hopeful in community–university partnerships and also to imagine the critical work that we might still undertake in these contexts.

I am heartened by the coursework that is central to this literacy endeavor. Since the University of California at Berkeley (UCB) mentors and tutors are simultaneously enrolled in "Social Issues of Literacy," they have the opportunity to construct, question, challenge, and rethink their notions of reading and writing, and to consider their multiple meanings in both the learning contexts of the university and of the YMCA community program. For undergraduates potentially without pedagogical grounding, the course offers a place to develop practical and theoretical knowledge, which is then informed and (re)shaped by their literacy experiences with the youth at the Y. Without a significant learning and reflection component, such as this course, we offer a disservice to both learning communities by implicitly sending the message that "inner-city" programs will take *whatever* services universities have to offer, whether or not they have been honed for a particular collaboration.

I am also excited by the "hybrid literacies" that are at the heart of this community program—literacies that are "created by, from, and for social interaction." The interactions between the Y youth and the UCB students provide opportunities to reach beyond the confines of "school literacy" and to create and construct texts that are potentially transformative. The vignette about Ruth and Thomas powerfully illustrates this point. Ruth's "invitation" to Thomas made him "realize that something he had to say mattered." He presented this message in a "literacy artifact that was part story, part newspaper movie review, part art." For Thomas, spurned by his peers and labeled by his teachers, literacy at the Y became a medium through which he was able to "redefine himself." In this way, persons rather than tasks fuel the significant processes of literacy.

236

I remain concerned, however, that these "collaborative efforts" are still designed with *university* life situated in the foreground. The university chooses the communities in which to initiate these kinds of literacy programs—this particular one portrayed as the "forgotten inner city" overshadowed by the infamous Oakland. Its efforts are always linked to widely publicized and broad-based initiatives, such as the "Berkeley Pledge," which highlight the university's commitment to its surrounding communities. The schedules of such programs, too, are invariably linked to university timetables. Students' and instructors' daily schedules are bounded by course time slots, and weekly schedules are directed by semesterly commitments. Thus busy undergraduates juggling these university-constructed versions of time can allot only *one* afternoon a week for *one* semester to the program at the Y. Even the concept of literacy itself is shaped primarily by a university course that seeks to examine theory and practice in the contexts of the academy and the community.

It is not that I question the university's social, political, and economic obligation to forge connections with the surrounding communities. It should undertake such endeavors. It must. It is not that I question the enthusiasm with which UCB students are received. Underresourced community program staff are always appreciative of capable assistance, and young students are often eager to occupy the center of undergraduate attention. It is not that I question the significance of the relationships that UCB and Y students form as they co-construct their literate selves. Through Ruth and Thomas, Sally and Tanisha, and Newman and Trisha, we realize the powerful connections among trust, patience, and literacy.

Yet I want to imagine what a program might look like if *community* life were situated in the foreground instead—where communities design university initiatives, where the daily and yearly school schedules of youth shape university commitments of time, and where university students begin their study of literacy in the context of the home lives of their young partners. Without this remapping of power, I wonder whether community-service programs will foster the kinds of long-term changes that will yield a more just and equitable society.

Part IV

REALITIES AND POSSIBILITIES IN THE COMMUNITY

8

Got Some Time, Got a Place, Got the Word

Collaborating for Literacy Learning and Youth Development

ELYSE EIDMAN-AADAHL

I can't say that I was thrilled to learn my first teaching assignment at West-minster Senior High School would include advising the student newspaper. I was nervous enough to be teaching literature—a subject I ostensibly knew something about. I knew nothing about producing a newspaper.

A weekend workshop sponsored by the Baltimore Sun Papers and filled with old hands at the adviser's game helped a bit. I learned a few things that seemed like actual journalism skills: counting headlines (a skill since made irrelevant by computers), a few principles of editing, a few principles of layout. But mostly the talk was about working with young people—my newspaper staff. I learned that my editorial board, a group of eight shaggy 16-year-olds, was expected to actually be in charge—not me. I learned the first issue had to get out by the end of September, so there was no time to teach first, publish later. We'd just have to get to work and learn together in the midst of the doing.

But mostly the old hands stressed that a newspaper ran on love. Not love for *me*, of course—love for *it*. My future editors, photographers, layout artists, and advertising execs would need to love being on the staff, to love the tradition of the paper itself, to love the responsibility, even to love just being in the newspaper office with its special smells and purposeful clutter. Being part of the newspaper would need to fill deeper needs than the osten-sible goals of learning to write, to think critically, to practice effective design. Nothing else would motivate the long hours, the endless rewrites, the tedious fund-raising. Nothing else would lead to more growth in literacy skills.

Over time I came to understand why and how our student newspaper was such a powerful learning environment for my students—including many young people not otherwise succeeding in school. Similar observations could be made about drama, art, athletics, and student government. We who were coaches and advisers saw unique opportunities in the hours after school when bells never rang in the middle of important work and when all of us could come and go without the heavy hand of schoolday surveillance. But we also appreciated that powerful literacy work could go on during the schoolday, albeit in smaller chunks of time and more restricted spaces, and worked to make that happen. After all, we were teacher and students together then, too.

Lately, I have come to reflect on those years with the student newspaper not just in the context of literacy learning but also in the context of "youth development." An emerging network of scholars and policy makers have since taught me to think of my "colleagues" more broadly than simply the close-at-hand network of teachers and literacy researchers I already knew. My colleagues are also those adults McLaughlin, Irby, and Langman (1994) call the *wizards*: Little League coaches and community drama producers, youth activists and Girls Inc. coordinators, detached youth workers and community health practitioners. As depicted in *Urban Sanctuaries: Neighborhood Organizations in the Lives and Futures of Inner-City Youth,* wizards are those passionate youth leaders who manage to create and sustain environments "that capture adolescents' time, attention, and loyalty" (McLaughlin et al., 1994, p. 37).

Looking at the past 30 years of literacy theory and practice, I wonder: How would we now understand literacy—what it is, what it could be for—if we and our theories had been in conversation with them? How might my own practice with young people have been different if our newspaper had been housed in a peer health clinic, a garage-based 'zine, or a community development agency?

School's Out! raises such questions. The authors and educators collected here advance sociocultural views of literacy that could not have been achieved unless researchers resisted the easy association of literacy and schooling and learned to look elsewhere. But now, having achieved these new understandings, what difference should they make? What would it mean for literacy practitioners to look elsewhere? The editors are clear about the implications:

> There is no better time for literacy theorists and researchers, long practiced in detailing successful literate practices that occur out of school, to put their

energies toward investigating potential relationships, collaborations, and help-ful divisions of labor between schools and formal classrooms and the informal learning that flourishes in a range of settings out of school. (Chapter 2, this volume)

Many agree there is no better time to investigate potential relationships and helpful divisions of labor among university-based, school-based, and community-based educators and researchers. No better time—no more challenging time. As a nation, we are currently in the midst of a frenzy of attention to *both* "school" and "after-school." The very partners we might seek are in the midst of historic realignments and escalating pressures. The pressures on schools in general and literacy curricula in particular are well known to teachers and researchers. Less well known is the policy work focusing on youth once school's out, work that presents extraordinary op-portunities and considerable risks. In this chapter, I summarize the political context for collaboration among in-school and out-of-school educators by looking at policy perspectives on non-school time, on youth organizations, and on school–community partnerships. I also raise several caveats that must be addressed if collaborations among researchers and educators work-ing across the school–community boundary are to serve the vision of liter-acy learning advocated in this book.

It's 5 O'clock. Do You Know Where Your Children Are?

It is not surprising that policies concerning youth and learning frequently start with schools. Schools are, after all, so easy to find. The American pub-lic school system enrolls more than 46.7 million students and employs 2.8 million teachers across a vast number of easily identifiable buildings.[1] The majority of these young people and adults are required to be located in a specific place for a specific time on specific days, and a substantial body of law details the nuances of these requirements. In contrast to 19th-century Americans, 21st-century Americans—including literacy researchers—can feel confident they know where to find young people and their teachers between the hours of 9:00 A.M. and 3:00 P.M. But when we shift the clock to the hours between 3:00 P.M. and 6:00 P.M., Americans are less sanguine.

Since the late 1970s, families and policy makers in the United States have become absorbed with the "problem" of young people during non-school hours. Set against a backdrop of fundamental changes in American family and community life from 1950 to the present, a range of studies and foundation reports have raised alarms about the quality of life for young people between the close of the schoolday and the return of parents from work. Foremost among them, the Carnegie Council on Adolescent Development's (1992b) report *A Matter of Time: Risk and Opportunity in the Non-school Hours* issued a clarion call to action that rivaled *A Nation at Risk*'s impact on school policy. What was the matter with young people's time? The report was clear: "By any standards, America's young adolescents have a great deal of discretionary time. Much of it is unstructured, unsupervised, and unproductive for the young person" (p. 10). Allowances for the diversity of adolescent lives aside, the report goes on to suggest that "only 60 percent of adolescents' waking hours are committed to such essentials as school, homework, eating, chores or paid employment, while fully 40 percent are discretionary" (p. 10).

Researchers documenting literate practices among young people in the non-school hours might be surprised to find themselves participating in a debate about the productivity of youth or the value of discretionary time, but they would be wise to prepare to do so. Since the 1980s attempts to characterize youth's "unproductive" time and to locate young people in time and space during the non-school hours have occupied researchers across a range of domains. As summarized in *A Matter of Time* (Carnegie Council on Adolescent Development, 1992b), we learn that the average junior high school student in America spends 28.7 hours per week in school and 3.2 hours studying, while a Japanese counterpart spends 46.6 hours in school and 16.2 hours studying. We learn that 27% of the 25,000 eighth-graders surveyed in the National Education Longitudinal Study spend 2 or more hours at home alone after school and that eighth-graders whose families are in the lowest socioeconomic group are home alone for 3 hours. We learn that many adolescents spend this time without the companionship of adults, while others are with adults who exploit them. We learn that young people might be variously located in private space, public space, commercial space, or stolen space—but that many report having no "safe" space. We learn that during the 3 hours after the close of school young people are at the greatest risk for criminal behavior, for engaging in self-harming or risky behaviors, or for simply enduring stultifying boredom. Virtually no reports suggest that young people might be using this time to "use writing to do social work" as Skilton-Sylvester (Chapter 3, this volume) reports of Nan. These private or self-sponsored literacy practices have no policy presence.

What does have policy presence in debates about out-of-school time is *absence*—the presence of time in the absence of space. Young people themselves speak to this issue, claiming in numerous polls and focus groups that they have nowhere to go. Younger children often find space in public libraries, many of which offer literacy programs and settings for the young people now known as latch-key kids (National Center for Education Statistics [NCES], 1990b). But older youth increasingly find themselves an unwelcome presence in many community spaces. Unlike other industrialized countries such as Great Britain, the United States has no national system of youth clubs, recreation centers, or programs with their attendant professionals bringing supervision to out-of-school time. Families are left to provide for their children out of their own resources, and an increasing number of families are hard-pressed to do so. Not surprisingly, recent polls such as those conducted by the Afterschool Alliance (2000, January) show strong support from families of all income levels for expanded programming for youth in the after-school hours, with access and affordability being their strongest concerns.

What are literacy practitioners and theorists to make of all this? Even a cursory reading of the political discourse around the concept of "out-of-school time" reveals that young people's time is characterized as open frontier, undisciplined and ownerless, waiting to be colonized. In the absence of contravening portrayals of how young people might spend their discretionary time, images of victimhood or representations of threat predominate. Like previous policy rhetoric about "youth," the current debate easily deconstructs to reveal "youth" as a container for adult fears and projections, racism and class bias (Fine & Mechling, 1993). It also deconstructs into similar dichotomies of work and play, consumption and production, currently shaping debates about youth in schools. Some might be tempted to withdraw from the fray rather than participate in a movement so permeated by stereotypical visions of youth. However, as Fine and Mechling (1993) argue, "to treat the child merely as a 'text' of adult anxieties and politics falls far short of our adult responsibilities for the lives of children" (p. 121). So how can literacy theorists and practitioners be helpful within the context of discourses around non-school time?

First, we might work with young people themselves to investigate the question of young people's discretionary time and the potential for literacy work in richer detail than the broad survey work most often referenced in reports. Any portrait of young people in their non-school hours must account for the complexities of family, ethnicity, and culture; expectations for different ages, genders, and economic locations; and the design of public and private spaces in particular communities. Such a portrait also needs to wrestle with questions of youth culture and youth employment in all their productive and reproductive aspects. Rather than assuming an open territory waiting to be filled with the desires and designs of adults, we might assume a territory already populated with the designs and desires of young people themselves, constructing literacy work around the borders and intersections. Rather than simply investigating the relationship of literacy to social and economic capital as conventionally defined by government indices or funding priorities, we might also support young people in exploring the relationship of literacy to outcomes valued by young people themselves.

Literacy theorists might also help enrich the policy discourses on *space*. Where are the spaces where productive literacy practices thrive? How are they designed? How can they be enriched? How do we conceptualize literacy work in cyberspace in relation to policies concerned with locating the adolescent body in actual space? Programs such as Fifth Dimension, described by McNamee and Sivright (Chapter 6, this volume), as well as the incredible number of youth-oriented and youth-controlled sites on the Internet, scramble questions of time, space, location, body, identity, and interaction. As a heavily text-dependent space, cyberspace pushes the boundaries of our understanding of the relationship between text and context—with implications for the literacy practices of young people. Similarly, the roles of media, popular culture, and commercial space, given their centrality in the "discretionary" lives of young people, may be richer sites for literacy theory and practice than many adults, including literacy researchers, imagine. Although we as a society invest heavily in the construction of young people as consumers of popular culture, we rarely take them seriously as producers of culture or view them as consumers capable of sophistication and discernment.

And finally, we might take seriously the question of *actual* space, public space, as a site for literacy practices. As we look at actual communities, we might consider whether it is possible within the construction of specific places for young people to be drawn in to literacy events as they move through public space. Do communities offer places where young people can experience "legitimate peripheral participation" (Lave & Wenger, 1991) in positive literacy practices constitutive of widening circles of interaction and influence?

Given the policy attention to out-of-school time, theorists and practitioners seeking to work with young people in the after-school hours are likely to find opportunities for funding, willing partners, and supportive policy environments. However, the goals these funders, partners, and policy makers value may or may not be the same as those of the communities and young people themselves. Who sponsors literacy work and why is a question for any literacy practitioner to consider. We may find that much is sponsored by the family and is highly dependent on the capacities of families to navigate larger systems. We may find that much is directly sponsored by media or linked to a commodity culture that constructs young people as consumers. Some might be sponsored by municipalities or philanthropists interested in invigorating public life. Still more will be sponsored, in effect, by the will and energies of young people themselves, particularly if we work to put ever more useful tools at their disposal. Theorizing and acting to enhance the potential of equity and access to more powerful literacy environments across all these spheres may have powerful effects.

Can You Count a Thousand Points of Light?

A significant sponsor of work with young people in the non-school hours is the loose network of nonprofit youth-serving organizations and agencies that are scattered across our communities. Through these organizations, many young people do find spaces where they can voluntarily spend their discretionary time. Increasingly, policy makers have sought to link concerns about out-of-school time with a growing interest in this nonprofit sector—that hazy and indistinct territory lit, in George Bush's memorable phrase, by "a thousand points of light."

In testimony before the House Select Committee on Children, Youth and Families, Karen Pittman (1991) characterized youth-serving agencies and organizations as an essential part of the web of supports that extends from the family outward. These are the organizations that offer young people a chance to take healthy risks, to make real choices and contributions, and to form lasting relationships. "These are organizations, programs and people across the country who are delivering what our youth—even our most vulnerable youth—need. Their knowledge, activities and achievements, however, have not been adequately documented," she noted (1991, p. 17).

At the time, the most recent *Directory of American Youth Organizations* listed more than 400 national youth-serving organizations and more than 17,000 nonprofits. The numbers have since grown. The diversity of these organizations is stunning: They range from multimillion-dollar national organizations such as Boys and Girls Clubs to voluntary neighborhood organizations operating without paid staff or facilities. They may be free-standing youth-serving organizations or may operate within larger organizations with a religious, ethnic, or dues-paying membership base. A number of programs cross sectors with juvenile justice, public health, or mental health agencies and are intended to work with youth under direction of the state. Others operate as enrichment programs—often for a fee, sometimes for a profit. Collectively, they touch the lives of many young people. The large national organizations such as 4-H, YWCA, and YMCA alone regularly enroll an estimated 30 million children and youth. Using the 1988 National Education Longitudinal Study (NCES, 1990a) as a window, over 70% of our nation's eighth-graders report participating in some sort of organized out-of-school activity.

What we know about these organizations comes from a growing body of program surveys and case study literature,[2] as well as from our experiences as youth, parents, and volunteers. Allowing for the wide variation in scale and capacity, some generalizations exist (Heath & McLaughlin, 1993; McLaughlin et al., 1994). These organizations tend to have broader missions than schools and to be strongly mission-driven. Many have distinct histories and reference their traditions in ways that define their organizational cultures and approach to service delivery (James, 1993). The activities they sponsor are extraordinarily diverse, including recreation, arts and cultural activities, homework help and tutoring services, health and therapeutic counseling, mentoring services, employment training, and community development projects. Apart from organizations related to the juvenile justice or child-care systems, most depend on the voluntary participation of young people and their families—and most therefore can give stronger attention to what their participants want, need, and can contribute than schools can or do.

In their local form, these organizations tend to be smaller and more loosely structured than schools, with a diverse funding base and significant presence of volunteers. Their structures make it likely, if not imperative, that young people themselves will exercise significant responsibilities and leadership roles. With a clear entrepreneurial imperative, these organizations need to maintain a flexible managerial design and can experiment with creative approaches to basic organizational issues. They may also be driven by the demon of constant fund-raising, buffeted by mercurial changes in priorities or falling assets in the local funding base and therefore unable to sustain long-term programming. Since organizational capacity is sometimes precarious, opportunities to expand programming or develop partnerships may actually be experienced as burdens, weakening systems rather than strengthening them (Langman & McLaughlin, 1993).

Paid staff and volunteers, particularly those who work directly with youth, are likely to be young, underpaid, and nonunionized. They are often drawn to youth work out of a spirit of deep commitment, much like the spiritual commitment that Long, Peck, and Baskins (Chapter 5, this volume) describe as the foundation of Pittsburgh's Community House. However, most staff will have little access to training and few opportunities for advancement; they are not likely to have participated in any certification programs (*Youth Development*, 1999). Staff morale and frequent turnover are often reported as core organizational challenges (McLaughlin et al., 1994). However, these same staff are more likely than teachers to match the ethnic and linguistic character of the communities they serve, to live in the communities where they work, and to position themselves as youth advocates. Case studies of successful programs consistently find that the quality of staff is key to programs young people find powerful and attractive (McLaughlin et al., 1994).

Collectively, these organizations are a significant site for literacy work. Indeed, literacy researchers and practitioners might be surprised at the eagerness with which many of these organizations respond to overtures and offers of help. Leaders of the most successful organizations are, as McLaughlin and colleagues suggest (1994), wizards at seeking and exploiting the resources of a community in favor of young people. They have to be. They are clear about what they need: more opportunities for their young participants, more resources, more space, more equipment, and especially more adults to take an active interest in the young people they work with. They are likely to have another set of needs as well: needs for evaluation expertise or technology planning, needs for routine clerical or bookkeeping help, needs for staff training or help with personnel plans, and certainly help with fund-raising. Educators used to the lumbering bureaucracy of a university or school district may be stunned at the speed with which these flexible organizations move toward action, quickly sealing "partnerships" with a handshake.

In contrast to the for-profit sector or the street settings of detached youth work, nonprofit and community-based organizations may be a more familiar home for literacy practitioners and researchers. However, before we rush to be of service to the nonprofits in our communities, we should give thought to how our efforts can be constituted within a mutually beneficial partnership, with real reciprocity and mutual learning that supports the organizational development of the host organization. Partnerships of this sort, be they constructed around volunteer action, community-driven literacy projects, or university outreach, are actual "contact zones," as Cushman and Emmons (Chapter 7, this volume) argue in their reflection on a university-based service-learning course conducted in partnership with a local YMCA. Their work examines the significance and challenge of hybrid *literacies*, but also points to the importance of crafting hybrid *organizational work practices*. Cushman and Emmons document a learning partnership between the YMCA staff and the university coordinators that stretched the boundaries of their communities of practice. They continue: "Our own experience suggests that such collaborations may be unfamiliar and uncomfortable for many—at least at first—as people redefine their roles and relationships, and as they reconsider their goals and values with new collaborations partners."

Stretching the boundaries of structures and expectations offers an opportunity for deep learning for partners with the luxury to reflect and explore; it may present a dangerous burden for partners at the limits of their organizational capacity. And, indeed, we must consider who stretches to meet whom? As the numerous scholars and advocates interested in the non-profit sector continue to repeat: These organizations survive and provide social value precisely because they can work in flexible, responsive ways with a constituent community. Literacy theorists and practitioners might follow Sarah Jewett's lead and "imagine what a program might look like if *community* life were situated in the foreground instead" (Chapter 7, this volume). Literacy researchers do these organizations, and the young people in them, a disservice by conceptualizing them simply as sites for research or placements for university students that we can enter and abandon as we choose. Universities or other sponsors do these organizations a disservice if they are unwilling to reconsider outreach policies to make it possible for literacy theorists and practitioners to work in real partnership with organizations in the community. These policies include not only funding and program design, but also decisions about how to document outreach efforts and evaluate them as part of tenure decisions (Boyer, 1990; Crosson, 1985; Lynton, 1995). Finally, literacy theorists and practitioners will find this an important moment to raise such questions as how escalating federal involvement in youth policy has made these organizations into centerpieces of public/private ventures into youth development.

From "Fixing Youth" to "Youth Development": A Foundation for Collaboration

Since the 1980s, as America has become increasingly critical of its public schools, programs and organizations outside of schools have become important as sites for federal, state, and foundation involvement. We can trace much of the current attention to youth development organizations to the active engagement of the Carnegie Corporation and its decision to form, in 1986, the Council on Adolescent Development. Seen as an heir to the tradition established by James Coleman's chairmanship of the Panel on Youth in the mid-1970s, the council began issuing a series of reports that aimed to expand the conversation about young people and their well-being far beyond the limited focus on academics characteristic of *A Nation at Risk*.

Beginning with the publication of *Turning Points: Preparing American Youth for the 21st Century* (Carnegie Council on Adolescent Development, 1989), a report of the Task Force on the Education of Young Adolescents, and *A Matter of Time: Risk and Opportunity in the Nonschool Hours* (Carnegie Council on Adolescent Development, 1992b), a report of the Task Force on Youth Development and Community Programs, Carnegie motivated renewed attention to youth policy among a broad range of national funders: the Ford Foundation, Annie E. Casey Foundation, DeWitt

Wallace—Reader's Digest Fund, Charles Stuart Mott Foundation, and others. Together, the work of these foundations has helped shape the current consensus that what the President's Science Advisory Committee, Panel on Youth (1974) had called "the institutional apparatus for maturation in the United States" must go well beyond the schoolday (p. 8). However, in recent years these policy makers and researchers have pushed further to define what that apparatus might look like and what frameworks for standards and accountability might guide it.

Addressing the policy implications of the new consensus, Pittman's (1991) testimony before the House Select Committee on Children, Youth, and Families introduced the term *youth development* into the vernacular of government. It has since become a central concept in the field. She argued:

> For years, Americans have accepted the notion that—with the exception of education—services for youth, particularly publicly funded services, exist to address youth problems. We have assumed that positive youth development occurs naturally in the absence of youth problems. Such thinking has created an assortment of youth services focused on "fixing" adolescents engaged in risky behaviors or preventing other youth from "getting into trouble." Preventing high risk behaviors, however, is not the same as preparation for the future. . . . What is needed is a massive conceptual shift—from thinking that youth problems are merely the principal barrier to youth development to seeing how youth development serves as the most effective strategy for the prevention of youth problems. Nothing short of a broad national initiative will accomplish this. (p. 3)

By the early 1990s a network of researchers and program officers were outlining the dimensions of this broad national initiative. The central pillar of this initiative would be the concept of youth development itself—a paradigm shift within youth services comparable to recent perspectives on literacy and learning. In an argument that resonates with Guerra and Farr's (Chapter 4, this volume) honoring of the competence and intentionality displayed by *mexicanas* in Chicago, youth development advocates argue that workers need to understand the competence, agency, and potential for resiliency of youth (Bernard, 1991; Werner & Smith, 1982). Youth development is defined as the central process young people engage in as they seek to meet their own needs and develop the competencies and skills they find useful and important. All young people could be understood as pursuing development, whether they do so in a supervised program, home alone, in a gang, or in school. Furthermore, if "develop" is what young people do (as opposed to what we do to them), then the role of youth organizations is to create the environments, the supports, and the opportunities that contribute to healthy development toward highly valued competencies. Although we must continue to question narrow or distorted views of healthy development or valued competencies, the shift away from viewing youth as a problem in need of professional solutions to seeing youth as a powerful agent and important resource is a significant new foundation for youth policy. It also provides a starting point for conversations about literacy in the out-of-school hours.

The concept of "youth development" is slowly gaining currency among youth-serving agencies and organizations, though certainly organizations differ in their awareness of and response to the concept. However, the youth development perspective offers literacy practitioners a compatible perspective on young people as agents who bring knowledge and capacities, and interests and desires, into any interaction. This common understanding of all persons as agents, rather than problems, can be a foundation for exploring collaborations across diverse specialties.

Fortunately so, since an expansion of public and private investment has created a complex and sometimes conflicting tangle of "collaborative and comprehensive" efforts. If the concept of youth development would be the foundation of the 1990s emphasis on youth organizations, collaboration and comprehensiveness would be twin pillars of policy. Arguing that young people need to be considered across the whole of their life worlds—school, community, family, peer group, as well as in the marketplace of media and youth culture—national funders advocated "comprehensive strategies" that would, in turn, require deep and systematic collaboration among the adults long charged with focusing on only one aspect of youth development (Dryfoos, 1990). As argued in *Great Transitions* (Carnegie Council on Adolescent Development, 1995):

> Given the complex influences on adolescents, the essential requirements for ensuring healthy development must be met through the joint efforts of a set of pivotal institutions that powerfully shape adolescents' experiences. These pivotal institutions must begin with the family and include schools, health care institutions, a wide array of neighborhood and community organizations, and the mass media.[3] (p. 5)

These collaborations would require professionals to move beyond single solutions to institutionally defined problems—delinquency, youth violence, substance abuse, or low literacy levels—to a comprehensive and positive vision of youth development. They would require professionals to grow beyond the histories of their specialties and professional allegiances, and to see their "clients" as agents.

Comprehensive partnerships are creative and challenging locations for literacy researchers and practitioners, offering opportunities to explore literacy as a practice in relationship to other professional fields, such as public health or community development, and to work with young people within settings that cut across disciplinary perspectives. In settings such as community health clinics, housing agencies, or youth advocacy organizations, the opportunities for literacy learning are rich as young people research and prepare materials for street outreach or mount campaigns on issues that concern them. Researchers and practitioners can work with diverse colleagues to deepen the learning potential of existing practices—creating a more educative environment without destroying the unique potential of the organization or the integrity of the work.

Once Again, Back in School

The notion of a system of overlapping comprehensive services for young people largely provided through the nonprofit sector fit well with the tenor of New Progressive strategies in the early 1990s. In keeping with the emerging "Third Way" characteristic of policies under Clinton (Giddens, 2000), youth organizations offered a way to link young people's "right" to supportive and safe environments with their "responsibility" to serve their communities through direct action and increasingly productive skills (Democratic Leadership Council, 1996). Initiatives as diverse as Bush's National and Community Service Act of 1990, the National Civilian Community Corps (part of an amendment to the 1992 defense appropriations bill), National and Community Service Trust Act of 1993, and the 21st Century Community Learning Centers (CLC) (authorized under Title X, Part I, of the Elementary and Secondary Education Act) were passed in quick succession. Service-learning programs, such as those described by Cushman and Emmons (Chapter 7, this volume), have become policy as well as program in many universities and school systems. And a range of private organizations with high-powered connections have also been created, foremost among them America's Promise, launched at the 1997 Presidents' Summit for America's Future and originally chaired by Colin Powell, and the Points of Light Foundation, championed and chaired by former president Bush.

Funding for the after-school arena grew dramatically during the 1990s. Appropriations for 21st Century CLCs, for example, have grown from $40 million in 1997 to $200 million in 1998 and $453 million in 1999, monies that are supplemented by services provided through federally funded regional labs and the U.S. Department of Education. Public investment has been augmented by private dollars; for example, the Mott Foundation has worked as a partner with government in support of the 21st Century CLCs, their support increasing from $2 million in the fall of 1997 to $83 million (over the course of 6 years) in the fall of 1999. The Mott Foundation currently reports their commitment at $95.2 million over seven years (www. mott.org/21stcentury). Through these initiatives, collaboration and comprehensiveness have been given the force of funding priorities with the surprising result that significant responsibility for out-of-school efforts has been given to the schools themselves.

Under the watchwords of *collaboration* and *comprehensiveness*, well-funded school–community initiatives have been sponsored by many municipalities. San Diego has created New Beginnings, a collaboration among five public agencies and the school district intended to better meet the service needs of children and families and to promote institutional change that would benefit young people throughout the day. New York has consistently expanded its Beacons initiative, begun with an appropriation of $5 million from Safe Streets, Safe Cities. Beacons "keep the light on" at schools by opening them for after-school, weekend, and summer programming for children and adults from the community. As of 1999, the program supported more than 75 school-based community centers receiving a base grant of $450,000 each (Warren, Brown, & Freudenberg, 1999). Other cities are launching school-based community centers: San Francisco has begun a Beacons initiative; Bridgeport, Connecticut, has formed 18 Lighthouse schools, and Chicago has funded Youth Nets. In many cases, these local efforts provide a solid foundation for researchers and practitioners interested in literacy and youth. Well funded and institutionally secure, at least in comparison with many community-based organizations, these efforts are as high profile as the school buildings that increasingly house them. Although as high-profile initiatives these policy actions are beginning to attract scrutiny by conservatives opposed to government incursions into "family life" by specifying programs for after-school hours (Olsen, 2000), there is evidence that the Bush administration will continue to support them.

Ironically, literacy practitioners and theorists interested in learning outside of schools may find themselves returning to the schools through the side door. The new youth development policies are creating opportunities, and in some cases critical needs, for literacy practitioners and theorists to work at the intersections of community-based organizations and schools. Many of the recent policy efforts mentioned above are deliberately constructed, along the lines of comprehensive service models, to require collaboration among community-based organizations and with schools. They may receive strong community support. Parents, who often report a lack of knowledge about after-school opportunities in their neighborhoods, frequently express a preference for the school to become the locus of information and collaborations (Philadelphia Citizens for Children and Youth, 1998). And community-based organizations, often with few facilities themselves, look with envy at the facilities, materials, and power of the school building and wonder why they can't just leave the light on.

Yet effecting meaningful collaborations often requires powerful "third parties" who can temper expected power imbalances and elucidate suitable conceptual frames that can allow partners to understand their work in relationship to each other. Since the late 1980s when funders, particularly the United Way, began rewarding collaborative proposals as a way of extending dwindling resources and managing an expanding set of applicant organizations, many community-based organizations have begun to see collaboration as challenging, time-consuming, and occasionally destabilizing (Langman & McLaughlin, 1993). Many have become wary, particularly of the more powerful partners in any collaboration who can create conditions favorable to their organizational ethos and strengths but less suitable for other partners. In this regard, the new policy initiatives present the challenge of working with a very powerful partner: local school districts. There are important roles for brokers, suitable "third parties" such as literacy theorists and practitioners, who can link literacy to youth development with a vision of powerful literacy learning and sensitivity to the unique qualities of each partner.

As a case in point, initial legislation behind the 21st Century Community Learning Centers (CLCs) specified that only school districts could apply for funds, with the requirement that schools create collaborations with community groups. Through the efforts of a coalition of national nonprofits, challenges to these restrictions opened new routes to funding in the next authorization of 21st Century CLCs.[4] Early predictions for George W. Bush's administration suggest a continued support for community-based organizations and faith-based youth groups, including access to federal funds (Boyle, 2001).

Yet despite focused offerings and proposed set-asides for community-based organizations, the power of school districts as a senior partner in many initiatives is virtually inescapable. School districts exercise fiscal authority, manage access to facilities, require reporting and evaluation processes commensurate with their own bureaucratic processes, and typically set goals and specify outcomes. Youth development organizations are justifiably sensitive to the very real danger that their special contribution to young people's lives will be lost in the rush to make the out-of-school hours "productive" of narrowly specified outcomes. They also worry they will lose the freedom and flexibility necessary to support youth leadership and to plan projects around the emerging interests of families and the community. Literacy researchers and practitioners with the ability to navigate a policy arena where schools and community organizations are positioned in opposition to each other's interests might be able to spot powerful opportunities for learning in the interstices.

Finally, partnerships with school districts dependent on public money often translate into an increased emphasis on standards-driven programs, academic outcomes, and results calibrated to scores on high-stakes tests. Youth development leaders complain about what one commentator called "the political grip of the give 'em more academics after 3 p.m. crowd" ("Newsmakers" editor, 2000, p. 36). As states pursue systemic reforms that increasingly seek to align expenditures for youth to standards and accountability packages, youth development leaders see the power base for their work shifting toward "the same education interests whose constituents' woeful performance before 3 p.m. makes them . . . uniquely qualified to dish out the same in what is labeled (with increasing inaccuracy) as out-of-school time" ("Newsmakers" editor, 2000, p. 36).

Although literacy practitioners who work in schools may find themselves the target of anger or suspicion by their out-of-school colleagues, it is important to temper emotions with the awareness that those powerful "education interests" are typically located somewhere outside the classroom, outside the local school, out of reach of *both* school-based and out-of-school educators. Such "interests" are likely to be drawn from the professional reform class, the education policy arena, the for-profit providers of curriculum materials, and the many public/private ventures specializing in technical assistance to the nonprofit sector. Already, the earliest examples of curricula and materials with a literacy focus developed explicitly for after-school settings are derived from adaptations of materials developed for in-school use, reformatted for the special contexts of voluntary after-school programs. If after-school becomes more like in-school, it will likely be because both are being co-constructed in relation to similar discourses on youth and productivity, and both are increasingly central as objects and markets for the business of educational reform. Indeed, educators in either setting who would link new literacy work and youth development would do better to see themselves as allies than adversaries, allies in the fight to maintain sufficient local freedom to innovate, to build on local assets, to meet the needs of actual communities, and to offer real leadership and responsibility to young people.

The new emphasis on the after-school hours has brought increased visibility, funding, opportunity, coordination, and professional development to youth-serving agencies and community-based organizations. It has also brought new pressures and conflicting priorities. With public money come increasingly complex funding and reporting requirements and new demands to produce academic outcomes, generally measurable in terms set by state school accountability plans. These goals may not represent the aspirations of local communities or the missions and capacities of these organizations. Similarly, the relentless attention given to schools in the years since *A Nation at Risk* has brought a wealth of resources yet has also served to limit options and exacerbate long-standing problems of equity. It will not help young people to accede to a discourse that constructs schools as places where they "work" to produce high test scores and after-school as the place where they "play" at what school, at its best, *should* be.

For this reason, there *is* real work to do if we are to rise to the challenge set for us in this volume. It may be necessary for literacy researchers and practitioners to take after-school and "discretionary" spaces very seriously, seriously enough to protect their unique potential. But ultimately, we may need to set the distinction aside and work to support the richest menu of educational practice in schools and out.

Conclusion

In the early 1980s, my colleagues and I were fortunate. Informed by emerging theory and research from the New Literacy Studies and the ethnography of communication—as well as by the budding writing process, whole-language, and writing across the curriculum movements—we had the freedom to reinvent curricula, to be the authors of our own practice. We had the freedom to apply the best of after-school during school. We were also fortunate that music, drama, art, publications work, and a wealth of student-initiated clubs were valued and supported as a necessary "co-curriculum."

By the end of the decade the picture was bleaker. Much of the "co-curriculum" would be labeled unnecessary in the push to achieve ever higher scores on state assessments. Teacher's options would be narrower; the happy climate of experimentation would suddenly look too risky, too suspect. More minutes during the day would be devoted to preparation before state tests or remediation after state tests. In the intervening decade since I left the high school classroom, I've heard many similar stories from teachers at all grade levels and in all regions of the United States. Although the picture is complex, they often say that "teaching writing as if the person matters," to use Cris Gutierrez's memorable phrase (Chapter 8, this volume), is getting harder to do—and certainly more important both in schools and out. Against this backdrop we have reason to consider what difference our new understandings of literacy can make to the lives of young people in this nation.

If current trends continue, researchers and practitioners will find a wealth of opportunities in the coming decade to put our hard-won new perspectives on literacy(ies) to work. What will that work be? Some of us may create the new programs and packages that current policies will seek out and scale up. These may, perhaps, be far superior to what is available now. Others of us, though, might take our knowledge out into the world in another way, to sit around the table with the parents, the teachers, the youth workers, and young people themselves to wonder: What is the potential in this time, in this space, with the word?

Notes

1. National Center for Education Statistics, *Common Core of Data* for 1999–2000 school year. (www.nces.ed.gov).

2. Early studies of the work of youth organizations include Hanson & Carlson (1972), Erickson (1986), James (1979), Kleinfeld & Shinkwin (1982), La Belle & Carroll (1981), Lipsitz (1986).

3. Core recommendation number 6; Executive Summary and abridged version available online at www.carnegie.org. As the concluding report of the Carnegie Council on Adolescent Development and the culmination of its work, *Great Transitions* draws heavily on previous publications, including its three major public policy reports: *Turning Points: Preparing Youth for the 21st Century* (Carnegie Council on Adolescent Development, 1989); *Fateful Choices: Healthy Youth for the 21st Century* (Carnegie Council on Adolescent Development, 1992a); and *A Matter of Time: Risk and Opportunity in the Nonschool Hours* (Carnegie Council on Adolescent Development, 1992b). The report also draws on a host of research syntheses, many supported through corporation funds. The council notes in particular Feldman & Elliott (1990).

4. For current reports on youth policy, see the website of the National Youth Development Information Center at www.nydic.org.

References

Afterschool Alliance. (2000, January). Poll Report. *Afterschool alert*, pp. 1–6.

Bernard, B. (1991). *Fostering resiliency in kids: Protective factors in the family, school and community.* Portland, OR: Northwest Regional Educational Laboratory.

Boyer, E. (1990). *Scholarship reconsidered: Priorities of the professoriate.* Princeton, NJ: Carnegie Foundation for the Advancement of Teaching.

Boyle, P. (2001). A peek at President Bush's youth policy. *Youth Today, 10*(1), 1, 50–51.

Carnegie Council on Adolescent Development. (1989). *Turning points: Preparing American youth for the 21st century.* New York: Carnegie Corporation.

Carnegie Council on Adolescent Development. (1992a). *Fateful choices: Healthy youth for the 21st century.* New York: Carnegie Corporation.

Carnegie Council on Adolescent Development. (1992b). *A matter of time: Risk and opportunity in the nonschool hours.* New York: Carnegie Corporation.

Carnegie Council on Adolescent Development. (1995). *Great transitions: Preparing adolescents for a new century.* New York: Carnegie Corporation.

Crosson, P. (1985). *Public service in higher education: Practices and priorities* (ASHE-ERIC Higher Education Report, No. 2). Washington, DC: ERIC Clearinghouse on Higher Education.

Democratic Leadership Council—Progressive Policy Institute. (1996). *The new progressive declaration.* Washington, DC: Democratic Leadership Council.

Dryfoos, J. (1990). *Adolescents at risk: Prevalence and prevention.* New York: Oxford University Press.

Erickson, J. (1986). Non-formal education in organizations for American Youth. *Children Today, 15*(1), 17–25.

Feldman, S. S., & Elliott, G. R. (Eds.). (1990). *At the threshold: The developing adolescent.* Cambridge, MA: Harvard University Press.

Fine, G. A., & Mechling, J. (1993). Child saving and children's cultures at century's end. In S. B. Heath & M. McLaughlin (Eds.), *Identity and inner-city youth: Beyond ethnicity and gender* (pp. 120–146). New York: Teachers College Press.

Giddens, A. (2000). *The Third Way and its critics.* Cambridge, UK: Polity Press.

Hanson, R. F., & Carlson, R. (1972). *Organizations for children and youth.* Englewood Cliffs, NJ: Prentice-Hall.

Heath, S. B., & McLaughlin, M. (Eds.). (1993). *Identity and inner-city youth: Beyond ethnicity and gender.* New York: Teachers College Press.

James, D. (1979). *Description study of selected national youth serving organizations.* Washington, DC: U.S. Department of Agriculture.

James, T. (1993). The winnowing of organizations. In S. B. Heath & M. McLaughlin (Eds.), *Identity and inner-city youth: Beyond ethnicity and gender* (pp. 176–195). New York: Teachers College Press.

Kleinfeld, J., & Shinkwin, A. (1982). *Youth organizations as a third educational environment particularly for minority group youth* (Final Report to the National Institute for Education). Washington, DC: U.S. Government Printing Office.

La Belle, T. J., & Carroll, J. (1981). An introduction to the nonformal education of children and youth. *Comparative Education Review, 25*, 313–329.

Langman, J., & McLaughlin, M. (1993). Collaborate or go it alone? Tough decisions for youth policy. In S. B. Heath & M. McLaughlin (Eds.), *Identity and inner-city youth: Beyond ethnicity and gender* (pp. 147–175). New York: Teachers College Press.

Lave, J., & Wenger, E. (1991). *Situated learning: Legitimate peripheral participation.* New York: Cambridge University Press.

Lipsitz, J. (1986). *After school: Young adolescents on the own.* Chapel Hill: Center for Early Adolescence, University of North Carolina.

Lynton, E. (1995). *Making the case for professional service.* Washington, DC: American Association for Higher Education.

McLaughlin, M., Irby, M., & Langman, J. (1994). *Urban sanctuaries: Neighborhood organizations in the lives and futures of inner-city youth.* San Francisco: Jossey-Bass.

National Center for Education Statistics (NCES). (1990a). *Profile of the American 8th grader* (National Longitudinal Study of 1988). Washington, DC: U.S. Department of Education.

National Center for Education Statistics (NCES). (1990b). *Services and resources for young adults in libraries, 1988–89*. Washington, DC: U.S. Department of Education.

"Newsmakers" editor. (2000, June). *Youth Today*, p. 36.

Olsen, D. (2000). 12-hour school days? Why government should leave afterschool arrangements to parents. (*www.cato.org*).

Philadelphia Citizens for Children and Youth. (1998). *Watching out for children in changing times: Safe, stimulated and supervised in the non-school hours: A report on youth programs*. Philadelphia: United Way of Southeastern Pennsylvania.

Pittman, K. (September, 1991). *A new vision: Promoting youth development* (Testimony of Karen J. Pittman before the House Select Committee on Children, Youth and Families). Washington, DC: Center for Youth Development and Policy Research/AED.

Pollack, S. (1995). *Youth organizations as educational partners* (Pew Forum on Educational Reform). California: Stanford University Press.

President's Science Advisory Committee, Panel on Youth. (1974). *Youth: Transition to adulthood*. Chicago: University of Chicago Press.

Warren, C., Brown, P., & Freudenberg. (1999). *Evaluation of the New York City Beacons: Summary of phase 1 findings*. New York: Academy for Educational Development.

Werner, E., & Smith, R. (1982). *Vulnerable but invincible: A longitudinal study of resilient children and youth*. New York: Adams, Bannister, & Cox.

Youth development: On the path towards professionalization. (1999). Washington, DC: National Assembly.

Mollie Blackburn Responds

As a former middle and high school language arts teacher and a current literacy practitioner and researcher in a youth-run center for lesbian, gay, bisexual, transgender, and questioning (LGBTQ) youth, I was inspired by Eidman-Aadahl's chapter. In some ways, she advocates for just the kind of work I have tried to do. I facilitated a literacy group that met weekly. In the group, youth brought their own reading and writing, as did I, to share with the group. Together we read, wrote, and told our stories. I also worked with youth on a speakers' bureau to talk with youth service providers, including teachers, about ways to better work with LGBTQ youth. Additionally—by default, really, because the youth knew I was a former English teacher—I often took on the role of editor-in-residence. This explicitly teacherlike role was the one that troubled me the most.

When I first came to the center—the very first day, when I was interviewed by youth to determine whether I could be a researcher and a volunteer at the center—they asked me whether I had worked with youth before, and I proudly said that I had been a teacher. At least one of the youth heard this with trepidation; she explained to me, quite plainly, that this was a *youth-run* center and asked me what I was going to do to *not* be a teacher in this center. Indeed, I was, as Eidman-Aadahl describes, "the target of anger or suspicion." Although I was taken aback, I explained that I understood that the space was theirs and that I respected that, but that, even as a teacher, I had worked hard to make classroom space *ours*, not *mine*. Several of the youth murmured comments about not having known any teachers like that. A few weeks later, I learned that the youth had accepted me into the center. Over time, I came to understand that many of the youth at the center have found schools to be heterosexist and homophobic places, and thus unsafe places for them; these experiences have, in some ways, implicated teachers. Because of this, it was important for me to *not* be a teacher. "Teacher" and teachers gave me a bad name at the center.

However, privately, youth asked me to help them write cover letters, shape résumés, apply to colleges, and edit and revise academic essays. In other words, just as I was asked to not be a teacher, I was asked to be a teacher—sometimes by the same youth. Sometimes I felt like an informant—like I had been to the other side, gathered secret information, and returned to share with the youth what I had gleaned. It seemed like school was the enemy, like I had to prove to the youth that I was not one of "them," and once I had, I could help the youth fight against "them" by revealing their battle plans. As long as I chose which side I was on and my loyalties were clear, I was on their side. This in-school/out-of-school dichotomy, I think, kept them safe, safe from the heterosexism and homophobia of the schools.

The dichotomy, was, of course, artificial. Their schoolwork found its way into the center, and work from the center made its way into schools. Eidman-Aadahl challenges us to recognize this dichotomy as false, to work together, to collaborate for literacy learning and youth development. When I read her chapter, I wrote "Yes!" in the margins, over and over again. The promise of educators listening, learning, and living on what is essentially youth's turf and terms gives me great hope for shifting power dynamics. This is work that needs to be done, it seems to me. However, it is risky work, and the consequences are important. What if the power dynamics don't shift? What if the educators come in and fail to relinquish power? What if the youth are not able to assert power? Eidman-Aadahl warns that as soon as "narrowly specified outcomes" are imposed on out-of-school contexts, "their special contribution to young people's lives will be lost"; and, as soon as these contexts become "sites for research or placements for university students that we can enter and abandon as we choose," they are no longer *for* youth. How can we ensure that collaboration will not come to these consequences? How can we become "allies in the fight to maintain sufficient local freedom to innovate, to build on local assets, to meet the needs of actual communities, and to offer real leadership and responsibilities to young people"? I believe that this work can be done, that it must be done, but that it is not just about sharing space and it is not necessarily about sharing work; rather, it is about sharing relationships. Ceglowski (2000) writes about "research as relationship," and she asserts that the people with whom she shares relationships in her research site will not only "teach [her] to interpret the phenomena [she] stud[ies], they will [also] teach [her] how to research" (p. 101). If literacy practitioner researchers have the time, energy, commitment, and passion necessary to share these relationships, then let's get to work.

Reference

Ceglowski, D. (2000). Research as relationship. *Qualitative Inquiry, 6*(1), 88–103.

About the Authors

JOYCE A. BASKINS is a community activist and community literacy practitioner. For the past 15 years, she has participated in community literacy projects and published work in the field of rhetoric. She frequently presents at both university and community forums the work of everyday people in community settings.

MOLLIE BLACKBURN is a doctoral candidate in the Language in Education Division at the University of Pennsylvania. She is a former middle and high school teacher of the language arts and a current instructor of teaching literacy and social studies in elementary classrooms. She is writing her dissertation on the literacy practices and identity work of queer youth in the youth-run center where she facilitates a literature discussion group, a women's group, and a speakers' bureau. Her previous work includes exploring race, class, and tracking sixth-graders in advanced language arts classes; as well as analyzing the role of African American vernacular in student writing.

ELLEN CUSHMAN, assistant professor of English at Michigan State University, studies literacy, critical pedagogy, activist methodologies, multimedia, and service learning. Author of *The Struggle and the Tools: Oral and Literate Strategies in an Inner City Community* and co-editor of *Literacy: A Critical Sourcebook*, she is currently researching visual rhetorics and the role of digital compositions in outreach initiatives.

VERDA DELP has taught English in the Berkeley schools for more than 30 years. She is a teacher consultant with the Bay Area Writing Project, presenting a summer course for new teachers of English. Her classroom research has been supported by membership in several practitioner research collaboratives over the past 10 years, including sponsorship by The Spencer Foundation. Her current research interest centers on the ways in which students in an academically heterogeneous eighth-grade English class appropriate interpretive thinking and writing skills.

ELYSE EIDMAN-AADAHL is co-director of the National Writing Project at the University of California, Berkeley, where she coordinates national program and research networks. Her current interests include projects that bring school-based educators and community-based youth workers together to enhance literacy learning across the school–community boundary.

CHALON EMMONS received her M.A. in Education in Language, Literacy, and Culture from the Graduate School of Education at the University of California, Berkeley. While a graduate student, she helped develop and teach courses that brought undergraduates to work and play with children in a local YMCA after-school program. She currently works as a researcher and writer for UC Links, a network of technology-based after-school programs connecting universities with communities.

MARCIA FARR is a sociolinguist who has published extensively on cultural variation in oral and written language use. She directed the funding of research on writing at the National Institute of Education from 1976 to 1982 and edited a research series on writing for Ablex and then Hampton Press. Two books are forthcoming. One is based on long-term ethnographic research with Mexican families in Chicago and in their Mexican village; the other is an edited volume on language and literacy in Chicago neighborhoods.

JUAN C. GUERRA is associate professor of English in Language and Rhetoric at the University of Washington, Seattle, where he teaches courses on writing pedagogy, language, literacy, and ethnography. His principal areas of research are highlighted in two books: *Writing in Multicultural Settings*, a collection of original essays he co-edited with Carol Severino and Johnnella E. Butler, and *Close to Home: Oral and Literate Practices in a Transnational Mexicano Community* (Teachers College Press, 1998). His current research examines a rhetorical practice he refers to as transcultural repositioning that is used as a coping mechanism by many Chicanos/as and *mexicanos/as* living in the United States.

LEIF GUSTAVSON is a Ph.D. candidate in Reading, Writing, and Literacy at the University of Pennsylvania. Before returning to school, he taught middle school language arts for 7 years. He is currently writing his dissertation— "Turntablism, graffiti, and zine writing: The out of school literacy projects of youth." This ethnographic case study of the out-of-school literacy projects of three ethnically and economically diverse youth examines the youths' literacy work in relation to space and place, as well as investigates the agency these youth have within their communities of practice. His most recent article is "Normalizing the Text: What Is Being Said, What Is Not and Why in Students' Conversations of E. L. Konigsburg's *A View from Saturday*," published in the *Journal of Children's Literature*.

CRIS GUTIERREZ, a peace educator, has worked with youth for 19 years in private and public schools as a teacher, coach, and adviser. With a focus on high school social studies and English, she seeks to develop powerful interdisicplinary scholars who think deeply and value themselves as a force for good in society. From 1988 to 1999 she taught in South Central Los Angeles at Thomas Jefferson High School's Humanitas Academy, part of the Los Angeles Unified School District. Now a K–12 Carnegie Scholar, she is documenting that practice in a retrospective study.

GLYNDA HULL is an associate professor of Education in Language, Literacy, and Culture at the University of California, Berkeley. Her research has included studies of underprepared student writers, technology and education, vocational training, and literacy at work. The latter interest led to two books, an edited volume called *Changing Work, Changing Workers: Critical Perspectives on Language, Literacy, and Skills* and *The New Work Order: Behind the Language of the New Capitalism*, co-authored with Jim Gee and Colin Lankshear. Her current research focuses on community-based, technology-centered job training programs for low-income youth and young adults, and how, within such settings, people may come to fashion new identities as students and professionals.

SARAH JEWETT is currently a doctoral student and an instructor in the elementary teacher education program in the Graduate School of Education at the University of Pennsylvania. Prior to her graduate study, she was a classroom teacher and a coordinator of an urban literacy project. Her research interests include urban education, school desegregation, and adolescent literacy.

PORFIRIO M. LOEZA has been a bilingual teacher in California for the past decade. His teaching experience reaches across all elementary grade levels. He currently serves as a "coach" for new teachers and provides them with in-service mentoring and professional development support. In combination with his professional responsibilities, he is also in the dissertation phase of a doctoral program in Language, Literacy and Culture at the University of California at Berkeley. His dissertation research centers on the examination of the literacy practices associated with the "retablo" in Mexican votive art. (A "retablo" is a small oil painting, usually made on tin, and most often made by a popular or untrained artist from the provinces.)

ELENORE LONG is an associate professor of rhetoric at Bay Path College in Longmeadow, Massachusetts. After completing a postdoctoral fellowship through the Community Literacy Center and Carnegie Mellon University, she stayed on at the Community House to direct the STRUGGLE initiative. At the same time, she taught communication courses and directed assessment efforts at Robert Morris College. Long was a finalist for the 1995 NCTE Promising Researcher Award for her dissertation, a version of which appears in *Inventing a Discipline: Rhetorical Scholarship in Honor of Richard Young*. With Linda Flower and Lorraine Higgins, she has recently published *Learning to Rival: A Literate Practice for Intercultural Inquiry*, an extended look at how students and professors use and adapt the practice of rivaling across the curriculum—in biology, history, and English—and how inner-city teens use rivaling to address problems such as substance abuse in their neighborhood.

GILLIAN DOWLEY McNAMEE is director of teacher education at Erikson Institute in Chicago. She has studied literacy development in home, school, and community contexts. She is co-author of *Early Literacy*. She has been a Spencer Fellow with the National Academy of Education and received a Sunny Days Award from Children's Television Workshop/Sesame Street Parents in 1998 for her work in developing an innovative early childhood teacher preparation program.

JULIA MENARD-WARWICK is a Ph.D. student in Language, Literacy and Culture in the School of Education, University of California at Berkeley. Previously she taught adult ESL for more than 10 years at the community college level. Her research interests include second-language acquisition, adult literacy, and immigrant education.

WAYNE C. PECK, a Rev. Dr., for the past 25 years has been the chair of the board of the Community House and the senior pastor of the First Allegheny Presbyterian Church on the North Side of Pittsburgh. For the past decade Dr. Peck has taught writing at Carnegie Mellon University and participated in writing research. He has published work in the field of rhetoric and is interested in translating rhetorical theory within practical contexts. Dr. Peck holds graduate degrees from Harvard University and Carnegie Mellon University.

MARSHA PINCUS has been an English teacher in the school district of Philadelphia for more than 25 years. She is currently on leave, serving as the executive director of the Philadelphia Young Playwrights Festival, a nonprofit arts in education organization that pairs professional playwrights with classroom teachers for the purpose of teaching students to write, revise, and perform their own original plays. She is a Ph.D. student in Reading, Writing, Literacy at the University of Pennsylvania and a fellow of the Carnegie Academy for the Scholarship of Teaching and Learning. Her research interests include the examination of possibilities for creating engaged, ethical classroom communities through playwriting and dramatic inquiry.

MARCI RESNICK has been an elementary school teacher with the school district of Philadelphia for 25 years. For the past 5 years she has served as director of the Philadelphia Writing Project of the University of Pennsylvania. In this capacity she has worked with other teachers, administrators, and parents to design and implement a variety of professional development opportunities focusing on literacy and leadership, including seminars, practicum schools, and teacher research communities. She is presently chairperson of the Urban Sites Network of the National Writing Project.

KATHERINE SCHULTZ is assistant professor in teacher education at the Graduate School of Education of the University of Pennsylvania. A former teacher and principal, she currently offers courses on literacy in the elementary school, urban education, and teacher education. In conjunction with her work with the Carnegie Academy for the Scholarship on Teaching and Learning, she is writing a book tentatively titled *Listening to Teach: Learning from Students How to Cross Cultural Boundaries*. She is currently involved in numerous research projects, including the documentation of a long-term, grassroots professional development network of teachers in Philadelphia. Her most recent article is "Democratizing Conversations: Discourses of 'Race' in a Post-Desegregated Middle School," co-authored with Patti Buck and Tricia Niesz, and published in the *American Education Research Journal*.

SARAH SIVRIGHT is presently a nursery school teacher at the University of Chicago Laboratory Schools. She has collaborated on research in computer-enriched after-school programs and has worked with school-age children as well as nursery schoolers, teaching a nature journaling summer course at the Chicago Lab School.

ELLEN SKILTON-SYLVESTER is an assistant professor in Temple University's College of Education. Her research focuses on sociocultural, contextual, and relational issues that surround bilingual and biliterate practices for immigrant, refugee, and international students in the United States. Connections between in-school and out-of-school language and literacy practices are of particular importance to her work. In 1999, she received the Council on Anthropology and Education's Outstanding Dissertation Award for her study of Cambodian women and girls in Philadelphia.

DIANE WAFF is a teacher leader/vice principal at Trenton Central High School in Trenton, New Jersey. Co-director of the Philadelphia Writing Project and a member of the National Writing Project Task Force, she facilitates Seeking Educational Equity and Diversity seminars for the National SEED Project in Philadelphia and New Jersey. The recent recipient of a 2-year Carnegie Foundation Fellowship awarded to school- and university-based scholars to conduct classroom-based research, she is also a doctoral candidate at the University of Pennsylvania.

MARTY WILLIAMS, a teacher-poet-activist, is currently co-director of the Bay Area Writing Project. Her education work grows out of her work for social justice. She has worked with young people and teachers in community-based literacy projects, taught writing at New College of California, and contributed to school reform efforts throughout the Bay Area. As a writer and teacher, she has a profound belief in the transformative power of the word in the world.

Index